MORE SAYINGS OF THE
DESERT FATHERS

T0382593

Most of the *Tales and Sayings of the Desert Fathers (apophthegms)* have survived in Greek, and most of them are now available in English, almost 2500 in number. A further 600 items in six languages have been available in French for some time, but often only in second- or even third-hand translations. These have now been newly translated directly from the original languages by scholars skilled in those languages and are presented, alongside an Introduction and brief notes, to the English reader who wishes to know more of those men and some women who rejected 'the world' and went to live in the desert regions of Egypt and elsewhere in the fourth to seventh centuries AD.

JOHN WORTLEY was born and educated in Britain, where he studied under Joan Hussey and Cyril Mango. Appointed Professor of Medieval History at the University of Manitoba in 1969, he developed a program of Byzantine studies there until his retirement in 2002, since when (as Professor Emeritus) he continues to research and publish, latterly concentrating on the *Apophthegmata Patrum*. In retirement he has held visiting fellowships at the Universities of Belfast (Queen's, twice), Princeton, and Durham. He has always maintained close ties with the Paris Byzantinists; it was at the instigation of the late Joseph Paramelle that he began work on the *Répertoire of Byzantine Beneficial Tales*. His translation of John Skylitzes' *Synopsis Historiarum* (Cambridge, 2010) was made in close cooperation with Bernard Flusin and Jean-Claude Cheynet. His pioneering work on the role of relics in Byzantine society can now be conveniently consulted in *Studies on the Cult of Relics in Byzantium up to 1204* (2009). He has produced a translation of the Systematic series of Sayings of the Fathers, *The Book of the Elders* (2012); a select edition and a translation of *The Anonymous Sayings of the Desert Fathers* (Cambridge, 2013); a new translation of the Alphabetical Sayings, *Give Me a Word* (2014); and a new translation of Palladius' *The Lausiac History* (2015). Ordained in the Church of England in 1959/60, he continues to serve as an honorary assistant priest in a city parish.

MORE SAYINGS OF THE DESERT FATHERS

An English Translation and Notes

EDITED BY

JOHN WORTLEY

University of Manitoba, Canada

with a preface by

SAMUEL RUBENSON

Lunds Universitet, Sweden

CAMBRIDGE
UNIVERSITY PRESS

Shaftesbury Road, Cambridge CB2 8EA, United Kingdom

One Liberty Plaza, 20th Floor, New York, NY 10006, USA

477 Williamstown Road, Port Melbourne, VIC 3207, Australia

314–321, 3rd Floor, Plot 3, Splendor Forum, Jasola District Centre, New Delhi – 110025, India

103 Penang Road, #05–06/07, Visioncrest Commercial, Singapore 238467

Cambridge University Press is part of Cambridge University Press & Assessment,
a department of the University of Cambridge.

We share the University's mission to contribute to society through the pursuit of
education, learning and research at the highest international levels of excellence.

www.cambridge.org
Information on this title: www.cambridge.org/9781108457071

DOI: 10.1017/9781108570411

First published 2019
First paperback edition 2023

A catalogue record for this publication is available from the British Library

Library of Congress Cataloging-in-Publication data
NAMES: Wortley, John, editor. | Rubenson, Samuel, writer of preface. | Kitchen, Robert A. |
Thomson, Robert W., 1934– | Vivian, Tim. | Witakowski, Witold.
TITLE: More sayings of the Desert Fathers : an English translation and notes / edited by
John Wortley, University of Manitoba, Canada ; with preface by Samuel Rubenson,
Lunds Universitet, Sweden.
DESCRIPTION: New York : Cambridge University Press, 2019. | Includes
bibliographical references and index.
IDENTIFIERS: LCCN 2018041952 | ISBN 9781108471084 (alk. paper)
SUBJECTS: LCSH: Desert Fathers – Quotations. | Spiritual life – Christianity – Quotations,
maxims, etc. | Monastic and religious life – Quotations, maxims, etc. | Spiritual life –
Christianity – Early works to 1800. | Monastic and religious life – Early works to 1800.
CLASSIFICATION: LCC BR60.A2 M67 2019 | DDC 270.2–dc23
LC record available at https://lccn.loc.gov/2018041952

ISBN   978-1-108-47108-4   Hardback
ISBN   978-1-108-45707-1   Paperback

For Kiera and Thea
εὐλογήσαι σε Κύριος καὶ φυλάξαι σε

Contents

Contributors

ROBERT KITCHEN recently retired as Minister at Knox-Metropolitan United Church, Regina. A prolific translator of Syriac texts he recently published a new translation of *The Discourses of Philoxenos of Mabbug* (Cistercian / Liturgical Press, 2013).

SAMUEL RUBENSON is Professor at the Centre for Theology and Religious Studies, Lund University, and Senior Professor of Eastern Christian Studies at Sankt Ignatios Academy and the University College, Stockholm. His main publications deal with early monasticism and he is the general editor of *Monastica*, an open access digital platform for research on the transmission of the Sayings of the Desert.

ROBERT W. THOMSON is Professor Emeritus (Armenian studies) at the Oriental Institute, Pembroke College, Oxford. He published most recently *The Lives of Saint Gregory: The Armenian, Greek, Arabic and Syriac Versions of the History Attributed to Agathangelos*, translated with introduction and commentary (Caravan Books, Ann Arbor, MI, 2010), as well as *Basil of Caesarea and Armenian Cosmology: A Study of the Armenian Version of Saint Basil's Hexaemeron and Its Influence on Medieval Armenian Views about the Cosmos*, CSCO 646, Subsidia 130 (Leuven, 2012).

TIM VIVIAN is currently Professor of Religious Studies at CSU, Bakersfield and priest-in-charge at St. Paul's Episcopal Church in Bakersfield. His most recent book (with Maged S. A. Mikhail) is *The Holy Workshop of Virtue: The Life of Saint John the Little* (Cistercian / Liturgical Press, 2010.) He and Prof. Mikhail are currently completing books on the *Life of Bishoy* and the *Life of Matthew the Poor*.

WITOLD WITAKOWSKI is a researcher in the Department of Linguistics and Philology, Uppsala University. He is presently working on (*inter alia*) *A Catalog of the Manuscripts of the Monastery of Gundä Gunde (Northeastern Ethiopia)*.

JOHN WORTLEY (Editor) spent his working life as Professor of Medieval (sc. Byzantine) History at the University of Manitoba. Still active as a priest of the Anglican / Episcopal Church, he continues to publish, including, most recently, *The Anonymous Sayings of the Desert Fathers, a Select Edition and Complete English Translation* (Cambridge, 2013) and a new translation of Palladius' *The Lausiac History* (Cistercian / Liturgical Press 2015).

Abbreviations

AP   *Apophthegmata Patrum*, Sayings [of the Desert] Fathers.

APalph The 'alphabetic' series of the above, *Apophthegmata Patrum, collectio alphabetica*, ed. Jean-Baptiste Cotelier, in *Monumenta Ecclesiae Graecae*, vol. 1 (Paris 1647); re-ed. Jacques-Paul Migne, *PG* 65:71–440; tr. John Wortley, *Give Me a Word* (Yonkers, NY 2014).

APanon The 'anonymous' sayings, ed. and trans. John Wortley, *The Anonymous Sayings of the Desert Fathers*, Cambridge, 2013.

APsys   The 'systematic' sayings, ed. and trans. Jean-Claude Guy, *Les apophtegmes des pères: Collection systématique*, 3 vols., SC 387, 474, and 498, Paris, 1993, 2003, 2005; tr. John Wortley, *The Book of the Elders*, Cistercian, 2012.

CSCO   *Corpus Scriptorum Christianorum Orientalium*

Guy   Jean-Claude Guy, *Recherches sur la tradition grecque des Apophthegmata Patrum*, Brussels, 1962, reprint 1984 with corrections.

HL   Palladius, *The Lausiac History*, ed. G. J. M. Bartelink, *Palladio, La Storia Lausiaca*, Mondadori, 1974; trans. John Wortley, *Palladius of Aspuna, Lausiac History*, Cistercian, 2015.

HME   *Historia Monachorum in Aegypto*, ed. André-Jean Festugière, Brussels, 1961; ed. Michelle Szkilnik, *Historia monachorum in Aegypto / L'histoire des moines d'Egypte; suivie de la vie de Saint Paul le Simple*, Geneva, 1993; tr. Festugière, *Les moines d'Orient*, Paris, 1964; tr. Norman Russell, *The Lives of the Desert Fathers*, Oxford and Kalamazoo, 1981.

PG	*Patrologia Graeca*
P&J	Pelagius and John, *Verba Seniorum*, ed. Heribert Rosweyde, *Vitae Patrum*, Antwerp, 1615, Books V and VI, reprinted in Jacques-Paul Migne, *PL* 73:855–1022; trans. Benedicta Ward, *The Desert Fathers: Sayings of the Early Christian Monks*, London: Penguin, 2003.
PL	*Patrologia Latina*
PO	*Patrologia Orientalis*
PS	John Moschos, *Pratum Spirituale*, ed. Jacques-Paul Migne, *PG* 87:2851–3112; tr. John Wortley, *The Spiritual Meadow*, Kalamazoo, 1992, reprint 1996, 2001; tr. Jean Bouchet, *Fioretti des moines d'orient*, Paris, 2006.
ROC	*Revue de l'Orient chrétien*
SC	*Sources chrétiennes*
Synagogê	Paul Evergetinos, *Synagogê*, Venice, 1783; 6th edition, 4 vols. Athens, 1980.
VA	*Vita Antonii,* ed. and tr. G. J. M. Bartelink, *Athanase d'Alexandrie, Vie d'Antoine*, SC 400, Paris, 1994; Athanasius of Alexandria, *The Life of Antony, the Coptic Life and the Greek Life*, tr. Tim Vivian and A. N. Athanasakis, Cistercian, 2003.

Preface

Samuel Rubenson

The sayings of the Desert Fathers, known as the *Apophthegmata Patrum*, are among the most widely read and frequently quoted texts in the history of Christianity. Originating in late fourth-century Egyptian monasticism and enriched by later generations of monks, collections of sayings rapidly spread throughout the ancient Christian world and were soon translated into all the languages of the early medieval Christian world. In the pointed sayings and dialogues, as well as in short, often witty, anecdotes, the wisdom and the experiences of the monastic tradition are transmitted. The often drastic and exaggerated words and deeds of the monastic figures are fashioned to be remembered, if not memorized. In a form similar to proverbs and caricatures, the sayings are both educational and entertaining. Although depicted against the background of the desert in the language of late antiquity and clothed in monastic garb, the sayings have a timeless quality, reflecting people's hopes, efforts, failures, and successes in relation to each other and to God.

Although the sayings are sometimes used as reliable evidence for the daily life of fourth-century monks in the deserts of Egypt and are even regarded as representing their authentic words, they should rather be seen as vehicles for conveying a tradition of formative wisdom. The precise location and identity of such-and-such a teacher or his/her disciples are clearly secondary to the maxim, dialogue or parable. This is evident in the textual transmission, for the context of each saying often differs, while the essence remains unchanged. The absence of any larger narrative or of direct connections between the sayings has resulted in a fluid tradition with innumerable variants. There are collections ranging from a few dozens to thousands of sayings, in which selection and sequence varies *ad infinitum*. The extant manuscripts indicate that each collection of sayings has its own logic and purpose. Every manuscript is an edition based on what was available to the scribe and prescribed by the interests and needs of the readers for whom it was intended.[1]

It is thus not as primary sources for historical research, nor as archaeological remains to be puzzled over, that the sayings have come down to us. The collections preserved are rather the result of conscious efforts to preserve an understanding of how an ideal life (or rather, the true life) can be formed, through spiritual and mental training; how virtues can be cultivated and vices be uprooted. The purpose is formative, not informative; and the kind of formation proposed is more concerned with self-knowledge than knowledge of the world. Although the sayings were created and transmitted within the monastic tradition, they do not deal exclusively with monastic issues or details of monastic life. They deal with those fundamental human issues identified by Evagrius Ponticus as the eight fundamental 'thoughts' or passions: gluttony, lust, and avarice, resentment, wrath, and despair, vainglory and pride.[2] The sayings do not, however, transmit a specific teaching on these, but rather a wide variety of examples of how to and how *not* to deal with them. Far from promoting any rules or even any confidence in rules, the sayings are designed to provoke reaction, repentance and renewal. Rather than teaching one standard to live by, they present an almost infinite number of examples, leaving it to the reader to discern which examples speak most directly to his/her own striving.

On the surface the impression gained from reading the sayings may deceive, and has deceived much of modern historically oriented scholarship. We encounter a radical and harsh desert environment in which the elders appear as figures larger than life, demonstrating a lifestyle with little, if any, concern for bodily needs or even for bodily health. But, as recent scholarship has been able to show, the image is largely a literary construct.[3] Just as icons are not, and are not intended to be, photographic reproductions, but images for contemplation, so are the sayings objects to be used for self-formation. The early monastic movement was not a movement of poor and uneducated radical Christians who turned their back on society to defeat their own weaknesses and become divine. It was rather an attempt to develop an educational setting for the Christian tradition.[4] The sayings were shaped, collected, and organized to

---

[1] Guy, pp. 231–3.

[2] Evagrius, *Practicus* cc. 6–14, Eng. tr. Robert Sinkewicz, *Evagrius of Pontus: The Greek Ascetic Corpus*, Oxford, 2003, pp. 97–100.

[3] James Goehring, 'The Encroaching Desert: Literary Production and Ascetic Space in Early Christian Egypt', *JECS* 1 (1993), 281–96.

[4] Lillian Larsen, 'The Apophthegmata Patrum and the Classical Rhetorical Tradition', *Studia Patristica* 39 (2006), 409–16.

transmit a formative tradition of wisdom, deeply rooted in the ancient world and now filled with Biblical references.[5]

Our earliest written evidence of a set of monastic sayings is found in the writings of Evagrius Ponticus, a Cappadocian monk who settled in Egypt in the late fourth century and died in 399. Many of his writings are themselves in the form of a series of gnomic sayings, and at the end of one of his most important works, the *Practicus,* he underlines his teaching by a series of sayings.[6] This, however, is probably not the beginning of the sayings-tradition but rather an example of it. Here we see how ascetic teachers adapted models of teaching inherited from the classical schools to their own ends. Sayings attributed to wise men and set in dialogues or short stories had been in use at all levels of teaching.[7] A generation before Evagrius both Basil of Caesarea in his *Rules*, and Gregory of Nyssa in his biography of his sister, mention the replacement of material from the classical myths by proverbs and other Biblical texts for teaching young Christians. The rules of Pachomius attest, moreover, to an emphasis on using the Bible for elementary teaching that most probably reaches back to the first decades of the monastic tradition.

The Biblical texts could not, however, satisfy the need for teaching materials capable of transmitting the legacy of the first monastic generations to the rapidly growing monastic community in Egypt and abroad. The roots of our collections of sayings and of hagiographic tales too are to be found in that need. Although the context for the majority of sayings in the early collections is the monastic environment of Lower Egypt, our earliest evidence of their use comes from Palestine. There are good reasons for regarding the monastic communities of the Gaza region as instrumental in the shaping of the literary tradition of the sayings. Here there was a strong connection with Egypt, as a number of influential monks had an Egyptian background; there were also close connections to the educational and literary traditions of the city of Gaza.[8] A further consideration is that the ecclesiastical conflicts of the later fifth and early

---

[5] For the use of the Bible, see Per Rönnegård, *Threads and Images: The Use of Scripture in Apophthegmata Patrum*, Winona Lake, IN, 2010.

[6] Evagrios, *Practicus* cc. 91–100, Eng. tr. Sinkewicz, pp. 112–13. (See the appendix to the Introduction, below.)

[7] Lillian Larsen, 'On Learning a New Alphabet: The Sayings of the Desert Fathers and the Monostichs of Menander', *Studia Patristica* 55 (2013), 59–77.

[8] Lucien Regnault, 'Les apophthegmes en Palestine aux ve–vie siècles', *Irénikon* 54 (1981), 320–30 and Samuel Rubenson, 'The Egyptian Relations of Early Palestinian Monasticism', in *The Christian Heritage in the Holy Land*, ed. Anthony O'Mahoney, Göran Gunner and Kevork Hintlian, London, 1995, pp. 35–46.

sixth centuries made it important to manifest an adherence to the tradition of the fathers of monasticism in Egypt.

As far as we can discern, the literary tradition of sayings developed first in Greek and was only subsequently translated into Coptic and other languages. Our earliest evidence of Greek collections (except for the writings of Evagrius) is found in certain early sixth-century authors from Palestine. These do not indicate what kind of collection they refer to, but there are good reasons to think that the original form of the two main and closely interrelated Greek collections, the systematic collection (GS),[9] with the sayings organized in thematic chapters, and the alphabetic collection (G),[10] with its attached anonymous sayings (GN),[11] in which the sayings are organized alphabetically according to the names of the fathers to whom they are attributed, were made at the end of the fifth century.[12] But although these two collections, with all their variations, dominate the manuscript tradition, and are the only Greek collections edited thus far, there is ample evidence that there have also been numerous other collections transmitting sayings in Greek, collections not necessarily dependent on the two main strands.[13]

The first translations of sayings collections date back to the same time as the early references to the Greek collections. A Latin translation of the early systematic collection is in the manuscripts attributed to Pelagius and John, identified as Pelagius, bishop of Rome in the mid-sixth century, and his disciple John, and thus usually referred to as the collection of Pelagius and John (PJ).[14] This collection is of great importance because both the text and the earliest manuscripts containing it predate the earliest Greek manuscripts of the same collection. PJ has been the most prominent collection in the Latin tradition, but there are manuscripts containing several other Latin collections, all most probably made in the

[9] Ed. Jean-Claude Guy, *Les apophtegmes des pères: Collection systématique*, 3 vols., SC 387, 474 and 498, Paris: Cerf, 1993–2005.
[10] Ed. Jean-Baptiste Cotelier, *Ecclesiae Graecae monumenta*, vol. 1, Paris, 1677, pp. 338–712, reprinted in *PG* 65:71–440.
[11] Ed. John Wortley, *The Anonymous Sayings of the Desert Fathers: A Select Edition and Complete English Translation*, Cambridge, 2013.
[12] Jean-Claude Guy, 'Introduction', *Les apophthegmes des pères I–IX*, SC 387, Paris: Cerf, 1993, pp. 79–84.
[13] Chiara Faraggiana di Sarzana, '*Apophthegmata Patrum*: Some Crucial Points of Their Textual Transmission and the Problem of a Critical Edition', in *Historica, Theologica et Philosophica, Critica et Philologica*, ed. E. A. Livingstone, *Studia Patristica* 29, Leuven: Peeters, 1997, pp. 455–67 and Britt Dahlman, 'The Collectio Scorialensis Parva: An Alphabetical Collection of Old Apophthegmatic and Hagiographic Material', in *Early Monasticism and Classical Paideia*, ed. S. Rubenson, *Studia Patristica* 55.3, Leuven: Peeters, 2013, pp. 23–33.
[14] Ed. Heribert Rosweyde, *Vitae Patrum V–VI*, Antwerpen, 1615, reprinted in *PL* 73:851–1024, 1060–2.

sixth century. Three of these, the collection of Martin of Braga (MD), that of Paschasius of Dumium (PA), and the one called *Commonitiones Sanctorum Patrum* (CSP), have been edited,[15] the fourth, preserved in a Darmstadt manuscript (LD) remains unedited.[16] Although strongly interrelated in content, all four present independent selections and organizations of the material.

The earliest manuscripts preserving the sayings are, however, a number of Syriac manuscripts dated to the 530s. These testify to one or more translations into Syriac in the same period. Although they contain more or less the same material as the early Greek and Latin collections, the Syriac manuscripts are clearly independent in their organization of their material. Thus they probably depend on Greek collections that predate the creation of the systematic and alphabetic collections.[17] These early Syriac collections were replaced in the seventh century by a huge collection of sayings edited by Paul Bedjan (Be) and E. A. W. Budge (Bu).[18]

Of the systematic collection known in both its Greek and its Latin form, there is also a Coptic translation (Ch), most probably from the sixth or seventh century. The text is unfortunately still unknown except for minor fragments, only identified as preserved in one manuscript – and this has ended up divided between a number of libraries.[19] Although mostly following the same text and sequence as the Greek and Latin, it includes a number of sayings not attested in any other known collection. A number of sayings attributed to St. Antony and St. Macarius are,

[15] MD–Barlow, ed. Claude W. Barlow, *Martini Episcopi Bracarensis Opera Omnia*, Papers and Monographs of the American Academy in Rome 12, New Haven: Yale University Press, 1950. CSP–Freire, ed. José Geraldes Freire, *Commonitiones Sanctorum Patrum. Uma nova colecção de Apotegmas, Estudio filológico, Texto critico*, Coimbra, 1974. PA–Freire, ed. José Geraldes Freire, *A versão latina por Pascásio de Dume dos Apophthegmata Patrum*, vols. 1–2, Coimbra, 1971.

[16] The manuscript was transcribed by the late René Draguet, but never published. It has now been thoroughly revised and published by Lund University as Darmstadt_1953 on http://monastica .ht.lu.se.

[17] Bo Holmberg, 'The Syriac Collection of *Apophthegmata Patrum* in MS Sin. syr. 46', in *Early Monasticism and Classical Paideia*, ed. S. Rubenson, *Studia Patristica* 55.3, Leuven: Peeters, 2013, pp. 35–57.

[18] Ed. Paul Bedjan, *Acta martyrum et sanctorum Syriace*, vol. 7, Paris, 1897 (repr. Hildesheim, 1968) and E. A. W. Budge, *The Book of Paradise, Being the Histories and Sayings of the Monks and Ascetics of the Egyptian Desert by Palladius, Hieronymus and Others. The Syriac Texts, According to the Recension of 'Anân-Îshô' of Bêth 'Âbhê*, Edited with an English Translation, vols. 1–2, London, 1904.

[19] Ed. Marius Chaine, *Le manuscrit de la version copte en dialecte sahidique des 'Apophthegmata Patrum'*, Bibliothèque d'études coptes 6, Cairo, 1960 and Alla I. Elanskaya, *The Literary Coptic Manuscripts in the A.S. Pushkin State Fine Arts Museum in Moscow*, Supplements to *Vigiliae Christianae*: Texts and Studies of Early Christian Life and Language, vol. 18, Leiden, 1994, pp. 11–40.

moreover, found in a Bohairic collection of material concerning these two central figures of the early monastic tradition.[20]

In addition to the very early translations into Latin, Syriac, and Coptic, we do also have evidence for an early translation into Palestinian Aramaic.[21] Collections of sayings were subsequently translated into Sogdian, Georgian, Armenian, Arabic, and Ethiopic, as well into Church Slavonic. Of the Sogdian version only fragments have come to light,[22] but for the others there is a substantial manuscript tradition and thus evidence for a wider use of the sayings. In Georgian both an alphabetic-anonymous collection (IA and IN) and a systematic collection (IS) have been critically edited from a number of manuscripts, in both cases similar to and clearly dependent on the Greek equivalents, but with significant variants.[23] In Armenian two different translations of a collection have been published (HSa and HSb),[24] the earlier one being significantly shorter than the second, but no studies based on the numerous manuscripts preserved have yet been undertaken.

The sayings also enjoyed a considerable popularity in Arabic, but until now only one Arabic manuscript has been studied in detail.[25] Studies on a number of Arabic manuscripts have shown that the transmission is very complex, not least due to the fact that the Arabic versions were made on the basis of Greek as well as Syriac and probably Coptic models.[26] In Ethiopic the sayings are preserved in a number of collections, often

---

[20] Ed. Émile Amélineau, *Monuments pour servir à l'histoire de l'Égypte chrétienne aux IVe et Ve siècles*, Mémoires de la mission archéologique française au Caire IV.2, Paris, 1895.

[21] The Palestinian Aramaic fragments have been edited by P. Kokowzoff, *Nouveaux fragments syro-palestiniens de la Bibliothèque Impériale publique de Saint-Pétersbourg*, Saint Petersburg, 1906 and H. Duensing, *Christlich-palästinensisch-aramäische Texte und Fragmente nebst einer Abhandlung über den Wert der palästinensischen Septuaginta*, Göttingen, 1906, pp. 38–41, as well as *Neu christlich-palästinensisch-aramäische Fragmente* (Nachrichten der Akademie der Wissenschaften in Göttingen, Philologisch-historische Klasse, Jahrgang 1944 no. 9), Göttingen, 1944, pp. 223–7.

[22] Ed. Nicholas Sims-Williams, *The Christian Sogdian Manuscript C2*, Schriften zur Geschichte und Kultur des Alten Orients, Berliner Turfantexte 12, Berlin: Akademie-Verlag, 1985.

[23] Ed. Manana Dvali, *Šua saukunet'a novelebis jveli k'art'uli t'argmanebi*, vol. 1, *K'art'uli paterikis ert'izveli redak'c'iis Ek'vt'ime At'onelis t'argmani XI s. xelnaceris mixedvit'*, Tbilisi, 1966 and vol. 2, *Abanur-anonimuri paterikebi*, Tbilisi, 1974.

[24] Nerses Sarkisian, *Vark' srbots' harants' ew k'aghak'avarut'iwnk' nots'in [Lives and Deeds of the Holy Fathers]*, vols. 1–2, Matenagrut'iwnk' naxneats' series, Venice, 1855.

[25] Ed. Jean Mansour, *Homélies et légendes religieuses: un florilège arabe chrétien du xe siècle (Ms. Strasbourg 4225)*, PhD dissertation, Strasbourg, 1972. A new edition of the Copto-Arabic version based on manuscripts held at the Monastery of St. Macarius was published by the monastery in 2013.

[26] Jean-Marie Sauget, *Une traduction arabe de la collection Apophthegmata Patrum de 'Enānīšō': Étude du ms. Paris arabe 253 et des témoins parallèles*, CSCO 495, Leuven, 1987.

mixed with material from other early monastic literature such as the *Historia Monachorum in Aegypto* and John Moschos' *Pratum spirituale.*[27] No comprehensive study of their transmission or models has, however, yet been done.

Since each individual saying is a verbal image of its own, sayings can be and have been combined freely. In the manuscript traditions in the various languages we thus find a very high degree of fluidity in transmission. The selection of sayings as well as their sequence varies from manuscript to manuscript, the variations indicating both what was available and what was of interest to the scribe of the manuscript. Individual sayings are often divided or combined in various ways, sometimes with change or even loss of attribution. Sayings are a living tradition that in every generation has been adapted to the needs of the people who used and transmitted them. Thus the manuscripts cannot provide a basis on which to reconstruct the original text or the order of the sayings; and they certainly cannot be organized into a simple stemma. What they do provide and what we are able to study is a variety of preserved glimpses of a rich tradition at diverse stages in its process of transmission.[28]

---

[27] Four Ethiopic collections have been published by Victor Arras, *Collectio Monastica*, CSCO 238–39, Script. Aeth. 45–46, Lovanii: Peeters, 1963; *Patericon Aethiopice*, CSCO 277–8, Script. Aeth. 53–54, Lovanii: Peeters, 1967; *Asceticon Aethipicae*, CSCO 459, Script Aeth. 78, Lovanii: Peeters, 1984; and *Geronticon*, CSCO 477, Script. Aeth. 80, Lovanii: Peeters, 1986.

[28] For a dynamic research tool for the *Apophthegmata Patrum*, see http://monastica.ht.lu.se.

CHAPTER I

Introduction

Outstanding among the scholars who advanced apophthegmatic studies in the second half of the last century was Dom Lucien Regnault (1924–2003), monk of Solesmes. The excellent translation of the major Greek collection of apophthegms that he and his colleagues published as *Les sentences des pères du désert* opened that corpus to a vast audience, while his *Table de la collection alphabético-anonyme* with its exhaustive indices[1] furnishes scholars with invaluable tools for further investigation. But, as Regnault was well aware, widely though the compilers of the major collection cast their nets, they did not succeed in catching all the extant *apophthegmata*. Nor of course could they have included sayings that were generated after their time. He and his colleagues at Solesmes therefore diligently applied themselves to identifying and translating items found in other collections, in other languages, that do not appear (or only appear in a very different form) in the major Greek collections. The fruits of their labours appeared as *Les sentences des pères du désert, nouveau recueil*, Solesmes, 1970, 2nd ed., 1977.

The present volume is not merely an attempt to make Dom Lucien's work available to English readers; there are a number of important differences. Thus (e.g.) the first section of *nouveau recueil*, 'Apophtegmes traduits du grec (Ms Coislin 126)' (pp. 13–162) has been wholly omitted here. That section provided translations of items in *APanon* not then available elsewhere. As both the Greek text and an English translation of the whole of *APanon* have now been published,[2] it would have been redundant to reproduce those items here.

Dom Lucien further developed the third section of his book, 'Apophtegmes traduits du Latin', in a subsequent publication, *Les*

---

[1] *Les sentences des pères du désert, troisième recueil et tables,* Solesmes, 1976, 201–308, 309–81.
[2] John Wortley, *The Anonymous Sayings of the Desert Fathers*, Cambridge, 2013.

sentences des pères du désert, troisième recueil et tables, Solesmes, 1976 (pp. 123–38), by taking advantage of José Geraldes Freire, *A Versão Latina por Pascásio de Dume dos Apophthegmata Patrum,* 2 vols., Coimbra, 1971. We have also profited from the same author's *Commonitiones Sanctorum Patrum,* 2nd ed., Coimbra, 2010, and brought Dom Lucien's two parts together.

However, the most important difference is that, whereas in several cases the monks of Solesmes were obliged to make their translations from translations of the original (usually into Latin), the translations appearing in the following pages have been made directly from the languages in which they have been preserved by persons familiar with those languages, working from the best available texts.

It will readily be appreciated that there is an obvious (and lamentable) omission in the list of languages from which translations have been made: Arabic. While it is well known that a considerable amount of apophthegmatic material has been preserved in Arabic, nobody has yet had the *courage* to determine how much of that material has not been preserved in any other language. That is a task which must await a future generation.

To facilitate reference to the sayings in this volume, the contents of each section have been numbered successively and provided with a letter identifying the language of the section, e.g. L24 is item 24 in the Latin section, S10 item 10 in the Syriac section, etc. (though see the note on p. 146 regarding numbering in the Ethiopic section).

The expression 'sayings (apophthegms) of the Desert Fathers' is a little misleading; 'sayings *and tales*' (or 'and anecdotes') would be more appropriate, and it would be good to add: 'of the monks associated with Antony the Great (ca. 260–356) and with the Nitrian Desert' (located in the northwest of what is today Egypt). For there was another and probably even more numerous monastic movement associated with Pachomius (290–346), further south, in the Thebaid, whose literary debris is negligible in comparison with the huge legacy of tales and sayings associated with the northern community.

The origins of the tales and sayings are obscure. Athanasius' *Life of Antony* [*VA*], written before 380, includes about 20 brief anecdotes about the saint: these are the earliest monastic tales on record. About half of them record visions seen by Anthony, the Ascent of Amoun (c. 60) being the best known. In many of the visions, demons appear in various guises, e.g. the Great Giant impeding souls that would fly upward (c. 66, see also *HL* 21). Most of the remaining anecdotes are miracle stories, usually about healings, but two at least are examples of Anthony's ability to be aware of what was happening elsewhere, or of what was about to happen (cc. 59, 62). There are also a few tales about the man himself: his aversion to cleanliness, how he ate, what he wore, how he created a garden to feed himself (cc. 45, 47, and 50). There are however no *sayings* in *VA*, which is odd considering how many sayings would eventually be attributed to Antony.

The earliest mention of sayings is by Evagrius Ponticus [*ob* 399]. At the end of *Practicus* [cc. 91–100] he writes: 'It is necessary also to interrogate the paths of the monks who have travelled rightly before us and set ourselves right by reference to them. There is much for us to discover that they spoke and did well' (ῥηθέντα τε καὶ πραχθέντα καλῶς, i.e. sayings and tales: theory and practice.) There follow nine sayings, one attributed to Antony, two to Macarius the Egyptian.[3]

But while Evagrius wrote in Greek, it is beyond doubt that the earliest monks spoke Coptic and that many of them knew no other language (including Antony himself). They were not sophisticated people, fellahin for the most part, yet their fame attracted visitors, two of whom left accounts of their experiences. One was an anonymous monk of the Mount of Olives who wrote A History of the Monks in Egypt [HME] recounting the experiences of himself and his brothers in the winter of 394–395. The other was Palladius, Bishop of Helenopolis, who had considerable experience of being a monk in Egypt. His exquisite Lausiac History [HL], written 419–420, is the most sophisticated of the extant monastic writings. Both works are in Greek, and both record a wealth of anecdotal material, but neither provides evidence of any sayings of the fathers.

By the end of the fifth century, however, there existed the comprehensive record of tales and sayings (apparently not the first of its kind)[4] the

---

[3] See the appendix to this Introduction.
[4] 'Those who have diligently labored on their account have set down in writing a few of their righteous sayings and deeds [. . .] Most have set out these sayings and righteous deeds of the holy elders in narrative form from time to time, in simple and uncontrived language, with only this one end in view: to benefit many [folk].' Prologue to *APalph, PG* 65:73B–C.

first part of which is known as the 'Alphabetic' collection [*APalph*].⁵ This is thought to have been compiled by members of a group of monks who had fled increasingly dangerous conditions in the Nitrian desert and religious controversy in Egypt. Taking refuge near Gaza, they sought to fix in writing the oral tradition they cherished of what the fathers of old had done and said. Whether they retained that tradition in Coptic or in Greek (or a little of both) we may never know: what is certain is that they set it down in Greek; and that they did it in an orderly fashion. The first part of their work is called 'Alphabetic' because its ca. 1000 items⁶ are arranged in more or less [Greek] alphabetical order, by reference to the ca. 125 fathers⁷ who allegedly uttered the sayings or are mentioned in the tales, ranging from Abba Antony to Abba Ôr (A–Ω).

However, by no means all the material they had collected lent itself to such a distribution: hence the compilers proceeded to assemble what is now known as the 'Anonymous' part of the collection [*APanon*], as the *Prologue* to the first part explains:

> Since there are also other words and deeds [λόγοι ... καὶ πράξεις] of the holy elders that do not indicate the names of those who spoke or performed them, we have set them out under headings [ἐν κεφαλαίοις] after the completion of the alphabetic sequence. But, after searching out and looking into many books, we set down as much as we were able to find at the end of the headings.⁸

There is little doubt that subsequent copyists added other material, some of which cannot be dated any earlier than the seventh century.

While a published version of *APalph* has been available since 1647, *APanon* remained virtually unknown until, at the beginning of the last century, François Nau transcribed the first 400 items of that collection from the venerable Cod. Paris. Coislin. 126 and published them, together with a partial French translation.⁹ Subsequently Dom Lucien Regnault

---

⁵ One version of the text of *APalph* has been available since the seventeenth century in the well-known edition with Latin translation by Jean-Baptiste Cotelier, *Monumenta Ecclesiae Graecae*, vol. 1, Paris, 1647, reprinted in *PG* 65:71–440, tr. Lucien Regnault (with Guy's supplement), *Les sentences des pères du désert: Collection alphabétique*, Solesmes, 1981; tr. Benedicta Ward, *The Sayings of the Desert Fathers: The Alphabetical Collection*, Kalamazoo, 1984; tr. John Wortley, *Give Me a Word: The Alphabetical Sayings of the Desert Fathers*, Yonkers, NY, 2014 (which includes Guy's additions).

⁶ There are 948 items in the edition; a further 53 were identified as such and printed in Guy.

⁷ Three of the 'fathers' are female: Theodora, Sarah, and Syncletica.

⁸ Such is the conclusion of Guy, pp. 182–4. Prologue to *APalph*, *PG* 65:73B–C.

⁹ *ROC* 12 (1907)–18 (1913), passim.

published a translation of the entire collection, apparently working directly from five manuscripts of the text.[10] Recently an edition of the complete Greek text with English translation has appeared[11] containing 765 items.

There is no reason to imagine that the compilation of the Alphabetic-Anonymous collection brought the oral tradition to a halt. Each manuscript represents the oral tradition at a different stage of its development. In fact, there is good reason to suppose that the oral tradition continued to grow and to diversify as the monastic movement spread beyond Egypt (which it did very rapidly) and as people speaking different languages visited and settled in the Wadi Natrun, where, in due course, monasteries were established (e.g.) for Ethiopians (Saint Elijah's) Armenians and Syrians (Deir el-Surian).[12]

One outstanding visitor to the Nitrian Desert was Rufinus of Aquileia [340–410], who not only became acquainted with some of the desert fathers (including Macarius the Egyptian, the founder of Scete) but also translated a large amount of monastic lore into Latin. There is no doubt that others did likewise, for many of the extant manuscripts of sayings in other languages show clear evidence of a Greek original. But they also contain many items not yet known to exist in any Greek manuscript, most of them bearing a striking resemblance to the material already known in Greek. Thus (e.g.) many sayings are attributed to the known pioneers of the monastic movement; many are references to Scete, and an equally large proportion of items is associated with the enigmatic Abba Poemen. And these 'additional' items are not few in number; there are almost 600 of them in this volume; others will probably come to light in due course. Already these items constitute about one quarter of the totality of the known apophthegms, and (as the reader will quickly discover) they are in no way inferior to ones he/she already knows. The same questions of authenticity arise with these as with any other sayings, but the truly important questions do not concern who really said what and so forth. They ask whether these sayings add anything to our understanding of the remarkable phenomenon we call the rise of Christian monasticism. Those who have worked on these new translations of the sayings that

---

[10] *Les sentences des pères du désert, série des anonymes*, Solesmes–Bellefontaine, 1985, mainly from Cod. Sinaï 448 and Cod. Paris. Coislin. 126.

[11] John Wortley, *The Anonymous Sayings of the Desert Fathers*, Cambridge, 2013.

[12] Mario Cappozzo, *I monasteri del deserto di Sceti*, Todi, 2009, passim.

Dom Lucien and his colleagues patiently isolated clearly believe that they
do. They are offered here in the hope that they will somewhat enhance
the English reader's appreciation of the Wisdom of the Desert Fathers.

Appendix to the Introduction

The earliest known sayings of the Christian monastic tradition are found
at the end of the work called *Practicus* [Λόγος πρᾱκτικός], written by
Evagrius Ponticus, who died in AD 399, Greek text ed. A & C.
Guillaumont, *Évagre le Pontique, Traité Pratique*, SC 171, Paris, Cerf,
1971, pp. 482–715, tr. here John Wortley.

Sayings of the Holy Monks

[**91**] It is imperative that we learn from the journeys of those who have
travelled the strait and narrow way before us, [Mt 7:14] keeping ourselves
on the right path by their example. There is much to be learned from the
excellent things they said and accomplished; among such things one of
those people says this: that when it is combined with love, a rather dry
and restrained diet brings a monk fairly quickly into the haven of *apatheia*.

The same [elder] released one of the brothers who was being troubled by
nocturnal visions by commanding him to wait upon the sick while fasting. When asked, he said that passions like those are suppressed by
mercy.

[**92**] One of the learned men of those days approached Antony the righteous and said: 'Father, how do you survive without the comfort of
books?' 'O philosopher', he said, 'my book is the nature of [all] that exists
and it is always there whenever I wish to read the word of God.'[13]

[**93**] Macarius the Egyptian, that elder who was a choice vessel, asked me:
'Why is it that we diminish the soul's ability to remember by bearing
grudges against men – but remain unharmed when we bear grudges
against demons?' At a loss how to answer, I sought to learn the explanation. 'It is because the first is contrary to nature', he said, 'whereas the
second is in accordance with the nature of wrath.'

[13] Cf. *VA* 3.7.

[94] I visited the holy father Macarius in the heat of the midday sun. As I was burning with thirst I asked for some water to drink. 'Be satisfied with shade', he said, 'for there are many on the road now or sailing along who are deprived of [shade].' Then, when I had recited some sayings about self-control, he said: 'Be of good courage my son; for all of 20 years I never took my fill of bread, of water or of sleep. I used to eat my bread by weight and drink water that was measured out. I used to snatch just a little sleep leaning my person against the walls.'

[95] One of the monks was apprised of the death of [his] father. To the person who reported this he said: 'Stop your blaspheming: my father is immortal.'

[96] One of the brothers enquired of one of the elders whether he would allow him to eat with his mother and his sisters when he visited [their] home. 'Eat not with woman', he said.

[97] One of the brothers was in possession of a copy of the Gospels [and nothing else]. This he sold and gave the proceeds to feed the hungry, making a memorable declaration: 'I have sold the text that tells me: "Sell your possessions and give to the poor".'[14]

[98] There is an island adjacent to Alexandria, in the northern part of the lake known as Maria [sc. Mareotis]. On it there lives a monk, a member of the gnostic sect, a well tried and tested monk who declares that everything done by monks is done for five reasons: for God, because it is natural or customary or necessary, or because it constitutes physical labour.

The same [monk] also said that virtue is one by nature but that it takes different forms in the powers of the soul. And sunlight is without form (he said) but is given form by the windows through which it shines.

[99] Then another of the monks said: 'I restrain [my] pleasures in order to restrain pretexts for anger, for I know that [anger] is always fighting for pleasures: that it troubles my mind, chasing away knowledge.'

One of the elders said that love does not countenance the hoarding of food or of money.

[14] Mt 19:21, cf. *APanon* 392, *APsys* 6.6.

The same elder said: 'I am not aware of having been taken in twice by demons.'

[100] It is impossible to love all the brothers equally, but it *is* possible to encounter them all dispassionately [*apathôs*], free of grudge-bearing and hatred.

Priests are to be loved next after the Lord for they cleanse us through the holy mysteries and they pray for us.

Our elders are to be revered like the angels for it is they who anoint us for the combat and heal the bites of wild beasts.

CHAPTER 2

Sayings Preserved in Greek

Translated by John Wortley

Source: Paul Euergetinos, *A Collection [Συναγωγή] of the inspired sayings of the godly and holy fathers gathered together from the entirety of divinely inspired literature appropriately and agreeably set forth by the most holy monk, PAUL, known as Euergetinos, the founder of the Monastery of the supremely holy Mother of God, she who does good deeds [εὐεργέτης]; taken from the library of the Imperial and Patriarchal Monastery known as Koutloumousiou* [. . .], Venice, 1783, 'παρὰ Ἀντωνίῳ Βόρτολι'.
Fifth edition: Athens, 4 vols., 1957–1966; sixth edition: Athens, 4 vols., 1980.

Before he died in 1054, Paul, founder and *higoumen* of the Monastery of Our Lady the Doer-of-good-deeds (*Euergetês*) at Constantinople, composed (or caused to be composed) a compendium of monastic lore that came to be known as the *Euergetinon* but is now more commonly referred to as the *Synagôgê*. The work consists of 200 *hypotheses* or propositions, each supported by a wealth of citations from a fairly restricted number of monastic works. The collection was edited from a number of Athonite manuscripts by Hieromonk Paul, Macarius of Corinth, and Nicodemus the Hagiorite, and published at Venice in 1783.

While most of the citations are identified, some are simply said to be found 'in the *geronticon*' [ἐν τῷ γεροντικῷ], indicating a collection of the tales and sayings of the [desert] elders. Many such collections exist in the manuscripts, varying in content and all diverging from each other to a greater or lesser degree. Not many of them have been published; some have yet to be recognized; and none has been identified as the *geronticon* of the Evergetes monastery. But this can be said of it with some certainty: that it contained a considerable number of items that are not found in any of the published collections. Dom Lucien was able to identify about 85 such pieces, some of which have since been published. The rest are here translated from the (by no means reliable) sixth edition (four vols., Athens, 1980) which includes a modern Greek translation. As there is no guarantee that the Euergetinos *geronticon* has survived, Paul's *Synagôgê* may well be the only witness to these texts.

N.B. The numbering of the items varies in recent editions; the numbering of the two most recent volumes is provided below.

Paul Euergetinos, *Synagôgê*

[G1] Abba Moses said to a brother: 'Brother, come to obedience in the truth where there is humility, where there is strength, where there is joy, where there is patient endurance, where there is long suffering, where there is brotherly love, where there is sorrow for sin, where there is love. For he who obeys well fulfils all the commandments of God.'
1.19.5 / 1.19.2.4

[G2] Abba Moses said: 'A monk who is under [the supervision] of a spiritual father yet does not possess obedience and humility, who fasts or does anything else of his own accord in order to appear righteous: such a person neither acquires a single virtue nor does he even know what it is to be a monk.'
1.20.9 / 1.20.3.6

[G3] A brother was embattled by the demon of *porneia* for a long time. He struggled hard but was unable to rid himself of it. One day when he was standing at the *synaxis* he felt himself being disturbed by the passion as before. He determined to overcome the insulting treatment of the demon and to ask the brothers to pray for him, that he might find some relief from the passion. Despising all shame, he stripped himself before all the brothers and placarded the activity of Satan saying: 'Pray for me, fathers and brothers, for it is now 14 years that I have been embattled like this' – and the battle immediately receded from him through the humility which he had demonstrated.
1.20.21 / 1.20.8.1

[G4] The disciples of Abba Eulogius recounted: 'When the elder sent us to Alexandria to sell [our] handiwork he gave us instructions not to stay more than three days. "If you stay more than three days", he said, "I am not responsible for your sins." We asked him how it is that monks in cities and villages, rubbing shoulders night and day with worldlings, are not damaged. "Believe me, my sons", he said; "after I became a monk, for 38 years I did not leave Scete. After that I went to Alexandria, to Pope Eusebius, with Abba Daniel for some necessity. Going into the city we saw many monks. I saw some of them being pecked by crows, some with naked women embracing them, speaking in their ears; others being beaten and smeared with human excrement by naked male youths. I saw some people with swords cutting up human flesh and giving it to the monks to eat. And I realized that each of the monks, whatever passion he had stumbled into, had that sort of demons escorting him and speaking to him in his mind. For that reason, my brothers, I do not want you ever to spend time in the city, lest you be molested by such *logismoi* – or rather by such demons".'

1.22.6 / 1.22.4.3

[G5] Seven brothers once came to Abba Macarius from Alexandria to put him to the test. 'Tell us father: how might we be saved?' they said. With a sigh the elder said: 'Brothers, each one of us knows how he is to be saved but we do not want to be saved.' But they said to him: 'We very much want to be saved but our evil *logismoi* do not let us; so what are we to do?' The elder answered them: 'If you are monks why are you going around with worldlings or approaching where there is a worldling? They are deceiving themselves, those who have renounced the world and have put on the holy habit but are [living] among worldlings. All their labour is in vain and they are far removed from the fear of God. They acquire nothing from worldlings other than physical repose; fear of God cannot dwell where there is physical repose, especially in a monk.

'A monk is deliberately called *monk* because he is speaking with God night and day and thinks only of what is God's, having nothing on the earth. But the monk who lives with worldlings or sometimes spends more than one or at the most two days with them – and that because of pressing need and the fact that he cannot live any other way, that is, because of selling his handiwork and purchasing his necessities – [he should be] in a hurry to return and then consciously apologize to God for the one or two days he spent in the world to supply his natural needs.[1]

---

[1] There is no main verb in this sentence in Greek.

'He is not really a monk who acts otherwise and is in frequent contact with wordlings without any compelling reason or wastes time with them. Nor will he ever reap any benefit, but rather shall acquire this from his dallying with worldlings: at first when he approaches them he holds his tongue, fasts and humbles himself. That is, until he becomes known and his reputation spreads – that so-and-so the monk is a servant of God. Then right away Satan prompts the worldlings to bring him everything he needs: wine, gold and all sorts of things, saying about him: "A saint, a saint!" On hearing the word *saint* the humble [monk] becomes puffed up and sits down with them, eating, drinking and taking repose. When he is standing up to sing the psalms he raises his voice so the worldlings will say: "So-and-so the monk is singing and keeping watch" – and will praise him. He is lifted up and exalted even more by their praise – and then humility departs from him altogether.

'Then if anybody says a slighting word to him, he replies even more slightingly and in this way his temper (helped along by vainglory) increases within him; desire is kindled more fervently in him as he continually sees women and children and hears worldly discourse. Thus he commits adultery every day, unaware that "Everyone who looks on a woman and desires her has committed adultery with her already in his heart". [Mt 5:28]

'Then, for his own sake and for the needs of those who come visiting, he undertakes to lay his hands on what he needs for a year; this for the greater refreshment, of course, of those who come, deriving gold and silver from this. He makes no end of adding to his own evils until the demons completely make a fool of him, having distanced him from God and thrown him to destruction over the precipice of loving money, "For the love of money is the root of all evil" the Apostle said [1 Tim 6:10] and as high as the heaven is from the earth, so far is a money-loving monk from the glory of God. There is no evil beyond the evil of a money-loving monk.

'A monk who entertains worldly contacts craves the immediate prayers of several holy fathers in the hope that they will be able to be some little benefit to him. But who will be of assistance to one who is throwing himself into death? Do we not hear the Apostle John saying: "Love not the world neither the things that are in the world. If one love the world the love of God is not in him"? [1 Jn 2:15] And James the [Lord's] brother declaring: "If someone seems to be a friend of the world, he becomes an enemy of God", [Jas 4:4] for friendship with the world is enmity with God? [cf. Rom 8:7]

'Let us fly from the world as one flees from a serpent, brothers. He who is bitten by a serpent either dies or only just recovers. It is to our advantage to have one battle, not many and innumerable battles, on our hands. Tell me, brothers, where did our fathers acquire their virtues: in the world or in the desert? Clearly, in the desert, untrod by worldlings. And we, if we are in the world, how shall we be able to acquire virtue? If we do not hunger and thirst and shiver; if we be not far from the material [delights] of the world and become dead to every desire of the flesh, how shall we live in the spirit? How shall we attain the Kingdom of Heaven? If the soldier does not fight and conquer and then get money he is not worthy of honour. If we are eating and drinking, living among the world-lings we used to be with before, how then shall we be made worthy of the Kingdom of Heaven?

'The monk who has gold or silver or material objects in his possession does not believe that God is able to sustain him: the God who feeds the wild beasts and the creatures in the sea. If he cannot provide us with bread, neither can he give us his Kingdom, so what are we labouring for? Tell me, brothers: is it gold and silver that the angels in heaven heap up, or the glory of God? And we, did we renounce the world to collect money and material goods again, or to become angels? Are you not aware that the rank [of angels] which fell from heaven is being replaced from among monks? That is proclaimed by our habit, which everybody calls *angelic*.'
1.22.6 / 1.22.10.1

[G6] An elder said: 'He who has sinned against God ought to remove himself from every human contact until he is convinced that God has become his friend, for the love of men obstructs us from the love of God.'
1.22.14 / 1.22.10.3

[G7] An elder said: 'Just as a dead person in a city neither hears the voice of those who are there nor perceives anything of what goes on there, but is removed to another place where the voices and rowdiness of the city do not penetrate, so the monk when he renounces [the world] and transfers himself to the monastic life ought to become dead to all attachment to the world and to the distraction and toil of the vain and soul-destroying life, becoming distant from them. For if he depart not from his home-land after renouncing [the world] but is in the midst of the former dis-turbances, such a person is like a corpse lying in a house and stinking, from which they all run far away who smell it.'
1.22.15 / 1.22.10.4

[G8] The same [elder] said: 'Just as unsalted meat goes bad for lack of salt and gives off a stench so that all who come by turn their eyes away from the bad odour, then worms are produced in it, crawling and burrowing into it while eating it; but if salt be put on it, the worms are eliminated and the bad odour is suppressed (for the nature of the salt causes the disappearance of both), so too does the monk go bad who devotes himself to earthly concerns and external distractions; who does not maintain *hêsychia* in his monastery nor fortify himself with the fear of God in order not to become relaxed through carelessness; who neither alerts himself by meditating on death and its attendant punishments nor strengthens his heart by prayer and vigils – [all of which activities] engender spiritual salt. Such a monk is rotten and is filled with the strong stench of unclean and wicked *logismoi* to the extent that the face of God is turned away from him; and the chosen angels, disgusted at the impurity of such a soul, distance themselves from it. Then the spiritual worms, the powers of darkness, ever rejoicing in such bad odours, burrow into [that soul] walking about there and feeding [on it], making pleasant food of the filthy and unclean *logismoi* and actions through which the wretched [soul] is destroyed and runs to perdition. But if the monk be aware that he is in such danger and cast aside the exterior distractions, committing himself entirely to God and putting his entire hope in him; if he change all his concern and occupation into pleasing [God]; then, not long after, God will send him the spiritual salt, the good and people-loving Spirit. At his coming all the passions and the demons who work in and through them immediately vanish and disappear like smoke.
1.22.16 / 1.22.10.5, cf. *APanon* 733

[G9] An elder said: 'One must run away from every worker of iniquity, be it a friend or a relative or one of priestly or princely dignity. Keeping our distance from the workers of iniquity bestows on us friendship with God and access to him.'
1.23.2 / 1.23.1.2

[G10] The same [elder] said: 'It is not advantageous to have close contact with the lawless in church, in a market place, in a council, or in any other situation. Rather should one totally disassociate himself from their company for every lawless one deserves to be rejected [as] a candidate for eternal punishment.'
1.23.3 / 1.23.1.3

[**G11**] An elder said: 'A monk who gives himself again to the distraction and hardship of this wretched life, to giving and receiving, once he has renounced the world, [such a monk] is like an indigent pauper lacking even the food he needs. Too idle to find the wherewithal to feed and clothe himself, he abandons himself to sleep and, in a dream, he sees himself as a rich man who had taken off his filthy clothes and put on gorgeous ones. Then he awakes from this joyful experience and finds he is empty-handed. The monk who is not vigilant is like that too, exhausting his days in distractions, mocked by *logismoi* and exhausted by demons who make a fool of him by suggesting that his distraction and hardship are from God and that he will have his reward on this account. When the time comes for his soul to be separated from his body such a monk will find himself indigent and impoverished, devoid of all virtue. Then will he realize how many good things being vigilant and paying attention to oneself provide: how much punishment the distractions of life bring about.'
1.24.4 / 1.24.2.3

[**G12**] An elder said: 'It is better to live with three who fear the Lord than with 10,000 who have no fear of God. For in the last days scarcely a few in 100 of those who live in *coenobia* will be found being saved and I do not know whether any will be found among 50. For all will turn aside in their love of dining and gluttony, their love of power and love of money. Hence: "Many are called but few are chosen".' [Mt 22:14]
1.25.2 / 1.25.1.2

[**G13**] The same [elder] said: 'If you are staying somewhere and you see some folk living comfortably, do not have anything to do with them. But if there be another person who is poor, have to do with him as long as he has no bread and you shall experience repose.'
1.25.3 / 1.25.1.3

[**G14**] A young man who wished to renounce the world went off into the desert. Seeing a tower, or rather a cell built in the form of a tower, he said to himself: 'Whoever I find in the tower, I will serve him until death.' He arrived and knocked. Out there came an elder, a monk who said to him: 'What do you want?' 'I came for the purpose of prayer', he replied. Taking him and entertaining him, the elder said to him: 'Have you nothing to do anywhere else?' He said: 'No; this is where I want to stay', and when the elder heard this, he left him: for the elder had fallen into *porneia*; he had the woman there with him. So he said to the brother: 'If you want to reap any benefit, get yourself into a monastery, for I have a woman.' The brother said: 'It is immaterial to me whether she is wife or sister; I will still serve you until death.' Some time went by and the brother performed all the duties of a servant without the least question or complaint. Then [the monk and the woman] said to each other: 'Are we not carrying a sufficient weight of sin as it is, without taking on the responsibility for this man's soul? Let us get away from this place and leave him the cell.' They took as much as they could of their belongings and said to the brother: 'We are going away to pray: do you look after the cell for us.' When they had gone a little way off, the brother realized what was their intent and went running after them. When they saw him, they were troubled and they said: 'How much longer are you going to condemn us? You have the cell; stay there and look to your own condition.' But he said: 'I did not come for the cell, but to serve you.' Their consciences troubled them when they heard this; they came to the conclusion that they should repent before God. For her part, the woman went to a monastery whilst the elder returned to his own cell: thus were they both saved by the patience of the brother.

1.27.3 / 1.27.3; *BHG* 1317s *iunior salvat seniorem*

Scholion in *PE*:

Do you see that the elder, being a spiritual entity, was not unaware of the law of the spirit, even though he had slipped and fallen into sin as a man? Thus he did not definitively turn away the brother who came to him, even though he had no wish to admit another person to the house. But after declining for a short time, when he saw that he was not content to go away, he received him against his will, as though he were impelled to do so by God. For he was afraid of offending the God who had moved the brother [in his direction] and who said: 'He who comes to me I will in no wise cast out.' [Jn 6:37] Likewise, after the brother had patiently remained there for some time and had unhesitatingly served him, because of this, he did not dare to send him away. He chose to abandon the cell himself rather than send away unjustly him who had come and remained [there] by the divine Providence which had also placed the conviction in him that [the elder] had deceitfully fled. May we too unwaveringly keep this rule.

[G15] Some brothers asked one of the fathers: 'How is it that the soul does not hasten towards the promises of God that are promised in the Scriptures but inclines towards the unclean?' 'I say that it has not yet

tasted the heavenly [things] and for that reason it longs for the unclean ones', the elder replied.
1.28.5 / 1.28.2.4

[**G16**] A brother asked an elder: 'How is it that they who spend their lives in the world do not fall, they who are negligent of fasts, despise prayer, absent themselves from vigils, filling themselves with all kinds of food, doing just what they want to in giving and receiving, devouring each other, passing the greater part of the day in swearing and perjuring themselves? They neither say: "We have sinned" nor do they exclude themselves from communion; whereas we monks, ever committed to fasts, vigils, sleeping on the bare earth, and a dry diet, deprived of all physical repose, mourn and lament saying: "We are lost and liable for Gehenna".' With a sigh the elder said: 'You are right to say that the worldlings do not fall, brother. They fall once: headlong and grievous is that fall. Neither can they rise again nor have they anywhere from which to fall. In their so great ignorance they are not even aware that they have fallen at first fall. Why should the devil trouble himself to wrestle with those who are always lying on the ground? Monks, on the other hand, in open opposition to the enemy, ever fight against him: wherefore sometimes they are victorious, sometimes vanquished. They make no end of falling and getting up, attacking and being attacked, striking and being struck – until they prevail over him by the grace of God, rendering him impotent and debilitated within themselves. Then, being completely at peace with God, continually enjoying his calm and joy within [themselves], they experience repose.'
1.29.8 / 1.29.5.2

[**G17**] An elder said: 'At first when the monk renounces the world the demons are not permitted to test him with violence lest, terrified and alarmed by the situation, he promptly return to the world. But as with time and effort the monk makes progress, then they unleash against him the conflicts with fleshly desires and the other delights; then soon after with anger, hatred, and other passions. Then must a man humble himself and lament, judging and blaming himself alone. In this way he learns patience, experience, discernment through temptations; and then he takes refuge in God with tears. Some, however, disturbed by the situation and overcome by unbearable sorrow, were borne down into the abyss of despair and returned to the world in their hearts, some in the body. But let us, brothers, never despair or be faint-hearted; let us patiently endure

temptations with courage and long suffering, giving thanks to God for everything that happens to us; for giving thanks to God undoes every machination of the enemy. He who has pitch on his hands can only get them clean with oil. So too we who are sullied by sin are made clean again by the mercy and the loving kindness of our Saviour Jesus Christ. So let us approach him in every temptation and fervently call upon his aid, giving thanks in all things. Then shall we see the enemy easily defeated, becoming debilitated and powerless with regard to us.'
1.29.12 / 1.29.5.6

[G18] Abba Isaiah said: 'We need humble-mindedness before all else, always being ready to say: "Forgive me" in response to any word we hear or deed, for all the devices of the adversary are destroyed by humble-mindedness.'
1.44.12 / 1.44.3.10

[G19] A man named Paul, *illoustrios* in rank, who had a wife and children and was very wealthy, wanted to become a monk. Calling his wife and children he explained his intention to them. When he found that they were of similar mind and were as attracted to the monastic life as he was, he said to them: 'If you really want to benefit in this way I will sell you as slaves at the monasteries' and to this they joyfully assented. So he took his wife (wearing simple clothes befitting a slave) and the portion of the estate that belonged to her and went to a women's monastery with her. He delivered her to the mother-superior [*hēgoumenissa*] to be a slave in the monastery, handing over her property too. Likewise, he took his children to another monastery and handed them over to the *higoumen* together with their share of the estate, to be slaves. Finally he came to another monastery himself and did likewise: he handed himself over as a slave. Then he said to the abba: 'If you please, I would like to go into the oratory alone.' The abba agreed and in he went. When the doors were firmly shut, he stretched out his hands and cried out saying: 'O God, you know that I have come to you with all my heart' and there came to him a voice saying: 'I too am aware of it and I have received you with all my heart.' He lived in the *coenobion* for a long time, performing all the mean service tasks like a slave and became the least of all. But he was raised up by God for his humility; after his death there flowed myrrh from his tomb and many signs and wonders took place at it.
2.1.18 / 2.1.8.3

[G20] [Abba Poemen] also said: 'By no means is the soul humbled unless you reduce its food [intake] or restrict it to feeding only when necessary.'
2.15.12 / 2.15.6.7

[G21] There was an elder living at the *coenobion* of the holy Theodosius the Coenobiarch who observed this rule for 30 years: he took bread and water once a week; he worked unceasingly; and he never went out of the church.
2.16.11 / 2.16.1.11

[G22] A brother asked an elder: 'To what extent ought one to fast?' and the elder said: 'No more than is stipulated. There are many who want to go beyond that but in the event, were not strong enough to complete even a little.'
2.18.13 / 2.18.3.10

[G23] Abba Paul the Cappadocian told us: 'When the devastation by the Persians[2] took place we too fled from our monastery and were dispersed. When I came to Constantinople I chanced upon a vessel about to depart for Alexandria. I paid my passage and went aboard; a few days later we came to Alexandria. Finding some monks from the Mountain of Nitria there I fell in with them. When I arrived at the Mountain, I shared a dwelling with one of the monks. When I had stayed with him a year and three months I went to the *higoumen* of the Mountain saying: "Take pity on me, abba, and give me a cell where I can live in *hêsychia*, for I cannot live with the elder as he follows neither the monastic nor the worldly way of life. He obliges me to fast on Sunday and the rest of the feasts including Pentecost. Worse still: he does not allow the singing of the canons and tropes which everybody is accustomed to sing. And in the days of the holy Lent (apart from Saturday and Sunday) we take no bread, wine, or oil: we were satisfied by feeding on fruit every second day." The elder who was the *higoumen* of the Mountain replied: "Go back there and stay with the elder if you wish to be saved, brother; for he who earnestly desires to be saved ought not to desist from glorifying God on feast-days or on Sunday, for that [practice] is strengthened and protected by fasts and vigils. Just as a fish cannot live without water, so neither can a monk live wholly and exist for God without continual prayer, fasts and vigils. To

---

[2] The monastery of Enaton was sacked by Persians in 617.

fast for two days is appropriate only for anchorites; likewise, to partake of fruit and refrain from bread is neither advantageous nor praiseworthy; it has the appearance of vainglory. To abstain for 40 days, during the holy Lent that is, then to relax and repose for 50 (meaning: in Pentecost) that is appropriate for worldlings and the rich, but not for monks. Likewise, to sing tropes and canons, to make melodies heard is fitting for priests and others in the world; that is why the people are accustomed to congregate in churches. But the like of it is not only inappropriate for monks, living far away from the disturbance of the world; it is often the cause of harm. Just as the fisherman catches the fish with a hook and a worm, so does the devil by these very tropes and the singing [of them] engulf the monk in vainglory, man-pleasing, love of pleasure, and soon even *porneia*. Singing is far removed from the monk who truly wishes to be saved.'"

2.19.5 / 2.19.1.5

[G24] An elder said: 'When you sit down to eat, conquer the demon of gluttony by restraint and hold him back, saying to him: "Just wait: you will not be hungry." Then eat slowly; and the more that one goads you on, eat yet more evenly; for he does goad a person into wanting to eat everything at one time.'

2.23.10 / 2.23.5.3

[G25] A brother asked Abba Palladius: 'Tell me what I am to do, father, because for three years I have fasted two days at a time then broken my fast on the third and I cannot escape from the demon of *porneia*.' The elder replied: 'My son, when God sent the prophet Isaiah to the Israelites he said to him: "Cry aloud and spare them not; announce their sins to the people. They seek me day after day and wish to come nigh me, saying: 'Why is it that we fasted and you are not aware of it? That we humbled our souls and you know it not?'" He answered them thus: "Because on your fast days you are found doing what you will. You wrong those who are in subjection to you, you annoy all your adversaries and you fast over disputes and confrontations so that the outcry becomes audible before the Lord. It is not such a fast as that that I have designated," says the Lord, "nor that you bow your neck like a bulrush nor lay yourself down in dust and ashes. An acceptable fast will not be described like that"[cf. Is 58:2–5]. So you, my son, if you fast from food but speak ill of somebody or judge him or bear a grudge or entertain evil *logismoi*; or if,

longing for one of the delights or for something that is forbidden, you fall in with the desire in your mind, how will you escape the battle with *porneia*? Or are you not aware that he who satisfies his desire in his mind is replete and intoxicated even without external food? If you want your fast to be acceptable to God, above all guard yourself against every evil word, against all back-biting, against passing judgment and do not accept a vain report as it is written: "Cleanse your heart from all defilement of flesh and spirit", [2 Cor 7:1] from all grudge-bearing and sordid greed. Tame your body by much repentance and watching and other labours; in secret meditation too and, when you are about to go to bed, do not lie down: sleep sitting up, for in such ways and their like can youth be trained (by the grace of God) to get the upper hand in the battle against *porneia*. This is why the fathers decreed that one should not stay in a cell or a place of *hêsychia* but live in a *coenobion*, there to be tamed by much toil. In addition to this they decreed old clothes and rags, not fine clothing, to be worn and that [the neophyte] be securely held and protected by those in charge. For leisure, relaxation, eating twice a day and plenty of sleep usually awaken in us not only the demon of *porneia* but also [the demons of] *accidie*, of vainglory, and of arrogance.'
2.25.10 / 2.25.9

[G26] An elder said: 'A little wormwood spoils a pot of honey and one physical sin distances one from the Kingdom of Heaven, sending him off towards the Gehenna of fire. O humble monk, flee from physical sin as though from fire, lest you be burned up by it.'
2.27.3 / 2.27.2.2

[G27] A brother embattled by *porneia* reproved the demon, saying: 'Get away into darkness, Satan; or are you not aware that, unworthy though I be, I bear the members of Christ?' And the burning was stilled at once like when one blows out a lamp. Amazed at this in his inner self he glorified the Lord.
2.28.19 / 2.28.8.2 [2.28.8 is headed: 'Of Saint Ephraim'.]

[G28] If the spirit of *porneia* troubles you when you are at work, do not hesitate to stretch out your hands in prayer and, if it attacks you with more intensity, stand up and bend your knee in prayer and the prayer [offered in] faith will go into battle on your behalf.
2.28.20 / 2.28.8.3

[G29] Brother, if you are counted worthy of a spiritual gift, do not go boasting, for you have no good thing but what you received from the Lord [cf. 1 Cor 4:7] and if you do not proceed according to his will, he will take away from you that which is his and give it to somebody who is better and humble-minded.

2.35.2.14 / 2.35.2.14

[G30] An elder said: 'Falsehood is the Old Man, destroyed by his appetite for deceit. But truth is the New Man, created in the image of God.'

2.45.2 / 2.45.1.2

[G31] He also said: 'The root of good works is truth; but falsehood is death.'

2.45.3 / 2.45.1.3

[G32] Two elders were at enmity with each other. It came about that one of them fell ill and a brother came to visit him. The elder besought the brother: 'There is bad blood between me and elder so-and-so; I would like you to invite him so we can be reconciled.' 'You have told me to do that, abba?' responded the brother; 'then I will [go and] invite him.' The brother went out then began to wonder within himself how he was to go about the matter, fearing that the [other] elder might refuse the invitation or become even more embittered. By the providence of God, one of the brothers brought him five figs and a few mulberries; the brother took them and put them in his own cell. Taking out one fig and a few mulberries, he brought them to the elder to whom he was intending to go, saying: 'Abba, somebody gave these to elder such-and-such who is ill. And as I happened to be there he said to me: "Take these and give them to elder so-and-so", so I brought them to you.' The elder stood speechless on hearing this; 'He sent these to me?' he said and the brother answered: 'Yes, abba.' The abba took them, saying: 'You are indeed welcome!' When the brother got back to his cell, he took two of the figs together with some mulberries and brought them to the other elder, the sick one. Prostrating himself to him, he said: 'Take these, abba; elder such-and-such sent them for you.' Suffused with joy, he said: 'Are we then reconciled?' 'Yes, abba, thanks to your prayers', said the brother and the elder said: 'Glory to God!' So, the elders were reconciled through the grace of God and through the astuteness of the brother who brought them together in peace by means of three figs and a few mulberries; and the elders had no idea what the brother had done.

2.45.10 / 2.45.7

[G33] An elder recounted that in the time of Isidore the Great, the priest of Scete, there was a brother who was a deacon. On account of his out-standing virtue [Isidore would have] made him a priest so he could succeed him after his death; but [the brother] was so devout he did not accept ordination and remained a deacon. Now by the machination of the enemy, one of the elders was envious of him. So, when everybody was in church for the *synaxis*, that elder went and put his own book in the cell of the deacon. Then he came and reported to Abba Isidore: 'One of the brothers stole my book.' Abba Isidore was amazed; 'Never has anything like this happened at Scete', he said. The elder who had placed the book said to the priest: 'Send two of the fathers with me to search the cells.' So off they went and first they examined the others' cells; then they came to the deacon's cell, found that very book and brought it to the priest in the church. In the presence and the hearing of the deacon they reported where they had found it. He prostrated himself to Abba Isidore before all the company, saying: 'I have sinned; give me a penance', and he gave him a penance: not to receive communion for three weeks. When the brother came to the *synaxis*, he stood before the congregation and fell down before all the company, saying: 'Forgive me for I have sinned.' After three weeks he was received back into communion and straightaway the elder who had falsely accused him was possessed of a demon. He began to confess, crying out and saying: 'I falsely accused the servant of God.' Although there was prayer for him on the part of the whole church, he was not healed. Then Isidore the Great said [to the deacon] before all the brothers: 'Pray for him; you were falsely accused and he is not going to be healed except through you', and when *he* prayed the elder promptly became whole.
2.46.6 / 2.46.4.3

[G34] An elder said: 'Do not entertain an accusation against your brother in your heart about anything whatsoever.'
3.1.3. / 3.1.4.3

[G35] Abba John Colobos said: 'There is no other virtue like not belittling.'
3.2.1 / 3.2.2.1, cf. John Colobos 22 and *APanon* 478

[G36] The blessed Syncletica said: 'Let the one who is standing up see that he not fall, while the fallen one has one concern: to get up. The one

who is standing should be on his guard against falling for there are different kinds of false steps. The fallen one is deprived of standing but he who is lying down was not hurt much. Let not the one who is standing be disparaged, lest when he fall he be brought into a deeper abyss and be completely lost. For his crying is overcome and concealed by the depth of the abyss, so that he cannot even ask for aid, as the great David says: "Let not the abyss devour me nor the well close its mouth upon me." [Ps 68:16] The one who fell first survived. Do you make sure you do not fall and become food for wild beasts. The fallen one does not make the door safe {on getting up again? – meaning obscure} but for your part do you not be dozing off at all but be forever singing that divine phrase which says: "Enlighten mine eyes that I sleep not in death." [Ps 12:4]
3.2.7 / 3.2.2.7

[G37] Abba Isaiah said: 'If a *logismos* comes upon you to judge your neighbour for some sin, first think to yourself that you are more of a sinner; then do not believe that the good things you are thinking of doing are pleasing to God – and you will not dare judge your neighbour.'
3.2B.6 / 3.2.8.6

[G38] He also said: 'Not to judge one's neighbour and to belittle oneself is a way of attaining repose for the conscience.'
3.2B.7 / 3.2.8.7

[G39] A brother who was in the desert practicing *hêsychia* in his cell was severely coerced by *accidie* to come out of his cell. He said to himself: 'Why are you in *accidie*, wretch, and wanting to come out of your cell? Is it not enough for you that, even though you do nothing good, you cause no offence or affliction to anybody? Think how many evils the Lord delivered you from. You do not speak stupidities, you do not hear what is inappropriate, you do not see damaging sights. You have one battle: against *accidie* and God is able to suppress it if you continually fall down before him in humility and with a broken heart, beseeching his assistance, for he knows your frailty in all things and he will not permit you to be tempted beyond what you can stand.' As the brother said these and similar things to himself, great comfort came upon him by the grace of God. He had this teaching from the holy fathers who had grown old in the desert and enjoyed great familiarity with God through their spiritual discipline.
3.13.8 / 3.13.7.8

[G40] An elder was asked: 'Why do you never become faint-hearted?' 'Because each day I expect to die', he replied.
3.13.9 / 3.13.7.9

[G41] Abba Palladius told us this: 'Once when I was going to Alexandria with Abba Daniel for some need, we met a young man coming out of the bathhouse, for he had been bathing. When he saw him, the elder sighed and said to me: "You see that brother? He is going to blaspheme the name of God on account of [the bathhouse] but let us follow him so we can see where he is staying." So, following, we went in behind him. The elder took him aside and said: "You are young and healthy, brother; you do not have to bathe. Believe me, my son, you offend many – not only worldlings, but monks too." That one answered the elder: "If I only wanted to please people, I would not be a servant of Christ; but it is writ-ten: 'Judge not and you will not be judged'." [Mt 7:1] Then the elder prostrated himself saying: "Forgive me for the Lord's sake; being a man, I have been mistaken." We came out of his place and I said to the elder: "Perhaps the brother is sick and there is no charge against him?" Sighing and weeping, the elder said: "The truth will convince you brother: I saw more than 50 demons around him, pouring mud on him; and a female burnt-faced-one sitting on his shoulders, kissing him; and another female burnt-faced-one in front of him manhandling him and teaching him shameless things. And the demons were accompanying him in a circle, rejoicing over him. [His] holy angel I did not see, neither nearby nor far away, from which I concluded that he was overwhelmed by all this inde-cency. [The young man's] very clothing bore witness to what I have to say (it was of goat's skin, soft, and with a lining) and so too did his shameless coming and going in the midst of this city into which they who have grown old in spiritual discipline come for indispensable needs then make haste to get out of it lest they undergo some spiritual harm. Moreover, if he were not in love with himself, with pleasure, and with *porneia,* would he not blush to make himself naked in the bathhouse and to see other people in the nude too, when our holy fathers Antony and Pachomius, Ammoun and Serapion, and the rest of the God-bearing fathers stipu-lated that none of the monks should make himself naked other than in great sickness and necessity? They themselves, when they wanted to cross rivers on account of some essential needs and there was no ferry, they would not consent to make themselves naked out of respect for the holy angel who had been sent along with them and the sun that was shining on them. Even though they were not in the sight of men they besought

God and crossed through the air; for God, the lover of people and all powerful, willingly accepted their just and pious request. He fulfilled it in a wondrous way, assisting their effort." The elder kept silence after he had said this to me. Not many days after we had returned to Scete, the brothers came from Alexandria and told us that brother so-and-so the priest (for he was ordained) who was at the church of Saint Isidore, recently come from Constantine (it was he of whom the elder spoke), had been taken in adultery with the wife of the Silentiary[3] whose servants and neighbours arrested him. His two testicles and the member were cut off from his body; he survived the excision for three days then died, a shame and a disgrace for all the monks. Getting up I went to Abba Daniel on hearing this and told him what had happened. The elder wept when he heard, saying: "[His] fall is a lesson for the arrogant." What the elder meant was: if that [fellow], sick with arrogance, had accepted [the elder's] advice, no such thing would have befallen him. Let it be a lesson to the rest of the arrogant, instructing them by his fall to avoid such an abyss.'
3.16.1–7 / 3.16.7.1–7; *BHG* 2102c, *de balneis*

[**G42**] An elder said: 'If some bodily sickness befall you, do not be discouraged; for if the Lord-and-master wishes that you be afflicted in body, who are you to complain? Does he not take care of you himself in all things? Could you live apart from him? So, be long-suffering and beseech him to grant you what is appropriate (that is his will); live patiently and eat what is freely given to you [*agapê*].'
3.18.5 / 3.18.7.5

[**G43**] An elder said: 'Through *apatheia* the holy ones who have God within themselves inherit both what is here and what is there. And since both what is here and what is there belong to Christ, they who possess him possess what is his too. He who possesses the world (the passions that is) even if he possess the world, he possesses nothing but the passions which rule over him.'
3.21.1 / 3.21.7.1

[**G44**] A brother embattled by the *logismos* of self-conceit said: 'You have already accomplished the virtues, [my] soul', but wishing to vanquish that [*logismos*] the brother put his hand under a cauldron that was being

---

[3] A court official who originally maintained law and order in the palace, then a rather low-ranking imperial servant.

heated, saying to himself: 'See, you are being burnt; no more boasting! The three children who were not burnt in the midst of the flames were not elated in their hearts; they were singing hymns to God in great humility in the midst of the furnace. With a broken soul and in a spirit of humility they were saying: "May we be accepted into your presence." [Dan 3:9] And do you have a high opinion of yourself, standing here at your ease?' In this way, he vanquished the demon of arrogance.
3.29.26–7 / 3.29.7.26–7

[G45] A brother asked one of the fathers about the *logismos* of blasphemy: 'Abba, my soul is afflicted by the demon of blasphemy. Take pity on me and tell me where it has come from and what I am to do.' The elder replied: 'A *logismos* like that comes upon us from back-biting, belittling, and passing judgment; even more so from arrogance and a person doing his own will and being neglectful of his prayers; from getting angry and enraged, all of which are symptoms of arrogance. [Arrogance] leads us towards the above-mentioned passions and from them the *logismos* of blasphemy is generated. And if *that* lingers in the soul for long, the demon of blasphemy hands the person over to the demon of *porneia* which often brings him to lose his senses. And, if a man regain them not, he is lost.'
3.30.4–5 / 3.30.1.4–5

[G46] An elder said: 'If we cultivated humble-mindedness we would be in no need of instruction. All the terrible things happen on account of our elation. If the angel of Satan was given to the Apostle to check him to prevent him from being elated, [2 Cor 12:7] how much more so will Satan himself be given to us who are elated to tread us down until we are humbled?'
3.33.2 / 3.33.7.2

[G47] A brother asked an elder: 'How is it that some people see revelations and visions of angels?' and the elder said: 'Blessed is he, my son, who sees his sins all the time because such a man is always alert.' 'Some days ago, father, I saw a brother casting some demon out of a brother' the brother said to him. 'I have no wish to cast out demons or to cure illnesses', the elder told him, 'but I do wish (and I beseech God) that no demon enter me and that I cleanse myself of impure *logismoi* – and here I am become great. For if one cleanse his heart of impure *logismoi* and unremittingly perform his service [*akolouthia*] he too will undoubtedly

be considered worthy of the Kingdom of Heaven in company with the miracle-working fathers.'
3.35.24–5 / 3.35.2.24–5

[G48] An anchorite stayed in the remoter desert for 30 years, getting his food from one fruit-tree. Later on, he began saying to himself: 'It is in vain that you wasted your time each day for so many years. Here I am for so many years not eating anything other than the fruit of this tree and I have neither seen a revelation, nor done a miracle as did the fathers who were monks before me. I am getting away from here and going off to the world.' While he was thinking these things, an angel of the Lord presented himself to him and said: 'What are you thinking?' – and he let the other know what he was turning over in his mind. Then the angel said to him: 'And what kind of miracle do you want to perform in excess of the patient endurance and the courage which God has given you? Bear in mind who it is that has empowered you to persevere for so many years in this place, nourished only by the fruit tree. So stay on and ask God to furnish you with humility.' Fortified by the angel he persevered there for the rest of his life.
3.35.29–30 / 3.35.2.29–30

[G49] There was an elder in Egypt who was always saying: 'There is no other way shorter than humility.'
3.38.44 / 3.38.1.44

[G50] Two brothers were combing out split linen during a vigil and one of the strands was continually breaking. *Logismoi* began to trouble the one brother whose strand was not breaking against the other one who was combing with him. Wishing to overcome his anger and not to distress his brother, he broke his own strand when his brother's strand began to pull – then they were both repairing [their strands]. In this way they stood up without distressing each other and the one was not aware of the deed that the other had done.[4]
3.39.5–6 / 3.39.2.5–6

[G51] To the brothers who visited him and had asked how to be saved, Abba Macarius said: 'My dear brothers, let us avoid contact with world-lings as much as possible. That does us the greatest benefit, because for

---

[4] The meaning of this piece is obscure. Maybe the brothers were actually *spinning* linen – during the vigil, interrupting their work to stand for prayer.

the most part their conversation is of nothing else but buying and selling, women and children, cattle and the like. Such contact separates the mind from God. Let us not eat with them either, for if only speaking with them separates the mind from God, what damage must there be in eating and drinking with them? I am not saying this to avoid them as unclean, indeed not! But because they are eating fine fare and meat two or three times a day while we are abstaining from meat and fine fare and eating once a day. Otherwise, if they see us eating our fill, they will immediately condemn us, saying: "Here are the monks filling themselves too", forgetting that we are clothed in flesh as they are. But if they see us disciplining ourselves in the matter of food, they immediately pass judgment on us and say: "Here are man-pleasers and they are losing their souls for our sake!" Then again, if they see us eating with unwashed hands or wearing dirty clothes, they immediately say: "What filth is here!" But then if they see us eating with washed hands, they say: "Here are the monks cleaning themselves. They are losing themselves for our sake, and we are becoming guilty and responsible for their loss." Fleeing then, let us flee their tables; let us seek their blame rather than their praise, for their blame is the procurer of crowns, their praise of perdition. What good does it do me if I please men and anger my Lord God? The godly Apostle bears witness, saying: "If I were still pleasing men, I would not be a servant of Christ." [Gal 1:10] Should we not be praying before the Lord, saying: "Jesus our God, deliver us from their praise and blame and let us do nothing to please them?" – for their praise cannot bring us to the Kingdom of Heaven nor is their blame strong enough to close off eternal life from us, but rather works together with us toward that end. Knowing then, dear brothers, that we are obliged to render an account for an idle word, let us flee from [worldlings] as one flees from a serpent.'
3.44.1–6 / 3.44.1.1–6

[G52] A brother asked an elder: 'If I find myself at a feast [*agapê*] with the fathers what am I to do?' The elder replied: 'Instead of fasting, concentrate on incessant prayer in humility.' The brother said: 'How can I eat and listen to them talking and pray [at the same time]?' The elder said to him: 'Coercion[5] is capable of everything and if you want to be a monk, always hold on to it; for he who has it not is not a monk.'
3.45.8 / 3.45.2.8

---

[5] Gk. *bia*, violence, force; maybe 'grim determination'.

[G53] Abba Macarius said: 'If I have what is sufficient for my needs and a person (especially a worldling) bring me something, I accept it not, knowing that it springs from a machination of the devil. But if I am in need of something which I do not possess and my *logismos* seeks once or twice to obtain it, then, knowing that I am in need, God will bring it to me by somebody – as he did for Daniel in the lions' den by the prophet Abbakoum. [Bel and the Dragon 33–9] If I possess the means to provide what I need (a little silver or a few coins) and do not spend it, hoarding my coins, waiting until somebody brings me what I need for nothing, then I become like Judas Iscariot who abandoned the grace that was given to him and ran into the passion of money-loving.'
3.49.4–6 / 3.49.1.4–6

[G54] An elder from Scete was living on Mount Paesios; a person possessed of a demon was brought to him and he healed him. That person brought him a basket full of gold but the elder was unwilling to accept it. Seeing the man sorrowing [the elder] retained the empty basket and said to him: 'Give charity to the poor with the gold.' The elder made a tunic with the basket (it was hairy and uncomfortable) and wore it for a long time – to wear down his flesh.
4.1A.2–3 / 4.1.9.2–3

[G55] I visited Abba Joseph one day at Enaton;[6] the sophist Sophronios[7] was there too and while we were speaking with the elder, here there came somebody from Aïla[8] and gave him three pieces of gold, saying: 'Take these, worthy father, so you will pray for my vessel, for I have loaded it and sent it off to Ethiopia', but the elder paid no attention to him. So Sophronios said to the elder: 'Take the money father and then give it to a brother in need.' The elder replied: 'My son, it would be a double disgrace if I took what I did not need and reaped another's thorns with my own hands. If only I could reap the thorns of my own soul! For it is written: "If you sow, sow what is yours", for another's tares are more bitter, especially when it is not a question concerning the soul.' Sophronios said to him: 'Well then, whatever a man does by way of alms-giving, is it not counted by God?' The elder answered: 'Alms-giving is done for many different

---

[6] I.e. 'ninth', an important monastic settlement on the coast at the ninth mile-post west of Alexandria.

[7] Possibly the future Patriarch of Jerusalem. This whole passage reads like a piece from John Moschos' *Pratum Spirituale*.

[8] Jerusalem.

reasons, my son. There is one who gives alms for his house to be blessed and God does bless his house. Another gives alms for his vessel and God gives his vessel a good passage; another for his children and God protects his children, another [gives] to be esteemed and God esteems him. God does not reject anybody, but grants each one what he desires, provided his soul is not adversely affected by it. These all attain their reward; for, according to the purpose of their almsgiving, God rewarded them and owed them nothing in the future. So then, if you are giving alms, do it for your soul's sake and God will grant what you desire, for it is written: "May the Lord grant you according to your heart['s desire]". [Ps 19:5] But there are some who seem to give alms but in fact enrage God.' 'Explain this to us', said Sophronios, and he said: 'God stipulated that the first fruits of what is born and of all the crops and the clean beasts be offered to him for the blessing of the remainder and the forgiveness of sins; and also, that they dedicate the firstborn of humans to him. But the rich do the opposite, retaining the useful things for themselves while distributing the useless ones among the poor and to their brothers. For example: they drink the good wine while providing widows and orphans with that which is bitter and malodorous. They eat well-preserved fruit themselves but give away that which is spoiled. And clothing: they assign that which is luxurious and serviceable for themselves, throwing old and ragged clothes to the poor. And of the children, the healthy and good-looking ones they get ready for marriages and alliances, taking great care of them; but the weak, the one-eyed, the ones lacking a limb, and the deformed, these they dedicate to God and hand over to monasteries, so their offering becomes unacceptable. In this way when Cain made his offering, he not only failed to please God: he actually angered him. [Gen 4.3–5] Such people ought to have thought like this: if when we wish to honour mortal men among us we endeavour to offer those things which seem to them to be very valuable, how much more then should be so the things we offer to God our maker, from whom we have the very things we offer? And since we wish him to be favourable to us on account of our almsgiving, we ought to offer him the more valuable things we possess, to ensure that our gift be not rejected and be returned to our breast in shame, our offering become an abomination and unacceptable. Just as the sacrifice of Noah consisting of savour and smoke was reckoned a sweet-smelling odour to God on account of the good disposition of him who offered, as it is written: "And the Lord smelled the sweet savour", [Gen 8:21] so an offering of fruit presented with evil intent, even if it looks well to the eye, is an abomination in the estimation of the Lord, like the sacrifices and the

incense of the Jews, for so spoke God to them through the prophet: "Incense is an abomination to me."' [Is 1:13] This is what the elder said to us; we went out having reaped much benefit. As he sent us on our way he said: 'Come to me next Saturday, my sons, for I shall need you.' As he had told them, they came on the Saturday at the third hour and found him dead. They buried him and went their way giving thanks to God who had counted them worthy to perform the funeral of such a holy man.
4.2.1–9 / 4.2.1.1–9, cf. *APanon* 571

[**G56**] [An elder] said: 'If a monk ever experience a physical disorder too he ought not to think anything of it but purchase his *hêsychia* by it.'
4.5.16 / 4.5.2.16

[**G57**] When a brother earnestly besought him to tell him a saying, Abba Sisoes said: 'Stay in your cell keeping watch and consign yourself to God with many tears and you will experience repose.'
4.5.28 / 4.5.2.28

[**G58**] An elder said: 'It is not necessary to be anxious about anything other than the fear of God. For my part', he said, 'even if I am obliged to be anxious about some physical need, I never take it into consideration until the time [comes].'
4.5.39 / 4.5.2.39

[**G59**] [Abba Moses] said: 'It is good for him who has God nearest to him and interacts with him not to bring a person into his cell.'
4.5.55 / 4.5.2.55

[**G60**] I once visited Abba Joseph at Enaton and said to him: 'Is the soul damaged by colluding with a passionate *logismos*?' The elder replied: 'If the soul benefits from pure and devout *logismoi*, clearly it is damaged by shameful and evil ones, if it persists in them.'
4.6.7 / 4.6.1.7

[**G61**] An elder said: 'There are two kinds of forgetting and the one militates against the other. The one who gets to the point of forgetting to eat his bread from the voice of his groaning [cf. Ps 101:5–6] is not dominated by the forgetting of the enemy.'[9]
4.7B.2 / 4.7.5.2

---

[9] Cf. *APanon* 65: 'The root of all evils is forgetting.'

[G62] A scorpion bit a brother who was standing in prayer in the foot and the pain so affected his heart that he was almost surrendering his soul. But in spite of the way things were, he who was in such pain did not stand down until he had completed his prayer.
4.9.8 / 4.9.3.8

[G63] A brother asked Abba Sisoes: 'How am I to be saved?' The elder said to him: 'If you wish to be well-pleasing to God, exit from the world, abandon the earth, leave creation, and approach the Creator, joining yourself with God by prayer and lamentation; then you will experience repose both now and in the age to come.'[10]
4.10.15 / 4.10.2.15

[G64] Abba Isaiah said: 'When you are performing your liturgy, if you do it in humility of mind as one who is unworthy, it has weight with God. But if you rise up in your heart and think of somebody who is sleeping or neglectful and you condemn him, your labour is in vain.' He also said: 'If one seek the Lord with the knowing of the heart, the Lord will listen to him if he ask in the knowing [of the heart] provided he be not involved with any of the things of this world and that he care for his soul, fearing to present it irreproachable at the judgment seat of **[G65]** Christ according to his power.' [cf. Phil 1:10] For according to all the Scriptures a man is not accorded a hearing by God other than by labour, toil, and exertion.
4.13.19 / 4.13.1.19–20

[G66] An elder said: '"The clean beast chews its food and has a cloven hoof." [Lev 11:3–4] So we who believe correctly and accept the two Testaments should ruminate on the good food, not at all on the bad. The beneficial food is good *logismoi* furnished by the tradition of the holy teachers and reading the Scriptures, upon which the God-loving soul must ever meditate. The bad food is unclean *logismoi* injected at the attack of the demons, to be rejected at their onset with no lingering in them.'
4.15.3 / 4.15.1.3, cf. 10.151, *APanon* 676 (*olim* 645)

[G67] An elder said: 'There are some who, while wasting the days of their life in negligence, seek to be saved in word and mind, but make no effort in deed. They read the *Lives of the Fathers* but do not imitate [the

---

[10] Cf. 'Abba Joseph asked Abba Poemen: "Tell me how I can become a monk." Said the elder to him: "If you want to find repose *here* [ὧδε] and in the age to come, say in every situation: 'I, who am I?' and do not pass judgment on anybody".' [Joseph of Panepho 2, 228C, 9.8]

Fathers'] humility, their indifference to possessions, their self-control, watchfulness, prayer, kneeling, sleeping on the ground, their *hêsychia*, and the rest of their spiritual discipline. But in their own opinion and negligence [such people] make the *Lives of the Fathers* a fiction, it being impossible (they say) for a man to endure such things – they failing to consider that where God dwells through the grace of baptism and the keeping of the commandments, supernatural gifts exist and actions take place.'
4.16.1–2 / 4.16.3.1–2

[G68] An elder said: 'A man cannot be good even if he wants to be good and strenuously applies himself [to being good] unless God dwell in him, for "None is good but one: God".' [Mk 10:18]
4.22.5 / 4.22.1.5

[G69] A brother asked an elder: 'What is the cultivation of the soul so that it produces fruit?' and the elder answered: 'The cultivation of the soul is the *hêsychia* of the body, much bodily prayer [εὐχὴ σωματική], not paying attention to the shortcomings of men but only to one's own. If a man persevere in these, his soul will not be long in producing fruit.'
4.24.2 / 4.24.1.2

[G70] Abba Serinos once went to Abba Poemen together with his disciple, Isaac, and said to him: 'What am I to do with this Isaac for he gladly hears what I say?' Abba Poemen answered him: 'If you want to be beneficial to him, show him virtue by deed. He who pays attention to the word remains slow; but if you show him by deed, that stays with him.'
4.38.3 / 4.38.3.3

[G71] Abba Peter asked Abba Isaiah: 'What is a servant of God?' The elder replied: 'As long as one serve any passion whatever he has not yet been reckoned a servant of God, for he is a servant of that [passion] by which he is dominated. And as long as he be detained by it, he is incapable of teaching one who is dominated by the same passion. Shame it is for him to teach before being set free from that [passion] or to intercede with God about it on his neighbour's behalf when he is still detained by it.'
4.38.17 / 4.38.3.17

[G72] [An elder] said: 'He who teaches others about the salvation of their own [souls] ought first to reap the fruit of teaching; for how can one who is not in control of himself teach another person to be self-controlled? How can one who is throttled by the love of money and dragged along by the demon of it teach another about almsgiving? And he who occupies himself with give-and-take and selling, wasting his days in earthly cares, how will he teach others about the good things to come? Especially as they who were taught by him would pay more attention to his deeds than to his words. They would learn to disregard things eternal and always be striving for the here-and-now, just as they saw their teacher doing. God says to such a one: "Why do you proclaim my judgments and restate my covenant with your mouth? You have hated instruction and thrown my words behind you" [Ps 49:16–17] and: "Woe to those through whom my name is blasphemed." [cf. Rom 2:24] Teaching is good if he who speaks so conduct himself that his actions agree with what he says and if he be known for matters on which he keeps silence. He who only teaches is not blessed, but he who does what he teaches.'
4.38.3–5 / 4.38.7.3–5

[G73] There was an elder who had 12 disciples. Now it came to pass through the temptation of the devil that one of them went into the village for some need and fell into *porneia*. Then, growing accustomed to the evil deed, he often went off to the village in secret after the early morning worship and returned whilst it was still early. The rest of the brothers were aware of what he was doing and eventually so was the abba himself, but he did not reprove [the brother] right away; he let him go on like that for the time being, pretending to be completely unaware of the matter. When the other brothers inveighed against that brother and questioned the silence of the *higoumen* as being inappropriate, the abba went to that brother's cell one day when it was early and it chanced that [the brother] came back from the village where, as I said, he had gone in secret for the shameful deed. But this time, making haste to return, he had put on the woman's shawl instead of his own cloak. Then when he got back he hung it in the corner of the wall of his own cell, neither bothering nor noticing what it was – for, realizing that the superior was coming towards him, all his attention was focused on meeting him and he was working out in his mind what explanation he would give him. The abba saw the woman's shawl hanging there when he entered the brother's cell but for the moment he kept quiet about it. He said to the brother: 'Where were you, brother?' He made up a reply: 'I went some-where on an errand.' 'Did you not go to the village?' said the abba. 'No, Lord-and-master' the other said. Then the abba said: 'Whose is this shawl hanging [here]?' As soon as he saw it the brother knew it was the wom-an's; he immediately threw himself at the abba's feet saying: 'Forgive me and I will not do this anymore.' [The abba] did forgive him; he raised him up and besought him saying: 'Pay attention to yourself from now on my son; what do you gain from that uncleanliness other than shame and dishonour among the men here and the unquenchable fire and the worm that does not die [cf. Mk 9:48] in the age to come? I beg of you my son never again to become involved in that foul and abominable practice.' Severely conscience-stricken, the brother fell again at the elder's feet, watering them well with his tears, fervently begging forgiveness of God. From that time he not only desisted from that shameful practice; he also demonstrated such fervent repentance that he became well-pleasing to God through his excellent endeavour and in short measure became a most experienced monk. This had the result that, when the rest of the brothers saw his repentance and his godly progress, they gave thanks to God. Once they came to the abba and asked him to tell them the reason why he had not reproved the brother when he was aware that he was sin-ning like that, but had patiently bided his time. In answer the elder said to them: 'I saw Satan holding one of the brother's hands, drawing him into the world. I was patiently holding his other hand lest, having been reproved, he would run right off to the world where the devil was drag-ging him. When it pleased God to save his own creation, here we have both his other hand and the whole of him, saved.'

4.48.1–11 / 4.48.3.1–11; *BHG* 1317u, *de longanimitate*

CHAPTER 3

Sayings Preserved in Latin

Translated by John Wortley

Sources:
Among the many translations that Rufinus (Tyrannius Rufinus of
Aquileia, 340/345–410) made from Greek (which include *Historia
Monachorum in Aegypto*) there is a collection of *Verba seniorum*. This was
edited by Heribert Rosweyde as Books 2 and 3 of *Vitae Patrum: De vita et
verbis seniorum libri x*, Lyon, 1615, reprinted in *PL* 73.

José Geraldes Freire, *A Versão Latina por Pascásio de Dume dos Apophthegmata
Patrum*, 2 vols., Coimbra, 1971, 1:157–333: Paschasii Dumiensis translatio,
Liber Geronticon de Octo Principalibus Vitiis.

José Geraldes Freire: *Commonitiones Sanctorum Patrum. Uma nova
colecção de apotegmas, Estudo filológico*, Coimbra, 2010, 2nd ed.

Some items in *De Vitis Patrum* liber 7, *Verba Seniorum*, translated by
Paschasius the deacon, ed. Heribert Rosweyde, reprinted in *PL* 73:1025–
62 that are not found in the edition noted above.

Appendix 3 to *Vitae Patrum* [*PL* 74:381–94]: 'Sayings of the Egyptian
Fathers by an unknown Greek author translated into Latin by Bishop
Martin Dumiensis.'

Rufinus, *Verba Seniorum* [*PL* 73:739–810]

[L1] When some monks questioned him on the reasons for abstinence
one of the holy elders and fathers said: 'Little sons, we ought to be averse
to all kinds of repose in this present life. Let us look neither for the
delights of the body nor for the satisfaction of the belly nor to be

honoured by men; and the Lord Jesus will give us heavenly honours, repose in eternal life, and glorious joy among his angels.' [R1]

[L2] The same elder said: 'It is natural for a man to eat, but he ought to take food for the necessary sustaining of the body, not out of passionate desire or to fill the belly. It is also natural for a man to sleep, but not until he has had enough sleep or his body is relaxed, but so we can suppress the passions and the vices of the flesh. Taking enough sleep dulls a man's mind and senses making them sluggish; but vigils render both the senses and the mind purer and finer. The holy father said that because holy vigils purify and enlighten the mind. It is natural for a man to be angry, not in a passionate outburst, but to be angry with himself and with his vices, so he can easily correct them and separate them from himself. And if we see others doing something evil and contrary to the precepts of God, we ought to be very angry at their vices – but diligently to correct the persons themselves; to reprimand and admonish them so that, having emended their lives, they may be saved and come to eternal life.' [R2]

[L3] Among the early fathers there was a hermit named Pior whom the blessed Antony had inducted (as a young man) into the monks' holy way of life; but he only stayed with Antony a few years. When he was 25 years old off he went to another secluded place in the desert to live alone. He did this with the goodwill and consent of the blessed Antony, for holy Antony said to him: 'Go and live where you will, Pior, and when the Lord reveals it to you in any reasonable way, come to me.' When this Pior arrived at a spot between Nitria and the Desert of Scete he dug a well, thinking to himself: 'Whatever kind of water I find, I ought to be content with it,' and when that was done, it became an occasion for him greatly to increase his merits. For the water he found was so salty and bitter that, if anybody came to visit him, that person would bring water for himself in his own flask. For 30 years he stayed in the same place. The brothers used to tell him that he should get away from that place because of the bitterness of the water but he said to them: 'If we run away from the bitterness and the toil of abstinence and want to experience repose in this world, after we have departed this life we shall neither acquire those eternal and truly sweet benefits nor enjoy those perpetual delights of blessed paradise.' The brothers used to say that the only food he took was one dry loaf and five olives, which he ate walking about outside. Many of the holy fathers also affirm this of him: that, having left his parents' house 30 years and more ago, he was never persuaded to go to find out about them or to visit the neighbours, even when he heard that his parents had died. Nevertheless, when his sister became a widow, as she had two sons already youths, she sent them into the desert to enquire for her brother Pior. After they had gone around the monasteries searching for him and finally only found him with difficulty, they said to him: 'We are your sister's sons and she would very much like to see you before she dies', but he would not acquiesce in their request. So the youths went to the blessed Antony, the man of God, and told him why they had come. Blessed Antony sent for [Pior] and said to him: 'Why have you not come to me in such a long time, brother?' In reply he said to him: 'Most blessed father, you directed me to come to you when the Lord revealed to me by some means and here it was not revealed to me until now.' Blessed Antony said to him: 'Go and see your sister.' Then, taking another monk with him, he went to the place and the house of his sister. He took up his station outside, before the gate of the atrium, and stood there with his eyes closed so he would not see his sister. But she came and threw herself at his feet, choking with excessive joy. Pior said to her: 'Here I am, your brother Pior; look at me as much as you like', and then he went back straight away to his cell in the desert. This he did to teach monks that they are not at liberty to visit their parents or neighbours at will. [R31]

[L4] Abba John who dwelt on the mountain called Calamus[1] had a sister who had been living in the holy estate of monks since infancy. It was she who educated and taught her brother – the same Abba John – to abandon the vanity of this age and to go into a monastery. Once he had entered the monastery, for 24 years he neither came out of the monastery nor visited his sister, while she earnestly desired to see him. She often wrote and sent a letter to him, begging him to come to her before she departed from this body, that in Christian charity she might rejoice in his presence. But he excused himself, unwilling to come out of the monastery. Yet again his sister, that venerable handmaid of God, wrote to him saying: 'If you are unwilling to come to me, I am going to have to come to you in order to revere your holy charity after such a long time.' When the above-mentioned John heard this he was extremely sad; he thought to himself: 'If I let my sister come to me, permission is being given for others, our parents and relations, to come and visit me', so he arranged with himself that he should rather go and visit his sister. Taking

---

[1] Presumably the Lavra of Calamon of Arsinoe in the Fayûm; see *APalph* Sisoes 32, 33, and 48.

two other brothers of the monastery with him he came to the gate of his sister's monastery and shouted: 'Bless and hear the pilgrims.' Out came his sister with another handmaid of God and opened the gate. She did not recognize her brother at all – but he recognized his sister; he said not a word, lest she recognize him by his voice. The monks who were with him said to her: 'We beg of you, lady mother, to order some water to be given to us to drink, for we are tired out by the journey.' Having received and drunk [water] they offered a prayer and, giving thanks to God, they withdrew and went back to their monastery. A few days later his sister wrote to him again [asking him] to come so she could see him before she died and so he could offer a prayer in her monastery. Then he wrote back to her (sending the letter with a monk of his monastery) and said: 'I came to you by the grace of Christ and nobody knew me. You came out to us and gave us water; I took it from your hands and drank; then, giving thanks to God, I came back to the monastery. So let it satisfy you that you saw me and do you trouble me no more; but pray constantly to our Lord Jesus Christ for me.' [R32]

[L5] Once a murder was committed in the area where blessed Macarius lived and a man who was in fact innocent was charged with the crime. He who was suffering from the false accusation rose up and fled to the cell of blessed Macarius, but they got there too who were pursuing him and tied him up, saying that they were themselves in danger if they did not arrest him and hand him over to the law as a murderer. But he who was charged with the crime affirmed with oaths that he was innocent of [the victim's] blood. And when the argument went back and forth for some time holy Macarius asked where the alleged victim was buried. When they indicated the place to him he went to the sepulchre with them and there, having invoked the name of Christ on bended knee, he said to those who were present: 'Now the Lord is going to show whether this man you are after is really guilty.' He raised his voice and called to the dead man by name. When he whom he had called replied to him from the sepulchre, holy Macarius said to him: 'By the faith we have in Christ I adjure you to say now whether you were slain by this man who is accused on your account.' Then he replied from the sepulchre with a loud voice saying that he was not killed by him. They all fell to the ground, astounded, embracing [Abba Macarius'] feet and they began asking him to enquire of him by whom he was killed. Then the holy man said: 'That I will not ask; it is enough for me that the innocent man is set free; it is not my concern that the culprit be detected. Perhaps he will yet feel compunction for the crime he committed and repent – for the salvation of his soul.' [R41]

[L6] 'Get up, Abba Macarius' said a demon appearing as a monk when he knocked at the gate of his cell one night – and the veracity of this was confirmed to us by those who heard it from his own mouth. 'Get up and let us go to the *synaxis* where the brothers are assembled for a vigil.' But he, full of the grace of God, was not to be deceived. Perceiving that it was a deception of the devil he said: 'O liar and enemy of truth; what contact and what association do you have with the *synaxis* and the congregating of the holy ones?' But the other said: 'Do you not realize, Macarius, that there can be no *synaxis,* no congregating of monks without us? So come along and you shall see our work there.' But holy Macarius said to him: 'May the Lord rebuke you [Jd 9], unclean demon' and, turning to prayer, he asked the Lord to show him if what the demon was boasting of was true. He went to the *synaxis* where a vigil was being held by the brothers and again, in prayer, he besought the Lord to show him the truth of what that one said – and here he saw what looked like some little black Ethiopian boys running here and there throughout the whole church in leaps and bounds. As they ran around these Ethiopian boys were playing games with some of the brothers as they prayed and sang psalms. If they pressed the eyes of one of them with two fingers, he immediately fell asleep. If they put a finger in the mouth of another, they would make him yawn. Then after the psalm, when the brothers prostrated themselves for prayer, they were running around individuals again. They would appear in the form of a woman before one [brother] as he lay praying; before another like builders carrying something or doing various things. And whatever the demons pretended to portray, those praying brothers were turning over in the thoughts of their hearts. But as soon as [the demons] began to do any of these things they were promptly rejected as though violently repulsed by some brothers, so that they dared neither to stand nor to pass before them; but they went on playing around the heads and backs of others. Holy Macarius sighed deeply when he saw this and, pouring out tears, he said to God: 'Look down O Lord and do not keep silent; let not God delay but arise and let your enemies be scattered; let them flee from your face, for our soul is filled with illusions.' [cf. Ps 67:1] After the prayer, in order to examine the truth, he summoned to his presence one by one the brothers before whose faces he had seen the demons playing in diverse costumes and appearances. He enquired of them whether in their prayer they had experienced thoughts of building or going on a journey or other types of activity which he had seen represented by the demons. Each one of them confessed to having thoughts in his heart such as he alleged. Then he understood very well that all bad, superfluous, and vain thoughts each one might conceive in his heart, whether in psalm-singing or at the time for prayer or for sleep, are illusions instigated by the demons. But those shady Ethiopians and the thoughts they project are repelled from those who keep their hearts well protected in the fear and love of the Lord. For the mind that is joined to Christ and is especially attentive at the time of prayer accepts nothing that is bad, nothing that is superfluous. [R43]

[**L7**] An elder said: 'Never eat what you would like to eat; but eat what the Lord has sent you, giving thanks without interruption.' [R49]

[**L8**] Abba Moses said: 'Passion is generated by these four things: plentiful food and drink, sleeping one's fill, free-time and jesting, going about in decorated clothing.' [R48]

[**L9**] Two brothers came to Abba Elijah embattled by their *logismoi*. Seeing that they were somewhat fat, as though speaking to his disciple the elder said with a smile: 'Brother, I really do blush for you who have so nourished your body though you profess to be a monk, since the honour of the monk is pallor and emaciation along with humility.' He also said: 'Let not the monk who eats much and is very active be confident; but let him who eats little, even if he does little, be confident and live courageously.' [R64]

[**L10**] Abba Agathon took care of his own needs and was prominent for his discretion in all things, as much in his handiwork as in his clothing. He wore clothes that seemed neither to be too good nor too bad to anybody. [R75]

[**L11**] An elder said: 'Anger arises from these four things: the cupidity of greed; giving and receiving; when one is attached to his own opinion and defends it though it seem neither good nor bad enough to somebody [else]; when one wishes to be elevated with honours or to be learned, hoping to be wiser than all. Anger also dulls a man's senses in these four ways: if he have hatred towards his neighbour or envy him or belittle him or disparage him. Likewise, there are four ways in which this passion can be remedied: first by the heart, second by the face, third by the tongue, fourth by deeds. If one can bear evil so that it not enter his heart it does not come into his face. But if it do come into his face, let him hold his tongue and not speak of it. But if he have spoken of it, let him keep it at that and not translate it into action, but rather soon let it go. There are three categories of men where the passion of anger is concerned: he who allows himself to be hurt and harmed yet pardons his neighbour, he partakes of the nature of Christ. He who neither wounds nor is inclined to be wounded, he partakes of the nature of Adam, while he who injures or harms or speaks ill or demands repayment of a loan is of the nature of the devil.' [R76]

[L12] There was another elder who, if someone spoke disparagingly of him, would personally go and recompense him well if he were near or, if he lived further away, send him a reward. [R81]

[L13] An elder said: 'If a person will not hold his tongue when he is angry he will never be able to restrain his physical passions.' [R91b]

[L14] Demons also frequently appeared to Abba Moses, cursing him and saying: 'You have conquered us, Moses; we can do nothing to you, for whenever we want to press you down into despair you exult and each time you are exalted, you humble yourself so that not one of us gets near you.' [R102]

[L15] One of the fathers used to say: 'Every deed of a monk [done] without humility is vain; for humility is the forerunner of love, just as John was the forerunner of Jesus, drawing everybody to him. So humility draws [us] to love: to God himself, that is, for God is love.' [R126]

[L16] A brother asked an elder: 'Abba, do you think holy men are aware of it when grace comes upon them?' The elder replied: 'They are not always aware of it; for when the disciple of a certain great elder sinned in some particular, the elder shouted at him in anger: "Go and die", and he immediately fell down dead. Mighty dread came upon the elder when he saw him dead and he prayed in profound humility, beseeching God and saying: "Lord Jesus Christ, bring him back to life and never again will I speak so inconsiderately to him." When he had said this, his disciple promptly got up.' [R182]

There are some items that are not part of *P&J* but are found in *De Vitis Patrum* liber vi.iv, *PL* 73:1014–24.

[20. A brother asked Abba Isidore of Scete about the *logismos* of *porneia* . . .]

[L17] The same elder replied to the brother concerning that *logismos*: 'If we do not have *logismoi* we are like wild beasts. But just as the enemy insists on having what is his, so too ought we to fulfil what is ours. If we are diligent in prayer the enemy runs away. Persist in meditating on [what pertains to] God and you will conquer: the perseverance of a good man is victory. Fight on – and you will be crowned.'
PL 73:1014–24, 21

[L18] Amma Syncletica said: 'Our adversary is more easily overcome by those who possess nothing, for he has nothing to wound them with. Most people mindful of spiritual difficulties and temptations that separated them from God have got themselves into the habit of sacrificing by abandoning riches and the rest of their goods.'
PL 73:1014–24, 23

[L19] An elder said: 'He who implants the remembrance of evil in his soul is like one who hides fire in straw.'
PL 73:1014–24, 25

[L20] A brother asked an elder: 'How is it that the soul delights in impurity?' The elder said to him: 'Most of the time the soul has a longing for bodily passions but it is the Spirit of God that restrains us. We should weep and be on the lookout for our impurities. You have seen how when Mary wept and bowed before the sepulchre of the Lord, the Lord called her. So will it be for the soul.'
PL 73:1014–24, 27

[L21] There was a brother at Kellia[2] who used to wait until everybody had gone out when the Eucharist was finished and the priest dismissed the congregation – in the hope that somebody would invite him to eat [with him]. But one day he came out before everybody else when the *synaxis* was over and went running to his cell; the priest was amazed to see him running. When that brother came to church for the *synaxis* at the end of the week, the priest said to him: 'Tell me the truth brother: why is it that you, who used to wait to be last of all at the *synaxeis* of the church, went out before everybody at this last *synaxis*?' The brother

---

[2] I.e. The Cells, ca. 12 Roman miles south of Nitria.

replied to him: 'I was freeing myself from cooking, so I was expecting somebody would take me to eat [with him]. But in the case of this *synaxis,* I cooked myself a few lentils before going to church; for that reason I went out before them all when the sacred mystery was over.' On hearing this the priest issued a directive in church, saying: 'Brothers, before you come to church for the *synaxis,* cook yourself a little dish so that, on account of that, you will make haste speedily to get back into your cells.'
PL 73:1014–24, 31

[L22] Some elders said: 'When Moses entered into the cloud he was speaking with God: when he came out of the cloud, with folk. So it is with the monk: when he is in his cell, he is speaking with God, but when he comes out of his cell he is among demons.'
PL 73:1014–24, 33

The following passages are translated from José Geraldes Freire, *A Versão Latina por Pascásio de Dume dos Apophthegmata Patrum,* 2 vols., Coimbra, 1971, 1:157–333:
Paschasii Dumiensis translatio, *Liber Geronticon de Octo Principalibus Vitiis.*[3]

[L23] A brother enquired of Abba Sisoes how he ought to remain in his own cell, to whom he said: 'Eat your bread and salt and let it not be necessary for you to cook anything.'
[Freire 1971, 1.1 /1.1]

[L24] A brother enquired of an elder: 'Of your charity, abba, tell me a saying: what ought I to appropriate in youth so that I will have it in old age?' To him the elder [said]: 'Either acquire Christ and think of yourself, or contend for money so you do not beg.'
[Freire 1971, 14.12 / 2.3]

---

[3] Gregory, *Dial.* 4.42 speaks of Paschasius (died 511/514). Note ad loc. says his highly praised book on monastic life is lost.

[L25] Abba Agathon frequently used to adjure his disciple: 'Never acquire anything that you would be reluctant to give to your brother if he asked for it and you be found transgressing the commandment of God.'
[Freire 1971, 14.13 / 2.4]

[L26] [Abba Macarius] said: 'It is a fault in a monk if, when he is mistreated or insulted by a brother, he be not the first to go before him with a heart purified by charity.'
[Freire 1971, 141.131 / 2.4 16a]

[L27] When one brother was hurt by another he went and reported it to an elder, who replied to him: 'Convince your *logismos* that the brother does not want to hurt you but your sins get the better of him. For in every temptation that comes upon you from a person, do not blame the person: just say: "This happened to me on account of my sins."'
[Freire 1971, 21.3]

[L28] A brother enquired of Abba Elias: 'If I have depressed somebody, in what way am I to ask [forgiveness]?' The elder replied: 'From the depth of your heart make your apology to him with sorrow and, seeing your intention, God will make it up to him.'
[Freire 1971, 28.2 / 10.2]

[L29] If, while staying in his cell, a monk recalls his sins, the Lord is his helper in all things and he will not suffer *accidie*.
[Freire 1971, 32c]

[L30] A brother enquired of Abba Poemen whether it were better to live further away from other folk. The elder replied: 'If a man blame himself, he can exist anywhere. But if he exalt himself, he never endures. Whatever good a man does let him not exult in it for he will soon lose it.'
[Freire 1971, 33.1 / 12.1]

[L31] Just as pride, if it raise us to heaven, is brought down to hell, so humility, if it descend to hell, then will it be exalted to heaven.
[Freire 1971, 34c]

[L32] [Abba Macarius] said: 'He who works under the impression that he is achieving something gets his reward right here.'
[Freire 1971, 35.6]

[L33] A brother said to an elder: 'My *logismos* tells me I am good.' The elder replied: 'He who does not see his sins always thinks he is one of the good; but he who sees them, a thousand *logismoi* cannot convince him that he is one of the good; he knows what he sees. Much hard work is needed so that each one might examine himself, for negligence, faint-heartedness, and relaxation blind us.'
[Freire 1971, 29.7 / 15.4]

[L34] Questioned by a brother how it is that the soul resists and refuses to fear God, Abba Pambo replied: 'The soul really does wish to fear God, but it is not yet time; for fear of God is perfection.'
[Freire 1971, 53.1]

[L35] There came a brother to Abba Poemen telling him that he had suffered a great temptation. 'Flee from this place', the elder replied; 'walk as far as you can in three days and three nights then spend a whole year there, fasting until nightfall.' The other said to him: 'What if I should die before one year has gone by; what would become of me?' Abba Poemen said to him: 'I trust in God that if you go out there with such an intention as I propose, as you live by it, your repentance will be acceptable with God, even if you be soon dead.'
[Freire 1971, 57.1 / 24.1]

[L36] [Abba Macarius] said: 'God often postpones [granting] our request with good reason, sometimes providing for us otherwise; and by what he provides he makes the one who asks to go on asking.'
[Freire 1971, 58.2]

[L37] When the time for psalm-singing arrived Abba Agathon would abandon his work, even though it were less than finished. He would not suffer the rule of worship to be transgressed even for the sake of handiwork.
[Freire 1971, 59.1]

[L38] A brother enquired of Abba Achilles in what way the demons are able to oppose us. The elder replied: 'Through our wills', and he added: 'The cedars of Lebanon said: "How magnificent and tall we are – yet a small piece of iron cuts us down. Let us grant it nothing that is ours,[4] then it will not be able to cut us down." But there came men and made a

---

[4] I.e. not supply a handle.

handle for the axe from the trees themselves and so cut them down. The trees are [our] souls, the axe the devil; the handle is our will. So we are cut down by our bad wills.'
[Freire 1971, 71.4 / 25.4]

[L39] Just as it often happens in war that when they see a stronghold held by the enemy they themselves choose a yet stronger position and, if it be possible to strike [their] head, the others run away and are defeated; so too do the *logismoi* have one head, whether of greed, avarice, wandering from place to place, or other things. And if you do not recognize that head right away and cast it away from you, they will deceive you and lead you astray in other *logismoi* yet to come. For when the head itself comes under attack, the other passions are brought into play, to deceive a man as he wanders from one to another. So, if you wish to conquer your passions always watch for the head of the *logismoi*; and, when you perceive which it is, do battle only against that one.
[Freire 1971, 73.5 / 26.1]

[L40] An elder said: 'Abhor your belly, the necessities of this world, and honours, and you will experience repose as though you were absent from this world.'
[Freire 1971, 76.4 / 26.4]

[L41] The same elder said: 'The monk should purchase repose for himself', meaning: he should despise the world, even if he suffer bodily harm. For if he find fault with others here, neither can he enjoy the repose of death.
[Freire 1971, 76.5]

[L42] An elder said: 'A man should toil on until he possess Christ, for he who has once acquired Christ toils no more. He is however free to toil on so that, keeping in mind the affliction of the toil, he protects himself on all sides, fearing the loss of such toils. For God so led the children of Israel around in the desert for 40 years that, recalling the affliction of the journey, they would refuse to go back.'
[Freire 1971, 78.1 / 28.1]

[L43] A brother enquired of an elder: 'In what way is there grace for toiling fathers?' and the elder said: 'Whereas those who have been toiling up to now making requests about remission of sins are pale and [remain]

in their toil before grace which bears with their toiling has reached them, yet those to whom the grace of Christ has already reached as a result of their previous endurance flourish, for the face of an exulting soul is clear. Just as the sun gives out light when it does not have clouds, but grows pale when it is covered by clouds, so also the soul grows pale as long as the passions darken it. [The soul] that is now clean through grace, however, is as it is written: "Great is his glory in your salvation." [Ps 20:6]
[Freire 1971, 78.2 / 28.2]

L44] When Amma Sarah leapt over a small stream while she was walking in the way, a worldling saw her and laughed. Unaware that the grace of God had come upon her, she said to the worldling: 'Be quiet: you are going to burst.' She turned around and saw him with his intestines spilled out. Stricken with fear, she prayed, saying: 'My Jesus, bring him back to life and I will never say such a thing again.'
[Freire 1971, 80.2]

L45] An elder said: 'He is not a monk who curses another. He is not a monk who renders evil for evil. He is not a monk who gets angry. He is not a monk who is greedy, proud, miserly, vain, or talkative. But the true monk is calm and full of charity, having the fear of God in his heart all the time.'
[Freire 1971, 82, cf. *APanon* 665]

[L46] An elder said: 'The monk ought not to enquire how this one is or how that one is doing; for by asking questions he is turned aside from prayer, turned toward distractions and much talking. So, nothing is better than keeping quiet.'
[Freire 1971, 86.1 / 30.1]

[L47] An elder said: 'If somebody speaks to you about the Scriptures or any other matter, do not dispute with him. If he speaks correctly, agree; if incorrectly, tell him: "You know what you are talking about." In this way, you will acquire humility and avoid ill-feelings. For if you persist in disputing and want to defend your point of view, offence is caused by that. Indeed, it often occurs that, even as you praise the other person, disagreement arises over his justification. Therefore, no matter what the subject, if you dispute vigorously you will experience no repose at all.'
[Freire 1971, 87.1]

[L48] A brother enquired of an elder: 'Until when should one keep
silent, father?' The elder replied: 'Until you are asked [a question], for it
is written: "Speak not until you hear." Even he who speaks a good word
ought not to speak unless he has formerly come to the conclusion that it
would be to his advantage to speak [it]. You will experience repose
anywhere, if you remain silent.'
[Freire 1971, 88.2 / 32.3]

[L49] An elder said: 'Voluntary exile [*perigrinatio* / ξενιτεία] undertaken
for God is a good thing if it be practiced in silence; for loose talk [*fiducia*
/ παρρησία] is not voluntary exile.'
[Freire 1971, 89.1 / 32.5]

[L50] Abba Moses used to address those who lived alone, saying: 'There
are four principal observances: keeping quiet, observing the
commandments of God, humbling oneself, and oppression by poverty.
But these three virtues a man acquires with difficulty: that is, by grieving
all the time, ever being mindful of his own sins, and always confronting
his eyes with death.'
[Freire 1971, 5.1 / 35.1]

[L51] An elder said: 'If you have a passion and you get free of it, then
pray to the Lord for another one, you will not be granted it. So, pray first
for your struggle and, when you have been spoken of for having
persisted, then make intercession for others.'
[Freire 1971, 36.2]

Some apophthegms that are found interspersed with Paschasius' text in
some manuscripts but which are to be considered spurious:

[L52] One of the fathers said: 'Whatever bitter or heavy thing you
tolerate for God, do not make it known to men and lose your
recompense. Let it be known only to God who sees in secret [Mt 4:6, 16]
and from whom you await the reward of your labour.'
[Freire 1971, App. 1]

[L53] Saint Hilarion said: 'He arranges his life well who for Christ's sake
keeps nothing back for himself.'
[Freire 1971, App. 2, from *Life of Hilarion* c. 18]

[L54] An elder said: 'Whatsoever you disburse in alms out of fear for God, do not lay it out as a hard and bitter thing to do, but look upon the poor man with joy in your soul and a calm face and thus you raise him up in honour above yourself, knowing that giving to the poor is the treasury of Christ and that "the Lord loves a cheerful giver".' [2 Cor 9:7]
[Freire 1971, App. 3]

[L55] A brother asked some elder: 'Tell me, father, what proportion ought I to have of that which is in the cell and is of the gifts of the Lord?' To him the elder replied: 'It is dangerous for one who serves the Lord to be given to avarice. But if you wish to experience repose, do not store anything up before time or any more than you need. Be more concerned about heavenly than about earthly things, as the Lord himself said: "Where your treasure is, there will your heart be also." [Mt 6:21] He who stores up does not know for whom he is collecting; but he who disburses undoubtedly sends a light before him. Therefore, we believe that nothing is more useful than freely to hand out the gifts of the Lord.'
[Freire 1971, App. 4]

[L56] He [Abba Agathon?] used to say to his disciples: 'Also let a monk's clothing be one that [covers] his nakedness and keeps out the cold, not one of added colour on account of which his soul wavers this way and that through boasting in pride or in vanity.'
[Freire 1971, App. 5]

[L57] The holy Abba Hilarion said: 'Cursed is the man who looks for physical food before the spiritual; whatever he does, he should ever meditate good things in his soul.'
[Freire 1971, App. 6, from *Life of Hilarion* c. 27]

[L58] When Abba Paul the Simple wanted to cure some sick person, he continued in prayer and fasting, saying: 'I will indeed not eat bread today unless you make him whole' – and all illness departed from the sick man.
[Freire 1971, App. 7, cf. *HL* 22:12]

[L59] There were also seven other well-tried men living in that desert close to the Saracens. [They occupied] cells not far removed from each other and were joined to each other by the link of love. One was called Peter, another Stephen, the third John, the fourth George, the fifth Theodore, the sixth Felix, the seventh Laurus. Living in this sterile and vast altitude, scarcely fit for human habitation, they permitted themselves

to see each other once a week. For on Saturday at the ninth hour they would come together, each one from his own place, at an agreed location, each one bringing what he had been able to find. One would bring nuts, one lettuce, one dates, one figs, one edible plants: cabbage, parsnips, cumin, and parsley. Such indeed was their usual nourishment, for they made no use of bread, oil, or drink; they were only sustained by the above-mentioned plants and by fruit. Only the palm provided them with clothing. Almost no water was to be found in those parts; they would only drink when setting out in the morning and, as they did their rounds, they would collect the dew which fell quite heavily on various plants – and that was the extent to which they used to drink. When, as we said, they assembled in one place, they would take food after giving thanks to God. After the meal, they would sit until evening meditating on the Holy Scriptures. No worldly conversation circulated among them, no concern for the world, nothing to do with earthly things; only spiritual discourse, a desirable recollection of the heavenly kingdom, the blessedness to come, the glory of the just and the sufferings of the sinful, the repose of all the saints which they are already enjoying in the blessed mansions of paradise. Thinking on these things they would sigh from the depths of their bosom and weep copiously. When they had kept vigil the whole night through, singing praises to the Lord, on the Sunday at the ninth hour they used to put an end to speaking with and seeing each other. Each one returned to his cell wherein he alone concerned himself with God alone, days and nights. Thus were they occupied when the Saracens, charging across the desert, discovered them, fell on them, and drove them out of the desert. They tied them and hung them up by their feet and, after afflicting them in many ways, they made a fire of the most bitter herbs beneath them. Tortured beyond belief, they lost the sight of their eyes on account of the bitterness of the smoke. After they had inflicted them with many tortures, they let them go, half dead. We know that one of them survived for a considerable time in a certain place but we have no idea where the others ended up.
[Freire 1971, App. 8]

'Reminders of the Holy Fathers who grew old in the study of the spiritual life, which they spoke by way of instruction to the younger brothers. Counsels of the holy fathers.'
[Freire 2010, p. 312]

[L60] The holy fathers also used to say of the holy Abba John also known as Colobus[5] that when he returned tired out from working at the harvest, he would present himself to the holy fathers then, when he had offered a prayer with them, go immediately to his cell. There he would spend a long time in silence; in prayers, readings of, and meditations on the Holy Scriptures. And while he was doing his handiwork each day he would not allow anybody to come to him. He used to say that at the time of working at the harvest, the concentration of the mind was dissipated and suffered by being set free, with the result that it became entangled in various thoughts. So, he would impose additional abstinence on himself, saying: 'Since in those days I used to eat my fill of bread each day because I was working at the harvest, now that I am enjoying respite in my cell, I ought to increase my abstinence and vigils to make up and compensate for what was omitted in those days.'
[Freire 2010, 1.2]

[*APalph* Benjamin 2, *APsys* 4.12: Abba Benjamin, the priest at Kellia, said: 'We visited an elder at Scete; we wanted to serve him some oil, and he said to us, "Look, there lies the small vessel [of oil] that you brought me three years ago; it stayed there where you put it." We were astounded at the elder's way of life when we heard this.']

[L61] When we heard this, we said to him: 'But why did you not taste this same oil at least on feast days, father?' He said to us in reply: 'I declined to use any of it in case I became accustomed to it and, from the sweetness of the oil, I might look for seasoned dishes. Then, in search of that agreeable seasoning, I might be obliged to go down into the town or into the villages to buy oil, then return to the desert only to go down again and come back to my cell. As I said, by this coming and going, my mind and my perception would begin to wander and I would lose the advantage of a life of withdrawal. The devil has many forms and he weaves a variety of nets to capture the minds of men.'
[Freire 2010, 1.9]

[*APalph* Benjamin 3: The same [elder] said: 'We visited another elder and he detained us to eat; he served us radish-oil and we said to him: "Father, rather do you serve us a little decent oil." When he heard this, he signed

---

5 Gk. κολοβός, maimed, curtailed, 'the dwarf'.

himself and said: "If there is any other kind of oil beside this, I do not know of it."']

[L62] The same elder [*senior*] had been raised in the desert from infancy and ever remained there with the holy elders [*seniores*] and never went out either into towns or villages.
[Freire 2010, 1.10]

[L63] An exhortation of holy Macarius to the monks. The holy Abba Macarius often used to remind his disciples and teach them, saying: 'Always remember that you are living in the sight of Almighty God who anticipates the *logismoi* of every man and scrutinizes the heart of each one. The Holy Scriptures also bear witness to this and the Apostle teaches saying: "The word of God is living and active and sharper than any two-edged sword, piercing even to the dividing of soul and spirit and discerns the thoughts and intents of the heart. There is no creature invisible in his sight for all things are naked and open to his eyes." [Heb 4:12–13] Therefore brothers, if carnal delight in the lust of *porneia* attack us, let us make haste to chase away and reject from our heart the most unclean and extremely detestable *logismos*, persistently invoking the help of our Lord Jesus Christ in prayers and fasts: that, by virtue of his strength, he might deliver and protect us and tread down Satan under our feet. We must both take hold of ourselves and say to our soul: "The physical delight that is charming you adversely lasts for a short time; while the afflictions and torturing of soul and body in the eternal fire of Gehenna are a punishment that endures for ever." And in admonishing our soul, let us say this too: "If you are ashamed for men (who are sinners like you) to see you sinning, why ought you not even more so to revere and fear the majesty of Almighty God, who closely observes the secrets in the hearts of all? As the Apostle says: 'All things are naked and open to his eyes.'" [Heb 4:13] If we make our own ears ring with such thoughts, the fear of the Lord comes into our heart right away and our soul is confirmed in the love of chastity. We are also moved to observe all the precepts of the Lord with the help of the grace of our Lord Jesus Christ who has promised to give heavenly and eternal [things] in that glorious life of the age to come to those who serve him in holiness and chastity, ever to rejoice with the holy angels in a perpetual splendour of light.'
[Freire 2010, 3.1]

[L64] One time very many monks came to holy Poemen. When he had explained various chapters of Holy Scripture to them, he asked them: 'Tell me, who sold holy Joseph?' In reply they said to him: 'His brothers sold him off.' The blessed elder [*senior*] said to them: 'Not so; his humility and patience sold him for, patiently enduring [the situation] through humility, he refused to resist his brothers. If he had been willing to say: "I am their brother" they could not have sold him; but he kept quiet and made no contradiction, committing everything to the judgment of Almighty God. So, it is clearly shown that his humility sold him off. Then again, the same grace of his humility (by the disposition of divine providence) made him king and prince of the entire land of Egypt. It was not only in this world that humility obtained him a kingdom, for he is also reigning gloriously in the heavenly and eternal kingdom with all the saints. So ought we, little sons, to hold fast and for ever embrace the virtue of humility, enduring afflictions and insults in all patience for the sake of righteousness, in order that we might attain eternal and heavenly glory.' [cf. John Colobos 20]
[Freire 2010, 4.5]

[L65] There was an old man [*senex*] in a *coenobion*, a highly experienced monk, who became sick with an extremely grave illness. Overwhelmed by this excessive and intolerable illness, he laboured on for a long time in great pain. The brothers were unable to find out how to treat the sickness, for they did not have what the gravity of his illness demanded in the monastery. But when a certain handmaid of God heard about the affliction of his illness, she asked the father of the monastery if she could take him to her cell and look after him, especially as she could more easily find in the town the things that the gravity of his illness seemed to require. So, the father of the monastery directed that the brothers were to carry him to the cell of the handmaid of God. For her part, she took the old man in very respectfully and looked after him in the name of the Lord for the recompense of the eternal reward which she believed she would receive from Christ our Lord. When she had sedulously cared for and looked after the servant of God for three years and more, men whose minds were corrupt began to suspect in the perversity of their own minds that the elder [*senior*] did not have a clear conscience concerning the virgin who was looking after him. When he heard this, the elder besought the divinity of Christ the Lord saying: 'You, Lord our God, you alone know everything; you see the great pain of my sickness and misery

and the affliction of so great an infirmity. This has consumed me for such a long time that the help and support of this your handmaid (which she offers me in your name) are essential to me. Grant her, Lord my God, an appropriate reward in eternal life such as you have deigned of your goodness to promise to those who care for the poor and the sick in your name.' [Mt 25:35–40] When the days of his demise drew nigh, very many holy elders and brothers of the monastery congregated around him. The elder said to them: 'Fathers and brothers, I beg of you sirs, that when I am dead, you take my staff and plant it on my grave. When it puts down roots and bears fruit, you will know that my conscience is clear concerning the servant of God who looked after me. But if it does not put out shoots, know that I am not innocent regarding her.' So, when the man of God departed from his body, the holy elders planted his staff over his own grave as he had specified; and it put out shoots! In the course of time, it produced fruit and they were all amazed and glorified God. At such a miracle many even came from the surrounding regions, glorifying the grace of the Saviour. We too have seen the actual bush and have blessed the Lord who in every way protects those who serve him in sincerity and truth.
[Freire 2010, 4.10; *APalph* Cassian 2 abbreviated]

[**L66**] One of the holy ones had a disciple named Peter who dwelt with him in solitude. One day he became angry with him, drove him out of the cell, and shut the gate after him. He however remained where he was and went no further away; he was praying and weeping. When the elder opened the gate two days later and found him standing there he was exceedingly glad, appreciating his patience and true humility. He embraced him and led him into the cell; and he persevered with the old man [*senex*] until his life's end.
[Freire 2010, 4.15; cf. *APalph*, The Roman 2, *APsys* 16.26]

[**L67**] In a monastery there was a brother named Eulalius distinguished by the abundant grace of humility. If rather negligent brothers admitted to some fault, making excuses for their faults as usual, they would affirm that the afore-mentioned brother was the guilty one. When he was brought to book by the elders, he did not deny it. He would prostrate himself on the ground, revering them, saying he had sinned and dealt negligently. But when [brothers] frequently accused him and [elders] imposed a two- and three-day fast on him according to the rule of the monastery, he would patiently endure it all. Unaware that he was

patiently enduring all this by virtue of humility, the brothers (especially the older ones) met with the father of the monastery and said to him: 'Think what is to be done, father; how long can we put up with the omissions and the damage that Brother Eulalius is inflicting on the monastery? Already nearly all the vessels and utensils of the monastery are broken and destroyed by his negligence; how is a person like that to be tolerated?' In reply the father of the monastery said: 'Let us put up with him for a few days, brothers, and then let it be determined what is to become of him.' This said, he dismissed the brothers; then he went into his cell and prostrated himself in prayer, beseeching the mercy of the Lord to deign to show him what one might determine or decide concerning the frequently mentioned brother. Then it was revealed to him what he should do; the abba called all the brothers together and said to them: 'Believe me, brothers, I greatly prefer the mat of Brother Eulalius with his patience and humility to all the handiwork of those who work in the monastery, murmuring in their hearts. I order you to bring me the mats of all the brothers so that the Lord can show you what standing this brother has with God.' When they had brought them, he ordered fire to be lit; then he threw the mats of all the brothers into it. They were all immediately burned up, except the mat of Brother Eulalius; his mat was recovered whole for it was not burnt. When all the brothers saw this, they were much afraid, prostrating themselves on the earth, asking for the pardon and mercy of Christ the Lord, praising and admiring the extraordinary patience and humility of Brother Eulalius. Thenceforth, as a result of that, they honoured and exalted him as one of the great fathers; but Brother Eulalius could not tolerate this honour and praise. 'Woe am I, unhappy man', he said, 'for I have lost the humility I hastened to acquire (with the help and support of Christ the Lord) for such a long time.' So, he rose up at night and, going out of the monastery, he fled into the desert where nobody recognized him and lived there in a cave. For he refused the fleeting praise of men but [chose] to acquire heavenly and eternal glory from our Saviour in the age to come.
[Freire 2010, 4.16]

[L68] One day somebody came to blessed Macarius wishing to serve Christ in the monastic profession. He besought the holy old man to instruct and teach him and, from the fount of salutary doctrine which flowed freely from him through the grace of the Holy Spirit, to strengthen him and to show him how he might be able (with the aid of the Lord) to avoid the snares and onslaughts of the evil one. Blessed

Macarius said to him in reply: 'If you really wish with all your heart to renounce the present world, my son, and to cling to the Lord [our] Saviour, as the Psalmist says: "My soul clings after you but your right hand receives me", [Ps 62:9] the right hand of the Lord is ready to receive those who take refuge in him. You have to renounce this present world and reject all its works, as the Apostle says writing to the Colossians: "You are dead to this present world and your life is hidden with Christ in the Lord. But when Christ, your life, appears, then shall you appear with him in glory."' [Col 3:3] On hearing this, the young man said: 'Believe me, most blessed father, I have isolated my mind from this world and from all that is in the world, so that I now exist as though dead in the life of present time. For I am aware that all the things that seem to be good in this world are fleeting, ephemeral, and corruptible.' Then the elder said to him: 'Listen to me, my son; go to the sepulchres of the dead and attack them with as many insults, reproofs, and curses as possible and stone them so they be provoked and moved to anger against you.' The younger man made his way to the tombs of the dead as soon as he heard this. When (in his opinion) he had assailed them with many insults, according to the order of the blessed elder, he came back to the holy Macarius and told him what he had done. The elder asked him if those dead had made any response; in reply he said: 'They said nothing at all, master.' [The elder] directed him again, saying: 'Tomorrow, go praise and exalt them with great admiration.' The brother went off again to the sepulchres of the dead and began to praise them and to exalt them in laudatory phrases, saying: 'You are great and holy, like apostolic men; there is great righteousness in you.' After he had spoken very many other praises to them, he returned to the elder's cell and said: 'Here, I have praised and glorified those dead ones according to your instructions and they said nothing to me at all.' Then holy Macarius said to him: 'Just think, my son, how you reproached those dead with insults and opprobrium and they said nothing to you. So it is with you; if you wish to be saved and to please our Saviour Christ in the holy profession, imitate our Lord and Saviour himself, as John the apostle and evangelist says: "Whoever says he is living in Christ should himself proceed in the way [Christ] proceeded." [1 Jn 2:6] And in the Gospel we read that the Jews uttered many insults against the Lord our Saviour at the instigation of the devil, [saying] he was a Samaritan and that he had a demon [Jn 8:48] and that it was by Beelzebub, prince of demons, that he cast out demons, for they dared to say that he led [people] astray. [Jn 7:12] Yet the Lord, the creator of heaven and earth, patiently endured all these [insults] to provide us with examples of patience and humility. If he had wanted to show the power of his majesty and be revenged for the insults, he would suddenly have reduced the entire world into chaos. Both the human race and the world itself would have disappeared and in a moment; everything would have ceased to exist. Yet the ineffable affection of Christ the Lord (who had come not to punish but to save the world) [Jn 3:17] declined to do this. So he patiently endured it all so he could show us examples of patience and humility. So he said to the disciples who were his followers: "Learn from me for I am meek and humble of heart and you shall find rest for your souls." [Mt 11:29] But all the saints in this world, prophets as much as apostles, when they were afflicted with outrages, insults, and various torments, always maintained immovable the virtues of patience and humility and never were they led astray by the praises of men. They repudiated the empty talk of the vainglory of this present life; they who wished to please Christ desired only that heavenly and eternal glory which is from God and remains for ever, the splendour of whose brightness no human tongue can exhibit. So then, my son, contemplating these examples of patience and humility, when gratuitous offences come upon you, most strongly maintain the virtues of patience and humility, imitating the prophet who said: "I am like a deaf man who cannot hear and have been made like a mute not opening his mouth and does not have a sharp retort in his mouth." [Ps 37:14–15] This is sung each day at the *synaxis* so it might remind our senses. Take care also not to delight in the vainglory and praises of men and lose all you have acquired by toiling away at good works. Thus would you not receive of the Lord the fruits of your fasting and abstinence, the reward of your vigils and prayers in eternal life. For he himself says in the Gospel of those who look for the praise of men: "I tell you in truth, they already have their reward." [Mt 6:2] In many another passage the Holy Scriptures do not stop warning us to be cautious where vainglory is concerned. So, be cautious my son and do not let your spirit go up in flames of hasty temper at gratuitous insults. And if your heart be moved to anger, do you yourself firmly restrain your spirit from anger in the fear of the Lord, so you can maintain the virtues of humility and patience. Then, if you make no angry response to those who insult you, you will truly display that which you promised when you said you are living in this world as one who is dead. You will be like those dead men in the tombs who said absolutely nothing back to you when you directed many insults and much abuse at them. For that reason we must firmly maintain the virtues of patience and humility so that we might attain the heavenly rewards and the glory

of eternal life, as the Lord says in the Apocalypse: "Hold on to what you have, lest another receive your crown.'" [Rev 3:11]
[Freire 2010, 4.19]

[**L69**] The holy and most blessed Antony, the true father in Christ of monks, directed his disciples and often urged them to cut off the remembrance of close natural parents and relatives from their hearts and to have no concern about their activities. [This he said] in order that the soul might be able to cleave to God with a free and unimpeded mind; without any physical concerns; without interruption and more intensely. For the stability of the mind is seriously disrupted and destroyed by concerns of that nature and the light of the heart is so dimmed that one does not realize to how great an extent the soul is wounded and pulled apart by various extravagant *logismoi*. It is necessary and extremely appropriate that monks never cease attentively interceding with the Lord for the souls of their natural parents and relatives, praying that he might deliver and save them from the eternal sentence of fire that is coming upon this world; praying that they might qualify to have a share in the true and eternal light of the righteous when Christ, the Son of God, the eternal king, shall come in the glory of his majesty with the holy angels and all the heavenly powers and authorities to judge the living and the dead in that great and awful day of the judgment of God. Monks ought also to intercede with and pray to the Lord for their parents, that they might qualify to receive eternal salvation in life without end; and that their lot be found in the reign of Jesus Christ our Lord. Amen.
[Freire 2010, 5.1]

[**L70**] This Arsenius, enflamed with the desire for divine love, abandoning all the temporal glory of this world, went into the desert of Scete in order to live his life among the holy fathers, isolated from all the hubbub of this world, so that, separated from physical attractions and delights, he could cleave to the Lord the Saviour with all his mind with concentration, as it is written: 'My soul cleaves to you; your right hand has received me.' [Ps 62:9]
[Freire 2010. 6.1(a)]

[**L71**] [Abba Sisoes] said: 'He who toils and concludes that he has achieved something receives his reward here.'
[*PL* 73:1025–62, 11.6]

[L72] An elder said: 'What is the point of beginning a task if one does not learn how to complete it? For that which is begun but not completed is nothing.'
[*PL* 73:1025–62, 27.2]

[L73] An elder said: 'To do an injury or to tell lies or to bear false witness is foreign to Christ. The soul is defiled by these four things: if one be in favour with powerful people, fulfil his carnal desires, disparage his neighbour, or fail to keep a guard on his eyes while walking through a town; and if he have any acquaintance whatsoever with a woman.'
[*PL* 73:1025–62, 36.2]

[L74] A brother enquired of holy Antony: 'What am I to do about my sins?' He replied: 'He who would be set free of sins will be freed of them through weeping and lamentation; and he who would be built up in virtues is built up through weeping tears. The very praise of the Psalms is lamentation. Remember the example of Hezekiah, king of Judah, according to what is written in [the Book of] the prophet Isaiah: by weeping he not only recovered his health, but qualified for a 15-year extension to his life. [Is 38:1–6] And through the flow of his tears the power of the Lord laid low in death an invading army of 185,000. By weeping Saint Peter the Apostle regained what he had lost in denying Christ. And Mary, because she watered the feet of the Lord with tears, was privileged to hear that she had chosen the better part. [Lk 10:38–42] Holy is the fear of the Lord and it abides for ever and ever.
[*PL* 73:1025–62, 28.1]

[L75] A brother enquired of holy Antony: 'How is it that when God promises the soul good things through diligent attention to the Scriptures, the soul is unwilling to remain in [those] good things but falls away towards what is transitory, unstable, and unclean?' He replied: 'What the Psalmist says accords with this: "If I have looked upon iniquity in my heart God will not hear me." [Ps 65:18] Are you not aware that great sins burst out when the belly is full of food, sins such as our Saviour foretold in the Gospel? "It is not that which goes into the mouth that defiles a man's soul" [Mt 15:11]; it is what come out of the heart that drown a man to death. Note what he says first: "Evil arguments, homicide, adultery, fornication, robbery, bearing false witness, and blasphemy." [Mt 15:19] Thus, he who has not yet tasted heavenly

sweetness so that he seeks after God with all his heart reverts indeed to
what is impure. Who will truly say: "I am become a beast of burden for
you and I am ever with you"?' [Ps 72:23]
[*PL* 73:1025–62, 40.1]

[**L76**] A brother enquired of an elder: 'What action shall I take against
logismoi of the passions, father?' 'Pray to the Lord that the eyes of your
mind may see the help which comes from God – who surrounds a man
and preserves him', he replied.
[*PL* 74:381–94, 4]

[**L77**] A brother asked an elder: 'What am I to do, for *logismoi* are
troubling me?' He replied: 'Go and talk to them [saying]: "Tell me what
I am seeking: what have I to do with you?" – and you will experience
repose. Be in low esteem, put your will behind you, do not be concerned
about anything and your *logismoi* will run away from you.'
[*PL* 74:381–94, 40]

[**L78**] A brother asked an elder: 'How is it that sometimes when I am
singing psalms I am in a hurry to get through them faster?' And he
replied: 'How will the man of God appear other than as one who is prey
to the demons? Then, we drive ourselves on with vigour, sustained by
fear of God and his love.'
[*PL* 74:381–94, 41]

[**L79**] A brother enquired of an elder: 'Do you think it is a good thing to
be highly regarded among people?' He replied: 'Their regard is of no
worth. Run away rather than wish to be highly regarded by your
brother.'
[*PL* 74:381–94, 55]

[**L80**] An elder said: 'The virtue of a monk is to be always accusing
himself.'
[*PL* 74:381–94, 62]

[**L81**] An elder said: 'The work of a monk is to see his *logismoi* from afar.'
[*PL* 74:381–94, 64]

[L82] An elder said: 'A man will become implicated again in everything that he has not cut away from himself.'
[*PL* 74:381–94, 67]

[L83] An elder said: 'He who gets the better of human fame and his belly experiences repose.'
[*PL* 74:381–94, 73]

[L84] An elder said: 'A monk ought to be courageous and single-hearted – then he will be saved.'
[*PL* 74:381–94, 74]

[L85] An elder said: 'We diverged from the straight and glowing path and are stepping in dark and thorny places; that is, we neglect to weep for ourselves and our sins and are always paying attention to the shortcomings of our neighbours.'
[*PL* 74:381–94, 81]

[L86] An elder said: 'It is all the same to a monk whether he wishes to take issue with one who has violently assaulted him or with the devil.'
[*PL* 74:381–94, 85]

[L87] An elder said: 'Whatever thing a person is doing, whether greater or smaller, let it all be held in contempt, whether in thought or deed.'
[*PL* 74:381–94, 86]

[L88] An elder said: 'Humility is not an expense but provides the seasoning in everything that is expensive.'
[*PL* 74:381–94, 87]

[L89] An elder said: 'To be humble and self-deprecatory is like a protective wall for a monk.'
[*PL* 74:381–94, 88]

[L90] An elder said: 'Speak as a free person, not as a slave.'
[*PL* 74:381–94, 95]

[L91] An elder said: 'It is impossible for a man to advance even in one virtue without custody of the tongue. Custody of the tongue is the primary virtue.'
[*PL* 74:381–94, 96]

[L92] An elder said: 'Decide never to do harm to anyone and be open-hearted towards all.'
[*PL* 74:381–94, 104]

[L93] Abba Moses asked Abba Silvanus: 'Is it possible for a man to begin again every day?' And he replied: 'A true workman can begin again every day. Each man ought to understand some little bit from all the virtues. On rising each day make a beginning in every virtue and in every commandment of God, in much patience and long suffering, in the fear and love of God, in humility of mind and body, in much forbearance, in tribulation, in staying in the cell, in prayer and intercession, with groaning, purity of heart and eyes, custody of tongue and speech, in denial of material things and carnal desires, in the warfare of the cross, that is: in mortification and poverty of spirit, in spiritual temperance and agonized battle, in penitence and mourning, simplicity of mind and few words, in fastings and nightly vigils and in manual work, as Saint Paul teaches when he says: "Workings with our hands, in hunger and thirst, in cold and nakedness, in labours and tribulations, in need and difficulties and persecutions, in ditches and caverns and caves of the earth." [2 Cor 11] "Be a doer of the word and not only a hearer." [Jas 1:22] Let your talent bring forth double, wearing the bridal garment, founded upon the firm rock and not on sand. [Mt 7:26] Be faithful in almsgiving, steadfast in faith, remembering every day that your death is at hand. Have no more care for the things of this world than as if you were already in the grave. Do not let shortage of food, humility, and sorrow pass from you. Let the fear of God be in you at all times. For it is written: "In the fear of God we have felt pain and given birth to the spirit of salvation even from the womb." [Is 26:9] If there be any virtue, look to these things. Do not reckon yourselves to be among the great but consider yourself to be lower than all other creatures, worse than any other human sinner, that is. Gain discretion; know yourself; do not judge your neighbour nor delight in other people's sins, but weep for your own sins, and do not scrutinize other people's actions. Be gentle in spirit and not angry. Think no evil in your heart about anyone, bear no enmity, and entertain no hatred towards anyone who bears enmity towards you without a cause. Neither be upset by his enmity nor look down on him in his need and tribulation. Render no evil for evil, but be at peace with all people, for this is the peace of God. Do not entrust yourself to an evildoer; do not rejoice with anyone who does evil to his neighbour. Slander no-one, for God knows all and sees each one of us. Do not believe the slanderer or

rejoice in his evil speech. Do not hate anyone because of his sin, for it is written: "Judge not and you will not be judged." [Mt 7:1] Do not look down on the sinner but pray for him that God will patiently turn him and have mercy on him, for the Lord is of great power. And if you hear about anyone doing evil things, say "Who am I to judge? For I too am a sinner, dead under my sins and mourning my own wicked deeds." He who is dead has no cause to trouble himself about anyone. Anyone then who thinks on all these things and earnestly pursues them is a worker for universal justice under the grace and virtue of our Lord.'
[*PL* 74:381–94, 108]

[L94] Abba Moses gave the following seven precepts to Abba Poemen which, if observed, will lead to salvation for anybody, whether in a *coenobion* or in solitude or in the world itself:

1.   In the first place, as it is written a man must love God with all your heart and with all your mind.
2.   A man must love his neighbour as himself.
3.   A man must do to death all evil in him.
4.   A man must not judge his brother in any dispute.
5.   A man must do no evil to another person.
6.   Before departing this life, a man must cleanse himself of every fault of mind or body.
7.   A man must always be of a humble and contrite heart.

This can be achieved by anyone who thinks of his own sins all the time and not of his neighbour's, with the assistance of the grace of our Lord Jesus Christ who with the Father and the Holy Spirit lives and reigns world without end. Amen.
[*PL* 74:381–94, 109]

CHAPTER 4

Sayings Preserved in Syriac

Translated by Robert Kitchen

The principal source of these Syriac additions to the Desert Fathers' reper-
toire is E. A. Wallis Budge's English translation of *The Paradise of the Holy
Fathers*, compiled by the seventh-century Church of the East author
'Anan-'Isho' in two volumes, London, 1907. The 109 sayings presented
here are all from the second volume and are numbered consecutively.
Budge had originally published an edition of the Syriac texts with English
translation in two large folio volumes, published privately and limited to
only 500 copies. Ostensibly, the Syriac text in volume 2 is the basis of
both of Budge's translation volumes. However, something seems to have
happened along the way from the 1904 edition to the more widely distrib-
uted 1907 volumes. Without the presence of the Syriac text, Budge
appeared to aim for a more popular audience and included all the sayings
and stories without comment. For the reader in English that is a simple
and excellent solution. For those who wish to consult the Syriac text,
however, there are several problems that confuse matters significantly. The
number assigned to the sayings in the 1907 translation only rarely matches
the number of the saying in the 1904 Syriac text. Many of the Syriac texts
do not come from the original manuscript and are given in the footnotes
of the English translation. A good number, particularly towards the end
of our selection, are found only in the Syriac edition edited by Paul
Bedjan, *Acta Martyrum et Sanctorum Syriace*, volume 7, Paris, 1897. Budge
sometimes notes that Bedjan's edition is his textual source, but towards
the end of the volume makes no mention at all of the whereabouts of the
text. In the English translation below I will list several sets of reference
numbers. The first will be the 1907 number of the saying or story with its
page number(s) in that edition; the second will be the number of the saying in the 1904 Syriac text, giving the location of the Syriac text in
Bedjan's edition where needed. There is a variance from 2 to 25 numbers
between the enumerations of the two editions. Of course, for the English
reader these problems do not affect the content of the sayings at all.

Sayings Reference Numbers:

E. A. W. Budge, *The Book of Paradise* [vol. 1, English translation; vol. 2, English translation continued and Syriac text] (London, 1904) [= B04]
E. A. Wallis Budge, *The Paradise of the Holy Fathers*, vol. 2 [English translation only] (London: Chatto & Windus, 1907) [= B07]
Paul Bedjan, *Acta Martyrum et Sanctorum Syriace*, vol. 7 [Syriac text only] (Paris/Leipzig: Harrasowitz, 1897) [= Bedjan]

B07 Volume number.Sayings number (Volume 2:Page number/s)
B04 Volume number.Sayings number (Volume number for Syriac text:Page number/s)
Bedjan Sayings number (Page number/s)

[S1] There once was an assembly in a large church, and all the elders in the assembly were asked, 'Which battle is the most powerful against the monks [solitaries][1]?' All of them confirmed this one: 'There is no battle stronger than this one: that a person might renounce his cell and move out [of it]. When this battle is won, all of the rest will be easily overcome.'
B07 1.23 (2:9); B04 1.23 (2:448)

[S2] It happened once that two elders were going up from Scete to Egypt and, from the arduousness of the road, they sat down at the bank of a river in order to eat. But one of them took his loaf in his hand and dipped it in the water. He then said to his companion, 'Abba, why do you not [also] dip your loaf in the water?' He answered him, 'It is written that when a possession becomes large do not set your heart upon it.'[2]
B07 1.72 (2:18); B04 1.72 (2:451)

[S3] They spoke about a certain monk that when he went out from the world and lived in a *coenobion* for several years, he was gentle with everyone through his subservience. All the brothers were amazed at his abstinence from food. Then he went into the wasteland and lived there for

---

[1] In Syriac ascetical literature, a monk is typically called a 'solitary' (*īḥīdāyā*). The same term is used for the 'Only-Begotten One', identifying monks as followers of Christ, the *Īḥīdāyā*.
[2] Ps 62:10.

many years, eating wild herbs. After a while he prayed to God to let him know what kind of reward he would be giving to him. An angel spoke to him, 'Depart from this desert and go out on the road and a shepherd will meet you, and according to [what] this person [says] you shall receive [as] a reward.' Departing straight away, he met that shepherd about whom he had been told and greeted him. When they sat down to converse with one another he saw the shepherd's bag in which were some herbs. That monk asked, 'What is this?' He said to him, 'It is my food.' He said to him, 'How long have you been eating these herbs?' The shepherd said to him, 'Thirty years more or less I have not tasted anything else except these herbs once in the evening of every day, while also drinking water in accordance with what I eat.[3] The wage which the owner of the flock gives to me I give to the poor.' When that monk heard these things, he fell down at the feet of that shepherd and said, 'I thought I had mastered[4] abstinence, but you through your discipline are worthy of a greater reward than me because, every herb that I encountered, I ate immediately.' Then that shepherd said to me, 'It is not right for rational human beings to imitate the animals, but at the correct and organized times to eat what is prepared for them, and afterwards to take up a fast from everything until the [next] correct time.' Having profited [from this], that monk added to his labour and was perfected. He praised God, marvelling at how many holy people there were in the world, unknown to human beings.

B07 1.104 (2:23–4); B04 1.103A (1:618n1) – Bedjan 103 (p. 478)

[S4] An elder said, 'Whenever a person reads in the divine books, the demons are afraid.'

B07 1.107 (2:24); B04 1.107 (2:458)

[S5] An elder said, 'I know a brother who sat with the brothers at the meal which was meant for the arrival of the brothers. While the brothers ate and drank, he did not distance himself from conversation with God through his prayer; not even one cup did he [drink]. That brother was marvellous in his way of life. Someone said, "Once I wanted to count the prayers he made, and I saw that he did not shorten his prayer night and day."'

B07 1.117 (2:26); B04 1.117 (2:461)

---

[3] Lit., 'according to my food'.
[4] Lit., 'grabbed hold of'.

[S6] Moreover [Abba Epiphanius] said, 'Whatever you do that is success-ful and may boast about, destroy that thing, for it is not right for a monk to boast of his excellent accomplishments. For if he boasts, he shall fall.'
B07 1.21 (2:27); B04 1.21 (2:462)

[S7] Abba Arsenius said that it is sufficient for a monk to sleep one hour, if he is vigorous. They spoke about a certain monk who lived in the mon-astery of the brotherhood. While he was very vigilant and [constantly] praying, he neglected the prayer of the assembly. During one of the eve-nings he was shown a glorious pillar of sparkling light in the midst of the brothers' assembly, and it reached up to heaven. Moreover, he saw some-thing like a tiny spark circling that pillar. Sometimes it was shining and sometimes it was extinguished. While he was marvelling at the vision, it was revealed to him by God who said, 'The pillar which you are seeing is the prayer of many people being gathered and ascending to God and giv-ing him pleasure. And the spark is the prayer of those who dwell in the assembly and despise the specific ministries of the brotherhood. If you also wish to be saved, fulfil with your brothers what is customary. Then if you desire and are capable of something distinctive, [do so].' Then he related all these things before the brotherhood and they praised God.
B07 1.135 (2:30–1); B04 1.134A (1:630n1) – Bedjan 128 (p. 488)

[S8] Some brothers went to an elder and showed him repentance and said to him, 'Abba, what should we do, because Satan is hunting for us?' He said to them, 'You should be alert and weeping continually. Indeed, my own thought is always standing where our Lord was crucified, sighing and weeping at all times.' So, having received a beautiful example of repentance, they went and became chosen instruments.
B07 1.141 (2:232); B04 1.140 (2:468)

[S9] An elder said, 'God dwells in a human being in whom nothing for-eign enters.'
B07 1.147 (2:33); B04 1.146 (2:469)

[S10] An elder said, 'It is a disgrace for a monk to enter into judgment against one who has harmed him.'
B07 1.210 (2:47); B04 1.209 (2:486)

[S11] One of the monks wished to go outside of the monastery and walk around for the purpose of a little pleasure and refreshment. When they

saw him, the elders said to him, 'Do not seek comfort in this world, my son, but toil; and persevere all the more in the invincible power of the Holy Trinity.'
B07 1.226 (2:50); B04 1.224 (2:491)

[S12] [Abba Moses] also said, 'Endure disgrace and affliction in the name of Jesus with humility and with a troubled heart, and show before him your weakness and he will become your strength.'
B07 1.228 (2:50); B04 1.226 (2:491)

[S13] One of the elders said, 'We went to the mountain of the blessed Antony to [visit] Abba Sisoes, and when we were sitting down to eat, a young man came in who was asking for alms. When we were beginning to eat, an elder said, "Ask that young man if he wishes to come in and eat with us." When he spoke to him, [the young man] did not wish [to do so]. The elder said, "Let us give to him whatever is left over from us to eat outside." The elder produced a pitcher of wine which was being kept for the Eucharist, and the elder mixed for each one a cup and gave that young man two. I was joking and said to him, "I will also go outside. Give me two [cups]." Abba Sisoes said, "If he had eaten with us he would have drunk equally, and he would have been convinced that we do not drink more. For now he will think to himself, 'These monks enjoy themselves more than me.' It is good, therefore, that our conscience should not condemn us."'
B07 1.258 (2:59); B04 1.256 (2:502)

[S14] An elder said, 'Do not eat before you are hungry. And do not sleep before you are sleepy. Do not speak before you are asked.'
B07 1.312 (2:69); B04 1.308 (2:515)

[S15] An elder said, 'I am waiting to die, in the evening, and in the morning and every day.'
B07 1.334 (2:76); B04 1.330 (2:524–5)

[S16] Abba Epiphanius said, 'Whenever a thought comes to fill your bosom, that is to say, your heart, vainglory or pride says to it, "See your fornication."'
B07 1.337 (2:77); B04 1.332A (1:697–8) – Bedjan 331 (p. 569)

[S17] The elders said, 'That a person would dare to blame his neighbour is similar to a person who overthrows the seat of the lawgiver or judge

and wishes to judge in his place. It is like one who blames and accuses the weakness of the judge. So then this is the rebellion of a servant against his lord, and against the judge of the living and of the dead.'
B07 1.357 (2:80); B04 1.351 (2:529–30)

[S18] A brother again said to Abba Poemen, 'My body is weak and I am not able to lead [an ascetical life]. Tell me a saying by which I may live.' The elder said to him, 'Are you able to control your thoughts, and not allow it to go to your neighbour in deceit?'
B07 1.365 (2:83); B04 1.359 (2:532)

[S19] Abba Paphnutius said, 'Not only a monk's body should become pure, but his soul should be pure of impure thoughts. We find that the body is strengthened by thoughts, but if the thoughts do not withdraw themselves, they will also sink the body. The way thoughts [work] is like this: they feed all the lusts of the flesh so that one will be controlled by them, and when they receive the lusts, these will also upset the body and cast it down like a pilot who is trapped in a storm, and the ship will sink. However, is it not self-evident to us that, if one person love another, he will not say anything evil about him? But if he do say [something evil] about him, he is no longer his friend. In the same way also, whoever loves lust[5] does not say anything evil against it. If he speak against it, he is not its friend. But if someone [speak] against what he does not know, or against whatever does not afflict him, but whatever causes him suffering and is tempted by the hateful one, he will speak evil about it, and does not speak about it as a friend, but as an enemy. In this way everyone who says that [lust] is evil and rejects lust is not a friend of the lusts.'
B07 1.386 (2:86); B04 380 (2:536–7)

[S20] He spoke again, 'In the same way, just as when judges execute those who are evil, so [ascetical] labours kill the evil lusts. Just as evil servants flee from their masters, so also lusts flee from the exhaustion of the labours. But the good workers honour their masters just as sons [honour their] fathers. For exhaustion engenders virtues, and from exhaustion virtues spring forth, just as passions [spring forth] from delicacies. Exhaustion produces virtues, for a person becomes weary with his soul and it generates virtues. It slays vices just as the righteous judge [executes the evil ones].'
B07 1.387 (2:86); B04 1.381 (2:537)

---

[5] Typographical error in Syriac text; read 'lust, desire'.

[S21] [The brothers] again said, 'There was a certain brother, a Nazirite and an ascetic. He wanted to go to the city to sell his handiwork and buy what he needed. He called a brother and said to him, "Come with me so that we may go and return together." When they went up as far as the gate of the city, that Nazirite said to his companion, "Sit here, my brother, and wait for me until I go in and complete my business, and I will return to you quickly." But when he entered the city and went around among the markets, a wealthy woman seduced him, and he took off his habit and took her as a wife. He sent [word] to his companion and said, "Get up and go back to your cell, because you will no longer see me." But the one who was sent to him related to him everything which had happened. He responded to that one who was sent and said to him, "God forbid that these things would be said concerning my holy brother. And God forbid for me to move from here until my brother comes back as he said to me."

'He was waiting there a long time and did not cease night and day from weeping and prayer. His report was heard throughout the entire city, and the clergy and monks and bishops of the city [tried to] persuade him to move back to his monastery, but he was not obedient to their advice. However, he said, "I will not violate the commandment of my brother and I will not move away from here until the two of us go back to the monastery together."

'He stayed there for a period of seven years. During the summer he was burning up from the heat and during the winter he was drying up from the cold and frost. He was in hunger and thirst and in weeping, but through vigils he was petitioning God on his [companion's] behalf. Then one day his companion came back to him, dressed in expensive clothing, and said to him, "So and so, I am the one who came with you, the monk so and so. Rise up, go back to your monastery." But when [the other] saw him he said, "You are not [him], because that one was a monk, and you are a worldly person." Once God saw the vexation of that brother, after seven years that wife died. Moved to remorse, that brother put on again the habit and went out to that mourner, his companion. When he saw him, he stood up [and] embraced and kissed him, and took him with joy and they went back to the monastery. He renewed his former ways of life and became worthy of the highest perfection. Through the patience of the one, that other one lives; and that which was said was fulfilled, "A brother is assisted by his brother, like a city [is assisted] by its fortress."'

B07 1.395 (2:89–90); B04 1.388(b) (1:716–18n1) – Bedjan 390 (p. 590)

[S22] A brother went to buy linen from a widow, and when she was selling it to him, she sighed. That brother said to her, 'What is the matter with you?' The widow said to him, 'God has sent you today so that my orphans may be fed.' When that brother heard [this] he was distressed, and secretly took from his own linen and threw[6] [it] on the widow's side of the scales until he had fulfilled [an act of] charity towards her.
B07 1.419 (2:97); B04 1.412 (2:549)

[S23] A brother came to Abba Or and said to him, 'Come with me to the village and buy for me a little wheat which I need.' But the elder was greatly shaken by this, because it was not his custom to enter the village. Being afraid of [disobeying] the command, he got up and went with him. When they entered the village the elder saw[7] a person passing by and called out to him and said, 'Perform [an act of] grace and guide this brother and fulfil his need.' In this way he fled back to the mountain.
B07 1.420 (2:97); B04 1.413 (2:549–50)

[S24] Abba Pior worked hard to be able to defeat that [inclination] to speak familiarly to a brother.
['à ne pas dire "tu" à un frère' – Dom Lucien]
B07 1.501 (2:116); B04 1.493 (2:573)

[S25] The elders said, 'If someone should say to his brother, "Forgive me" while humbling himself, this comes from the perfection of the monk.'
B07 1.521 (2:118); B04 1.512 (2:575–6)

[S26] Once seven brothers came to visit Abba Arsenius, and they were asking him, 'Tell us, what is the work of monks?' The elder answered, 'When I came to dwell in this place, I went to two elders, and I asked them this [same question]. They answered me, "Do you believe us?" I said, "Yes." They said to me, "Go and whatever you see us doing, you should also do."' The brothers asked him afterwards, 'Tell us, Abba, what was their work?' The elder said to them, 'One acquired great humility and that other one obedience.' But they said to him, 'Tell us about your work as well.' The elder said to them, 'According to my will and mind, this is what is important: A person should not restrict[8] himself in any situation.' Having profited, they moved on with joy, praising God.
B07 1.527 (2:120); B04 1.517 (2:578)

---

[6] Typographical error: Syriac text has 'called'; 'threw, tossed' is the verb required.
[7] Syriac text has 'answered' or 'conversed'; 'saw' fits the context.
[8] Typographical error: the verb should be 'confine, bind, restrict', not 'consider'.

[S27] An elder said, 'Be careful, with all of your strength, not to do something worthy of blame, and do not desire to adorn yourself.'
B07 1.533 (2:121); B04 1.523 (2:579)

[S28] They said about Abba Poemen that he never insisted on his own opinion and that his knowledge was superior to [any] one of the elders.
B07 1.537 (2:121); B04 1.527 (2:589)

[S29] Again the elder said, 'If a person should exert himself to become a teacher, this is [an act] of labour.'
B07 1.545 (2:123); B04 1.535 (2:582)

[S30] One of the brothers asked Abba Zeno, for he had freedom [of speech] with him, and said to him, 'See, you have grown old; how is the matter of fornication?' The elder said to him, 'It knocks, but it passes by.' One of the brothers asked him, 'What is it that knocks and what is it that passes by?' The elder said, 'Suppose that the memory of such-and-such a woman is brought up, and you say, "Oh." Then you do not allow it to ascend up into your mind. However, the young men are excited by it.'
B07 1.587 (2:132); B04 1.576 (2:594–5)

[S31] One of the elders related [this story]: 'A certain monk dwelt in the wilderness and conducted himself in an excellent way of life. He was famous among people in the way he drove away demons and healed the sick. Then by the work of Satan it happened that the passion of fornication was aroused against him, and because he was not humble enough to reveal his battle to the elders around him, in a few days he fell into fornication with a woman who had constantly been coming to him to receive help. But when he fell, he gave up hope for himself and rose up to go back to the world, being sad and distressed concerning his fall. He thought again, "I will go into the inner wilderness [far away] from me, and I will see no one, nor be seen by anyone, and there I will die like the animals." And going, he wandered in the wildernesses and mountains, crying out during the night and during the day and saying, "Woe is me! Woe is me!" He did not cease from weeping and from groans. There was in that wilderness an older monk who dwelt in the cleft of a rock. When he heard the sound of weeping and lamentation, his compassion revealed to him about him and he went out to encounter him. They greeted one another, and he addressed him, "Why are you crying like this?" He said,

"Because I have angered God [and] have fallen into fornication." That elder was surprised and said, "O how much I feared and trembled at your quivering voice because I thought that you had been entrusted with the governance of the brothers and had governed unjustly, or scandalously squandered the work of the community of brothers. For the prostitute repented[9] and the unbeliever became the foundation[10] and the robber became the royal heir,[11] yet Ananias and Sapphira were killed because they had stolen from the money of the community of brothers.[12] In this way the soul of everyone is killed who dishonestly or disdainfully squanders the affairs of the monasteries. But you, my brother, take heart and return again to your cell, and pray to God while repenting, and [God] will restore you to your former status." Then he returned to his place and shut himself in it and no longer allowed himself to talk with anyone, except with that person who handed him food through the small window [in the cell]. He remained there until the end of his life, having attained the highest [level] of perfection.'

B07 1.602 (2:138–9); B04 1.590A (1:788–90) – Bedjan 594 (pp. 673–4)

[S32] Abba Amoun of Rhaithou[13] asked Abba Poemen regarding the impure thoughts and vain lusts which are generated from a person. Abba Poemen said to him, 'It is Satan's [undertaking] to sow, but ours not to receive.'

B07 1.603 (2:139); B04 1.590A1 (1:790) – Bedjan 596 (p. 676)

[S33] The elder Antony said, 'Many are those who fall and rise up to uprightness. There are some who fall from good actions to polluted things. Therefore, better is the one who falls down and gets back up than one who stands up and then falls down.'

B07 1.607 (2:140); B04 1.594 (2:605)

[S34] There was once a person among the brothers who at the beginning [of his ascetical life] took great care of his soul, but when a little while had passed, he began to despise the salvation of his life. His abba ordered him to take off the habit of the monks and to dress in worldly clothes and to depart from being among the brothers. Then he fell down at his feet and pleaded with him, saying, 'If you would forgive me this one

---

[9] Mary Magdalene.
[10] Jn 20:24–9.
[11] Lk 23:39–43.
[12] Acts 5:1–10.
[13] Possibly Tor.

time, abba, you will gain me from now on, for I will repent of those things I have done through negligence.' When he had greatly extended [his] plea and earnestly promised that he would become upright from then on, he became worthy of forgiveness and in this way struggled with all his soul in order to be a model for those great and small.
B07 1.613 (2:141); B04 1.599 (1:792–3n1) – Bedjan 606 (p. 678)

[S35] A brother asked an elder, 'My brother is abusing me and I am no longer able to endure it. What then should I do? Shall I rebuke him or speak nastily to him?' The elder said to him, 'Both things are evil: that one should rebuke him or that one should speak nastily to him.' [The brother] said to him, 'What should I do, for I am not able to bear either of these things?' The elder said to him, 'If you are not able to bear either of these things, speak to him, but do not rebuke him. For if you speak nastily to him and he hears, you may be able to calm him down, saying, "I did not say such and such a word," and it may be possible that the matter between both of you may be healed. But if you rebuke him to his face, you will make an ulcer which cannot be healed.'
B07 2.55 (2:168); B04 1.675 (2:632)

[S36] The brothers spoke about an elder who had a disciple who, when he sat down to eat, placed his legs upon the table. For many years the elder had this conflict, but did not rebuke him. Finally, [the elder] went to another elder and spoke to him about that brother. The elder said to him, 'Fulfil love and send him to me.' When the brother came to that elder, the elder stood up at meal time and set the table. As they were sitting down, [the elder] immediately placed his two feet upon the table, and that brother said to him, 'Abba, it is not proper to place your feet upon the table.' That elder said to him, 'Forgive me, my son, you have spoken well, for it is a sin.' He turned back and came to his teacher and told him [about it]. When the elder learned this, he discerned that this matter had been corrected for [his disciple]. From then on, that brother did not do it [again].
B07 2.64 (2:170–1); B04 1.684 (2:635–6)

[S37] A brother asked Abba Amoun, 'Why does one toil and ask in prayer, yet is not given what he is asking for?' The elder said to him, 'Listen, as much as Jacob laboured to receive, he did not receive what he was seeking, but what he was not seeking. Later on, he again worked and

laboured and at last received what he loved.[14] So also is the monk who shall be fasting and keeping vigil and not receiving what he is asking for. But he keeps on labouring with fasting and vigil and will receive the grace which he asks for.'
Bo7 2.68 (2:171–2); Bo4 1.688 (2:637)

[S38] Abba Poemen said, 'Everything which happens through the passions is sin.' Moreover, he said, 'Everything which is done[15] for the sake of God is a confession.'
Bo7 2.72 (2:172); Bo4 1.692 (2:638)

[S39] Another elder spoke about a passage of the Psalms, which was written, '"I will place his hand on the sea and his right [hand] upon the rivers."[16] This was spoken concerning our Saviour, who [places] his left hand on the sea which is the world, and his right hand on the rivers. This was spoken concerning the apostles for they water the entire world by faith.'
Bo7 2.98 (2.175); Bo4 1.716 (2.641–2)

[S40] Abba Sisoes showed us about Abba Antony and said, 'So then, in the cave of a lion a fox dwells.'
Bo7 2.103 (2:176); Bo4 1.721 (2:642)

[S41] Someone asked an elder from Thebes, 'Tell me how to be saved.' He said to him, 'There are three words: Sit in your cell and be silent. Examine your sins and fulfil your soul while not judging anyone else. And do not accept a favour from anyone, but may your hands be sufficient for your own provisions. If you are not able to grant a favour from your own labour, at least supply the need of your body by your own hands.'
Bo7 2.106 (2.176); Bo4 1.102 (2:643)

[S42] A brother asked one of the fathers, 'What shall I do for I am disturbed whenever I go up to fulfil the office of the deacon?' He said to him, 'It is not good for you to be disturbed whenever you go up to serve. But if not, and you are disturbed in your cell, then you should be labouring while giving thanks and receiving the wage of which you are worthy.' That brother said to him, 'If I find someone who will serve for me with

---

[14] Gn 29–31.
[15] Lit., 'bound'.
[16] Ps 89:25.

pleasure, while not being deceitful with him, can I do this?' He said to him, 'If a worldly person is able to fulfill your ministry and receive his wage, yes. But, a monk, no.'
Bo7 2.117 (2:179); Bo4 1.113 (2:656–7)

[S43] A brother asked an elder, 'Abba, what reply should I give to those who revile us that we do not return [to the world] on account of laziness, and through our manual work [and] labour of our souls we do not give comfort to strangers?' The elder said to him, 'While we have many things from the Law and from the commandments of our Lord to reply concerning the crown of perfection, yet in humility let us answer this. "Indeed, beloved, show us that when the Ninevites were in need of repentance, which one of them did these things for the world's need and requirements? Or did not even the king cease from doing that and took the same course of the ancient ones and the later ones and of those before them? He became quiet and was silent according to all the worldly qualities, and still no one has spoken regarding the punishment which was fitting for them.[17] Such is the case with ourselves: because we sin and violate natural and written law, we bring to naught all these worldly [qualities] until we sense that reconciliation has occurred and the penalty from former rights and commandments has been dissolved. Oh, did not also Paul teach us this: whoever is involved in a struggle, restrains his mind from everything else?[18] One does not rest until the Lord blots out the seed from Babel."'
Bo7 2.129 (2:182); Bo4 1.116 (2:649–50)

[S44] A brother asked an elder, 'What should I do with my thought which fights [against me]? Would it be better and also greater for me to go back into the world and teach and make disciples of many people and become a model of the Apostles?' The elder said, 'If there is nothing in your mind that makes you become less than all that has been commanded and you perceive and have encountered the haven of rest, and there is no passion of any kind in your mind, go. If these things are [not] gathered together, [the desire in you is due to] the working of evil that urges [you] on in order to cast you down from your stability.'
Bo7 2.130 (2:232); Bo4 1.117 (2:650)

---

[17] Jn 3:6–10.
[18] 1 Cor 9:24–5.

[S45] A brother asked Abba Marcianus, 'What should I do so that I may live?' The elder replied to him, 'Whoever looks above does not see what is below. And whoever is involved in what is below is not knowledgeable of these things that are above. Whoever understands these things that are above is not attentive to the things that are below. For it is written, "Turn towards [me] and know that I am God."'[19]

B07 2.150 (2:185); B04 1.136 (2:654)

[S46] Abba Poemen said about Abba John, 'He cultivated all the virtues.'

B07 2.160 (2:189); B04 1.145 (2:658–9)

[S47] An elder said, 'Wisdom and simplicity are the perfect order of the apostles and of those who examine their ways of life, to which Christ urged them when he said, "Be innocent as doves and wily like serpents."[20] The Apostle was also admonishing the Corinthians in this same matter, saying, "My brothers, do not be childish in your minds, but be infants to evil things and in your minds be perfect."[21] Wisdom without simplicity is evil cunning, and this is the craft of philosophers among the pagans of whom it is said, "He seizes the sages by their cunning."[22] Moreover, "The Lord knows the thoughts of the wise that are vain."[23] Simplicity without wisdom is foolishness which is prone to error. Concerning [simplicity] the Apostle also wrote to those who possessed it, "I fear lest, just as the serpent made Eve go astray through his deception, so your minds may be corrupted away from your simplicity towards Christ."[24] Because they received every word without scrutiny as it is said in [the Book of] Proverbs, "The childish person believes every word."'[25]

B07 2.168 (2:232–3); B04 1.153 (2:660)

[S48] The elder Macarius said, 'These three matters are of the greatest importance and a person must place them before himself at all times. These shall be found with him: the remembrance of his death at every hour, and to die from every person, and that at all times he should be constant in his thought towards our Lord. Therefore, if the memory of a

---

[19] Ps 45:11.
[20] Mt 10:16.
[21] 1 Cor 14:20.
[22] Job 5:13; 1 Cor 3:19.
[23] Ps 94:11; 1 Cor 3:20.
[24] 2 Cor 11:3.
[25] Prov 14:15.

person's death is not before him at all times, he is not able to die from every person, and if he does not die from every person, he is not able to be constantly before God.'
B07 2.172 (2:192); B04 1.157 (2:662)

[S49] Again the elder Macarius said, 'Fight for every kind of death on account of physical death, that is, if you do not have the spiritual death, fight for the sake of physical death, and then the death which is spiritual will be added to you. The death such as this will make you die from every person. From then on you will acquire also the ability to be with God constantly in stillness.'[26]
B07 2.173 (2:192); B04 1.158 (2:662–3)

[S50] A brother questioned an elder, 'Why am I remembering my sins, but am not pained by them?' The elder said to him, 'This happens to us by contempt and negligence. When a person wishes to boil some [food] for his own need,[27] he finds in his fireplaces some small fiery embers, and wishes to care for and preserve them, lighting a large flame from them. But if he should neglect them they will fade and extinguish. So also it is with us, for if, however much God has bestowed upon us, we remember our sins, if we desire to come to stillness and acquire persistence remembering our sins, we will achieve great mourning in our hearts. But if we neglect them and do not even remember them, we will be rejected.'
B07 2.175 (2:192); B04 1.160 (2:663)

[S51] An elder said, 'Do not do anything without prayer, and afterwards you will not be sorry.'
B07 2.192 (2:196); B04 1.176 (1:873n1) – Bedjan 190 (p. 773)

[S52] A brother questioned an elder, 'What is the cultivation of the soul so that it may produce the best fruits?' The elder said to him, 'According to my own mind, this is the cultivation of the soul: stillness and perseverance, asceticism and toil, humility of the body and constant prayer. A person should not be observing the faults of [other] people, but keeping watch over his own offences. Therefore, if a person perseveres in these things, the soul will show virtuous fruits after not a great deal of time.'
B07 2.213 (2:234); B04 1.197 (2:672)

---

[26] Syriac – *shelya*; the highest form of contemplative silent prayer.
[27] Lit., 'for the use of his need'.

[S53] Once some brothers saw that Abba Joseph was gloomy and greatly distressed and they asked him to tell them what his sadness was about. But he was not able to speak to them. Each one of them began to speak to his companion, 'What in fact is the passion and sadness that the elder has? For we have been dwelling with him for many years, and never have we seen him with suffering and depression such as this. Are we causing offense to the elder by something?' They threw themselves down on their faces before the feet of the elder, saying, 'Have we impeded you in something, Abba? Forgive us for the sake of Jesus.' But the elder, being sad, replied, 'Forgive me, my brothers, I am not offended on account of you, but I am sad on account of myself, because I see that I am going backwards more than [I am] going forwards. I am the cause of offense and harm not only to myself, but also to the rest of the others. For I see that in this way we are earning much more harm for our soul than what we once gained in the profit of the fear of our Lord, because shamelessness and fearlessness have power over us. For sometimes when the fathers were gathered together with one another they formed companies and ascended to heaven. But we are dissolute ones and are dead in our[28] sins. Whenever we approach one another, we come to talk spitefully about one another and one by one we are being dragged down to the deepest abyss. Not only do we sink ourselves and one another, but also the fathers who come to us and the strangers who collect around us and also the worldly people who come to us, as if to solitaries and holy men. We are the cause of offense and harm. For Abba Sylvanus and Abba Lot spoke to me in this way, "We can no longer remain here." When I asked them, "Why are you moving away from us?" they said this to me, "Up to today we have prospered in our residence with the fathers. But since Abba Pambo and Abba Agathon and Abba Peter and Abba John have died, they have despised the commandments of the fathers and we do not keep the orders and laws which our fathers established for us. In our gathering with one another, we double the harm by the frivolous things spoken among us. When we sit at the table, instead of [doing so] with the fear of God and with thanksgiving and praise and with inner confession, while we are eating something God has prepared for us, we are engrossed with one another in conversation of tasteless stories. In this way we are in such an uproar sitting at the table that nothing being read to us is heard due to the noise of unprofitable conversation which we are conducting with one another. Moreover, after we get up from eating we keep engaging in empty talk. What is the benefit of our residing in the

---

[28] Syriac text: 'their [sins]'.

wilderness, when we do not profit anything?" Abba Lot said, "Many times I have heard from foreign brothers and from worldly people who come to visit us that we greatly despise the commandments of the fathers, and so they do not believe that we are monks." One of the foreign brothers said, "Many times I have come to visit the fathers, and year by year we have greatly deteriorated from the original ways of the fathers." So then, what do you want [to do]? Do you want to correct your dissolute ways and observe the commandments of our fathers? Or should I also depart from being with you?' When those brothers heard these things, they sent out notice and assembled the entire brotherhood and Abba Joseph said all these words [written] above. When the brothers heard all the words of Abba Joseph and learned about his suffering and about his depression and that he wished to depart from them, they threw themselves down on the ground, weeping and made penance to Abba Joseph, 'Forgive us, our Father, for the sake of Jesus. We have angered God through our deeds as well as grieved your holiness.' Each one of the fathers said, 'If only from the first day that you heard from our upright fathers [about us] and they had not departed from us, we would have been roused from our sleepiness in our laxities. But what do we do? As for the elder and priests who do not teach us, not even they organize themselves in our assembly with one another, and in our sitting down at table. For many of us desire to hear the stories and commandments of the fathers which are read at table or between one sitting and the next, but we are not able to hear the sound of their speaking.' Abba Elijah said, 'Abba Abraham and Abba John talked a lot at the table during the time of reading and during the time of worship.' They began to perturb one another, and one said, 'Father, so-and-so is [too] excited,' and the other one said, 'So-and-so is bothering everyone.' When Abba Joseph saw that the whole brotherhood was upset, he entreated them, saying, 'I beg you, my brothers, silence your commotion, for God has called us to peace. On account of this I beg you, come, let us pray and supplicate to God so that he may make the legions and the host of the enemy pass over from our midst. For look, I see that they are standing in anger and rage, their swords being drawn and seeking to destroy all of us if God does not stand up in assistance of our wretchedness.' After he said these things, with difficulty he was able to silence them and Abba Joseph began[29] [to sing] from the words of the harpist David, saying in the following way, 'Then their sword shall enter into their heart and their bows shall be broken, and God made them like a potter's wheel and like straw

---

[29] Typographical error: read 'he began' instead of the text's 'he changed'.

before the wind. God will rise up and all his enemies will be scattered. God, deliver me; Lord, remain to help me.'[30] After all of them had said together the spiritual Psalms, they completed worship. They said, 'Holy God, Holy Almighty, Holy Immortal One, have mercy upon us.' All of them knelt down in prayer and, while they were praying, they heard the voices of the demons from the air and the sound of armour and of horses and of many soldiers. They heard again the sound of the demons themselves who were saying to one another, 'Do not give them any mercy.' Moreover, they said, 'O you unfortunate monks, why are you resisting us? If we were to do [something] to you, not one of you would be found upon the face of the earth. We will never cease and desist from [bothering] you.' After the filthy[31] legion was driven away through the hidden power and the evil demons rested from their wickedness, all the fathers rose up from [the ground] upon which they had been shedding [tears] in prayer, because the ground was damp with their tears. All of them offered penance to Abba Joseph, saying, 'Forgive us and pray for us so that our Lord, whom we have sinned against and angered, will forgive us.' Abba Joseph said to them, 'Be alert, my brothers, and take care of yourselves. For look, with your own ears you have heard the sound of the chariots of the Enemy who threatens and seeks to destroy us. Therefore, may every person reconcile with his neighbour and forgive everyone [his] offense from your heart. Bind yourselves in the love of our Lord with a strong mind and a pure heart with our Lord and with one another. Come near to God and he will approach you. Stand up against the Enemy who is Satan, and he will flee from you. Therefore, if [you] observe the commandment of the fathers, I will pledge myself to you so that Satan is not able to injure [you]. Nor will the barbarians come here. But if you do not keep [the commandments], believe me, my brothers, this place will be destroyed.' Everyone offered penance to each other and reconciled themselves with one another and lived in love and in great peace. They established canons among them on that day, so that from then on a person might not conduct himself through negligence and fearlessness and might not be doing or saying something foreign [to their way of life] at the table. If someone should be found later on ignoring and despising the commandments of the fathers, and it is a cause of offense and harm, firstly to himself and then to those who are residing with him, as well as to the strangers who come to visit us, let him know that this [offense] will bring punishment upon himself, while becoming

---

[30] A composite citation from Ps 37:5, 83:13, 68:1, 7:1.

[31] Typographical error: read 'filthy [ones]' instead of text's 'virtuous [ones]'.

a foreigner to the entire brotherhood. Abba Joseph sent the brothers after Abba Sylvanus and Abba Lot to bring them back. When Abba Sylvanus and Abba Lot heard what had happened among them, that they had established canons to guard the commandments of the fathers, they praised God. They rose up to come and see Abba Joseph [and] greeted him while weeping. Abba Joseph told them everything that had happened and they praised God who does not abandon those who fear him. As for the canons and ordinances they had established among themselves, they kept and fulfilled them all the days of their lives. They died at a good old age and in ways of life that pleased God.
B07 2.256 (2:206–10); B04 1.240 (2:681–5)

[S54] A person related about an elder from Scete who went up to Thebes to dwell there. As was the custom for those who were from Scete, he made bread for [several] days. Then, some people from Thebes came to him and said, 'How are you keeping the word of the Gospel which commands one not to be anxious for tomorrow?'[32] The elder said to them, 'Your custom, how does it work?' They said to him, 'We labour day by day with our hands and we sell [what we make] and from the market we buy food for ourselves.' The elder said to them, 'My market is my cell. Whenever I need something, I set to work with my hands and I take food for myself.'
B07 2.280 (2:215–16); B04 1.262 (2:692–3)

[S55] An elder said, 'A person who boasts in the name of God, but does not do work worthy of that name is similar to a poor man who, when the feast comes, asks for some clothes and puts them on. When the feast has passed, he takes off the clothes which are not his and gives them back to their owners.'
B07 2.304 (2:219); B04 1.284 (2:697)

[S56] An elder was asked, 'Why is it that when I am sitting in my cell my heart wanders?' The elder said to him, 'Because your external lusts are feeling the movements in [your] hearing and breathing and taste, for from these, if possible, one has pure labour and will make them become healthy and satisfied within.'
B07 2.320 (2:220–1); B04 1.300 (2:698)

---

[32] Mt 6:25–33.

[S57] [Abba Benjamin] also said, 'This is the abstinence of the soul: one should make straight its ways, and cut off the passions of the soul.'
B07 2.324 (2:221); B04 1.304 (2:699)

[S58] An elder again said, 'In this way you should be afraid: like one who is going to endure tortures.'
B07 2.326 (2:221); B04 1.304 (1:910n1) – Bedjan 320 (p. 818)

[S59] An elder said once again, 'You should wish to become a eunuch; this will help you.'
B07 2.328 (2:221); B04 1.307 (2:699)

[S60] An elder said, 'I have not yet tolerated my body to fulfil all my desire.'
B07 2.309 (2:221); B04 1.309 (2:669)

[S61] One of the elders said, 'The love of [manual] work is the fall of the soul, but its establishment is stillness in God.'
B07 2.334 (2:221); B04 1.313 (2:699)

[S62] Another [elder] said, 'I have not allowed error to have control over me, even for one hour.'
B07 2.338 (2:222); B04 1.317 (2:700)

[S63] An elder said, 'It is necessary to investigate spiritual works so that through them we may progress in excellence. For it is great toil for us to venture from the body so that we do not perform physical works.'
B07 2.340 (2:222); B04 1.319 (2:700)

[S64] An elder said as well, 'Affliction and poverty are the tools of the monks by which one labours in his craft.'
B07 2.341 (2:222); B04 1.330 (2:700)

[S65] An elder saw a brother sitting in the midst of the brothers, and [the brother] was pretending, 'I am not like [them].' He said to him, 'How can you walk in a country that is not yours?'
B07 2.349 (2:223); B04 1.338 (2:701)

[S66] There was a monk who exercised great [ascetical] disciplines and harsh labours, and the devil schemed to make him reduce and stop from

doing them. The monk would not give him any hearing at all, but he would act valiantly even more strenuously and resisted his wiles. But as that devil had spent a great deal of time in the struggle with him, another devil came to help him. When he asked his companion [what] kind of struggle and battle he should set up against him, and [how this holy man] was disrupting and diminishing [whatever the devil was doing], that cursed devil who had just arrived answered with the advice of the evil one, 'Do not lift yourself up below him, but raise yourself above him and so you will be able to be stronger than him.'
B07 2.351 (2:223); B04 1.340 (2:701–2)

[S67] Abba Poemen said, 'Abba Athanasius said that if one does not acquire good works before God gives him a gift on account of himself, then it is evident that not even one person becomes perfect by the fatigue of his own accord. But if he should reveal it to his neighbour, then he will receive a gift on account of his neighbour and be satisfied.'
B07 2.362 (2:225); B04 1.350 (2:704)

[S68] Abba Copres said, 'Anyone who loves the comfort of his own desire more than the comfort of the will of God does not fear God.'
B07 2.371 (2:226); B04 2.358 (2:706)

[S69] A brother asked Abba Ammonas, 'How should one act when he desires to begin in some work, or to go or to come, or to move from one place to another, so that his action may be according to the will of God, being free of the error of the demons?' The elder said to him, 'First, one should consider in his mind and see what is the purpose of whatever he wishes to do, from where it comes, whether from God or from Satan or from himself, and then let him do whatever [he wants to do]. But let him flee from these two things [coming and going, and moving around]. If he does not, inevitably he will be laughed at by the demons. Nevertheless, afterwards, let him pray and seek from God to do what is his own [work] which is God's, and then begin in the work and afterwards boast about God.'
B07 2.372 (2:227); B04 2.358A (2:706) – Bedjan 367 (pp. 828–9)

[S70] He also said, 'In this way bear with everyone as much as God bears with you.'
B07 2.373 (2:227); B04 2.359 (2:706) – Bedjan 366 (p. 828)

[S71] An elder said, 'Delicacies distance one from heavenly honours. For satiety and extravagance here [in this world] along with numerous forms of lusts shut the door in our faces so that we may not enter the comforts of God. But think about the story of that rich man and Lazarus. For who was it that carried Lazarus into the bosom of Abraham? Was it not those incalculable vexations in which he was raised up? What was it that brought the rich man to Gehenna? Was it not those comforts and lusts burning in his body?[33] Therefore, each one of us, according to his stature by the indication of fire found within him, will have use [of delicacies] in the world to come. But each one of us, therefore, if he is not cautious, will be unsettled by the wood, the straw, and the stubble. Since it is necessary to extinguish carefully the fire of the lusts being stirred up in us, we have need of water, and not of wine.'
Bo7 2.379 (2:229); Bo4 2.364 (2:708–9)

[S72] Again an elder said, 'True obedience is in the example of a chaste bride who is not lured away by foreign voices; and the ear which strays a little from the truth is like an adulteress who strays from her partner. The mind which is led to every teaching of error is similar to a prostitute who is persuaded by everyone who calls her. Therefore, let us render obedient the wandering [mind] which is led astray by foreign voices; which, instead of the name of the true bridegroom, loves the name of its seducer. For it has accepted in its mind to be called by the name of a stranger and not the name of Christ.'
Bo7 2.380 (2:229); Bo4 2.365 (2:709)

[S73] One of the holy men spoke in this way, 'For the past 20 years I have struggled not to allow a strange thought to enter my heart and I have seen Satan up until the ninth hour and his bow was stretched out in order to shoot an arrow into my heart. When he could not find an opportunity, he was disheartened and went away every day being ashamed.'
Bo7 2.382 (2:229–30); Bo4 2.367 (2:710)

[S74] An elder said, 'If you are repentant, do not [have anything to do] with those who are in this world.'
Bo7 2.383 (2:230); Bo4 2.367 (2:710n1) – Bedjan 3 (p. 834)

[33] Lk 16:19–31.

[S75] They said concerning bishop Serapion that when someone came to him to receive the monastic habit, he said to him this word, 'When you pray, say, "Lord, teach me that I may do your will."'
B07 2.386 (2:231); B04 2.369 (2:711–12)

[S76] One of the fathers related, 'Two natural brothers once came to the wilderness to [visit] the solitaries. They conducted themselves superbly and were praised by the entire community. Then one of them became ill for not a few years and his brother ministered to him. Some of the fathers came to visit him and they began to praise the one who was serving him, and said, "Your worthiness and your abstinence have made you excellent before the entire community." But he replied, "In great humility, forgive me, my fathers, because I have not yet begun in the ways of life such as these. But my brother is the one who is living in these [ways]. And so that you may learn truly that such is the case, follow me and see." He brought them to his brother in the cell in which he was laying and said to him, "Abba, where is that axe that I gave you yesterday?" He began to look for it and said to him, "See, my brother, do me a favour and look with me." That brother who was sick took it upon himself to be asked for that thing which he had not taken. Having profited, the fathers went away from there.'
B07 2.388 (2:231); B04 2.371 (2:712)

[S77] An elder said, 'Flee from that love which persists by the means of destructive things. For with them [a person] also passes away and is destroyed.'
B07 2.389 (2:232); B04 2.372 (2:712–13)

[S78] Abba Elijah said, 'The friendship which a person possesses towards his neighbour, since its cause is on account of a temporal matter, with time will be turned around to harsh enmity.'
B07 2.390 (2:232); B04 2.373 (2:713)

[S79] Again he said, 'Everything which happens for God's sake is what remains and endures forever with those who are true.'
B07 2.391 (2:232); 2.374 (2:713)

[S80] An elder said, 'If you wish to learn about a neighbour, praise him more than you criticize him.'
B07 2.400 (2:234); B04 2.383 (2:715)

[S81] Moreover, another of the elders held a book above him when he lay down so that when he fell asleep the book would fall [upon him] and wake him up.
B07 2.402 (2:234); B04 2.385 (2:715)

[S82] One of the elders, while urging the brothers concerning the toil of virtue, said, 'Vexations are difficult for those who are not aware of them. But they are easy for those who are practiced in them. Vexations are like dogs. Just as dogs bite those who are not familiar to them, and wag [their tails] at those who are familiar to them, so also are the labours, giving pain to those who are not spending time with them. They benefit those who are practiced in them. But aside from this, lusts help them to engender vexations and miseries. But vexations are the cause of comforts and pleasures.'
B07 2.404 (2:234); B04 2.387 (2:715–16)

[S83] Once the governor of Scete went up to Constantinople and when the king saw him, he asked him, 'How are the fathers who are in Egypt?' He bowed and replied to the king, 'See, they are eating one another and they live.' Upon hearing this the king was amazed and asked him, 'What does this mean, "they are eating one another"?' He said to him, '[The meaning] of "they eat one another" is this. If it happens that one of them is dying, he orders that whatever he has will be given to each one according to what he needs. Another one when he labours brings [the produce] from his gardening and gives comfort to all of them – and in this way they live.' The king said to him, 'You are truly blessed, for you are delivered from the cares of the world and freed also from the judgment of Gehenna. But as for us, the cares of the world plague us and Gehenna is prepared for us because of our sins.'
B07 2.413 (2:237); B04 2.396 (2:719)

[S84] Abba Gregory gave a response against the thoughts, saying to the brothers, 'My brothers, just as we have surpassed the age of youths, let us also cease from the mind of youths. That is, let us flee from dissolute customs of impure lusts. For it is a shame that the youthful age should have passed from us and old age has arrived and overtaken us, yet something shameful has not passed away from us.'
B07 2.418 (2:238); B04 2.396a (2:721)

[S85] There was one of the holy men who was seeing visions. This one related, 'Once when I was standing in prayer, I heard a demon complaining to his companion, saying, "I am in great toil and agitation." When [the other demon] began to ascertain from him the cause of his turmoil, he started to say to him, "This is the work assigned to me: when I bring these monks who are in Jerusalem and its environs to the mountain of Sinai, I have to bring these who are on the mountain of Sinai to Jerusalem, and there is no rest for me, not even a little."'
B07 2.420 (2:239); B04 2.398 (2:722)

[S86] There was a solitary who dwelt in a cell in the remote wilderness. He had a brother who lived in the world and was reaching the end [of his life] and was about to die. [The brother] sent for him, saying, 'For the sake of God, perform [an act of] grace and come, so that I may see you before I die.' When he heard [this request] he closed the door of his cell and set out to go. As he was walking in the wilderness he saw an elder sitting by the side of the road, mending nets. He was, however, the Accuser preparing his snares to trap with them those who were traveling on that road of excellence. He wanted to cast his nets on that brother and entangle him, [for] his leg had not only not been caught in his snares, but he had also cut off and broken his snares through the remembrance of God. That solitary, not knowing that it was Satan sitting beside the road and mending his nets, said to the elder, 'Why are you sitting here in the arid wilderness? And what are you doing here?' The Accuser said to him, 'I am mending my nets, for I wish to catch in them the gazelles in the wilderness.' That solitary said to him, 'Make a net also for me, for I wish to catch in it these gazelles that are entering and ruining my garden.' The demon said to him, 'You go on. I will make for you a net that is better than this one you are looking at now.' When that solitary went to his brother and saw him, he remained with him for two days, and on the third day [the brother] died. He prepared him [for burial] and buried him with the honour due to the faithful. When he lay down there in the house of his brother, his brother's wife stood before him during the night and came to lay down next to him through the working of the Accuser. She began speaking to him in this way, 'God has sent you here in order that you might care for your brother's children and raise them. But now take me as a wife and take care of your brother's house and children and remain peacefully in your house.' When that solitary heard what she had said to him, he was stirred up to anger against her and said to her, 'Woe upon you, woman. Get behind me, Satan.' He immediately got up and

picked up his staff and set out to go back to his cell in the wilderness. While he was walking on the road, he saw that elder sitting in his place and mending his nets. That solitary said to him, 'Elder, are you still sitting here? Have you fashioned for me that net of which I spoke to you?' Then Satan was indignant against him, and looked at him with fierce anger and said, 'Get away from me. Yes, because of this you have broken that net which I had made for you. But did you not know that I [was using] another net better than the [first] one which [again] you broke and cut off during this night? I am not able to make [a net to catch] you.' While he was speaking with him he changed himself and became like a great dragon. When that solitary saw [it], then he understood that this was Satan who had appeared to him. He fled from there afraid and went back to his cell praising God who had rescued him from the snare of Satan, that one who wished to hide and trap him through his brother's wife.
B07 2.421 (2:239–40); B04 2.399 (2:722–4)

[S87] A brother was bothering an elder many times, saying to him, 'What should I do, for evil and diverse and impure thoughts of all kinds are moving through me?' The elder answered him, 'You are a stagnant cistern which sometimes is filled with water, and sometimes water is drawn out from it. But why do you not imitate rather the spring which never dries out? Patience is victory and victory is persistence and persistence is life and life is the kingdom and the kingdom is God.'
B07 2.437 (2:245); B04 2.414 – Bedjan 57 (p. 861)

[S88] Again he said, 'Know yourself, and you shall never fall. Give work to your soul, that is, constant prayer and the love which is in God, before another will give it evil thoughts. And pray that the spirit of error will be distant from you.'
B07 2.439 (2:245); B04 2.417 – Bedjan 59 (p. 862)

[S89] The sons of Eli, Hophni and Phineas, were priests of the Lord, but they did not fear God and they perished with all of their household.
B07 2.443 (2:246); B04 2.421 – Bedjan 63 (p. 863)

[S90] [Abba Epiphanius] also said, 'If we do evil things, God will ignore his patience. But if we do good things, it will not help us very much, for in order for freedom's profit to increase and that the will's merchandise may not be spoiled, one must rejoice in conflict.'
B07 2.447 (2:246); B04 2.425 – Bedjan 67 (p. 863)

[S91] The brothers once persuaded Abba Epiphanius, saying, 'Speak to us, father, something by which we shall live, even if you speak and we do not hold on to the seed of your word because ours is a salty land.' The elder answered them, 'Whoever does not accept all brothers, but distinguishes [between them], whoever is like this, is not able to become perfect.'
B07 2.448 (2:246); B04 2.426 – Bedjan 68 (p. 864)

[S92] The way of life of one who loves God should be without blame.
B07 2.452 (2:247); B04 2.430 – Bedjan 72 (pp. 864–5)

[S93] An elder said, 'God gives an opportunity to a human being to repent as long as he wishes and as much as he desires. For it is written, "You shall first admit your sins and [then] you will be justified."'
B07 2.458 (2:248); B04 2.436 – Bedjan 78 (p. 866)

[S94] An elder said, 'Complete silence is full of life and too much talk has death hidden in it.'
B07 2.459 (2:248); B04 2.437 – Bedjan 79 (pp. 866–7)

[S95] Again the elder said, 'Falsehood and sin in words that are long and wide are laying out an ambush.'
B07 2.460 (2:248); B04 2.438 – Bedjan 80 (p. 867)

[S96] One of the elders said, 'Love does not know [how] to keep a storehouse of possessions.'
B07 2.467 (2:248); B04 2.445 – Bedjan 87 (pp. 867–8)

[S97] Abba Poemen said, 'There are four main passions.' A brother said to him, 'Which are these?' The elder said to him, 'Worldly sadness towards many unexpected things, the love of money, vainglory, and fornication. We should be cautious of these before everything [else].'
B07 2.478 (2:250); B04 2.456 – Bedjan 98 (p. 870)

[S98] Abba Agathon said again, 'Whoever removes from his eyes accusation and disgrace and loss is able to live.'
B07 2.484 (2:251); B04 2.462 – Bedjan 104 (p. 872)

[S99] One of the brothers asked a great elder and said, 'Abba, what should I do for, whenever I see the face of a woman, a battle of fornication is stirred up against me?' The elder answered, 'My son, guard your

eyes so that you do not look at one of them, and then you will no longer be afraid.' That brother said to him, 'Look, how many times does it happen that one might meet them unintentionally, by chance?' The elder said to him, 'As much as you are capable, keep watch carefully from within and without. But [the fact] that one meets them unintentionally by chance, [see,] passion does not even have the power to stir itself up. But you should be cautious so that this does not happen from your own will. For the holy book condemns this, saying, "Anyone who looks at a woman in order to desire her, at once he has committed adultery with her in his heart."[34] For although you do not intend to meet them, passion is [still] being stirred up against you, [so] lift up your thought quickly to God and he will help you.' Wishing especially to affirm that brother, he answered him, 'You should know, my son, that you have been with me for two years and I have not yet seen your face as it is, whether spiteful or good. [It was] this, my son, that has urged me to say to you to guard your eyes from their sight.' After this he offered a prayer for him and sent him to go back to the *coenobion* because that brother was dwelling in the church.
B07 2.491 (2:252); B04 2.469 – Bedjan III (pp. 874–5)

[S100] A brother asked an elder, 'If I am in a beautiful place and the time of worship has arrived, should I return?' The elder said to him, 'Who is it that, when he remembers wealth, returns to poverty?'
B07 2.494 (2:252); B04 2.472 – Bedjan 114 (p. 875)

[S101] Again that same elder said, 'If you call out to God in your prayer with a pure heart, your prayer will not return without fruit.'
B07 2.505 (2:254); B04 2.483 – Bedjan 125 (p. 877)

[S102] Again that elder said, 'Just as one is not able to speak two words with one voice and be understood and received, so is mixed prayer that is spoken by a person before God.'
B07 2.506 (2:254); B04 2.484 – Bedjan 126 (pp. 877–8)

[S103] Again he said, 'If you see the wings of ravens that are flying, so as well [you will see] the prayer of a disheartened mind being lifted up.'
B07 2.507 (2:254); B04 2.485 – Bedjan 127 (p. 878)

[34] Mt 5:28.

[S104] Again he said, 'If you are determined to ask from God, but will not repay as much as you are able, you will hear that [saying], "You will ask and not receive, for you have borrowed and not paid back."'
Bo7 2.508 (2:254); Bo4 2.486 – Bedjan 128 (p. 878)

[S105] Again the same one said, 'Whoever prays in a pure manner before God, the words of his mouth are a chain by which he will bind the demons under his feet like a sparrow, and like those tied down who tremble in the presence of one who has power over them; so also they will shudder from the words of his prayer.'
Bo7 2.509 (2:254); Bo4 2.487 – Bedjan 129 (p. 878)

[S106] He said again, 'Just as when the rain falls upon the earth, it takes the place of a key for its lock and opens and brings forth outwardly the growth of the seeds and roots in it; so also are the soul and the mind of one who receives and tastes from that heavenly drop, for through the words of his lips his hidden way of life before God will be evident to [others]. What I mean to say is that when a person's request and petition concerning everything are [offered] through the words of his pure prayer, he opens the door of the treasury of the Trinity, the Lord of treasures, and brings out from there the treasures hidden for those who are worthy of them.'
Bo7 2.510 (2:254); Bo4 2.488 – Bedjan 130 (p. 878)

[S107] A brother asked an elder, 'Which indeed is the best action that I should do and live by?' The elder said to him, 'God knows what is best, but listen. One of the elders spoke about a thought that rebukes a person, for it is his [best] adversary. For it confronts one who wishes to do his flesh's desires, and to rebel against God and not obey him, and delivers him to his enemies.'
Bo7 2.519 (2:256); Bo4 2.497 – Bedjan 139 (p. 882)

[S108] Again the elder said, 'In this way it is necessary for the soul to be worshiping day and night like Huldah the prophetess who sat in the house of the Lord in supplication and worship;[35] and also like Hannah who did not cease in her worship for 80 years.'[36]
Bo7 2.520 (2:256); Bo4 2.498 – Bedjan 140 (p. 882)

[35] 2 Kgs 22:14–20.
[36] Lk 2:36–8.

[S109] Brothers: 'Which is the pure prayer?' Elder: 'That which is smallest in word and greatest in action. For if it were not so, work would be more valuable than supplication. [....] But if it is not so, why do we ask and not receive when its gracious mercies are flowing? But the method of penitents is different, as is the labour of the humble ones. The penitents are hired hands, and the humble ones are sons.'[37]
B07 2.563 (2:266); B04 2.540 (2:975) – 2:732: 7–12

[37] Lk 15:11–32.

CHAPTER 5

Sayings Preserved in Armenian

Translated by Robert W. Thomson

The following translations are from the printed text of the Armenian Paterica: *Vark' srboc' Haranc'*, 2 vols., Mechitarist Press, Venice, 1855. The items are those identified by Dom Lucien Regnault, *Les sentences de pères*, Solesmes, 1970, pp. 253–75, as being only attested in Armenian, or having a better text in Armenian than other tongues. The references to Leloir are to the volumes and pages of L. Leloir, *Paterica Armeniaca a P.P. Mechitaristis edita (1855) nunc Latine reddita*, CSCO, Subsidia 42, 43, 47, and 51, Louvain, 1974–1976.

Armenian Paterica

[A1] 1 432: One of the fathers asked a wise doctor and said: 'Do you know the medicine for all pains, O wise one?' The doctor said: 'I know very well if you listen to me. Take the sugar of repentance and the flower of brotherly love and the leaf of poverty and the fruit of humility and fill the mortar of mercy. Pound it on your knees and strain it into the napkin of suffering and drink it mingled with tears in the middle of every night. This is the medicine of all pains, which not only cures the inner man but also purifies and renews and cleanses the outer [man].'
Leloir 1974–1976, 1 24

[A2] 1 461–2: 'But you should know, my son, that we who reckon that we are monks,[1] although we are, yet we are far from the way of life of monks and we must always mourn. And the greatest fathers and the ascetics and the withdrawn[2] and the hermits[3] and the perfect must also weep and mourn. Now if [you wish to know] why, listen wisely. God said that lying

[1] Monks: *krawnawork'*, lit. 'religious'.
[2] Withdrawn: *heṙac'ealk'*, lit. 'those who remove or separate themselves'.
[3] Hermits: *anapatawork'*, lit. 'those of the desert'.

is from Satan;[4] and who looks at a woman and desires her is a complete adulterer;[5] and to be angry at one's brother is murder;[6] and it is necessary to respond to one who speaks idle words.[7] But who would be suchlike, or where would we find such a man who is removed from all passions, and has not experienced lying; whose mind has never been crossed by desire and has never wrongly been angry with his brother, nor has an idle word emerged from his mouth, so that he would have no need of repentance? Know this: that who does not crucify himself completely and give himself to humility and contempt and subject himself to all ridicule so that everyone would despise and mock him, and he himself will endure it with thanks and humbleness for the sake of God; and he would not seek anything human at all, not glory, not food, not drink nor clothing—then he will be able to become a true monk. But do you try to do good and not fear your weakness.'
Leloir 1974–1976, I 55

[A3] I 510: [Father Nilus said:] 'For if sadness and anger are regulated, desire is extinguished, and, that I may express it briefly, all passions are diminished. And with the lengthy passage of time, good things become habitual naturally and passions will be forgotten and natural goodness will increase and sins will cease from those who are solitary.' Again he said:[8] 'For that reason, to be calm is good, so that it will not see any evil things, then how will the mind seek them? [By] what the mind does not investigate it will not be deluded, nor will it move the body and passions will not be able to rise up against the soul.[9] Now as long as it will be undisturbed by evils, it will be very calm, and the inner man will possess complete peace.'
Leloir 1974–1976, I 107

[A4] I 520: The elder said: 'O, what will happen at the future coming of the Son of God? For after the resurrection the souls[10] of men will come forth from the fear that will come upon the whole world, as the Lord said,[11] and they will be agitated at what is to come.'
Leloir 1974–1976, I 117

---

4 Jn 8:44.
5 Mt 5:28.
6 1 Jn 3:15.
7 Mt 12:36.
8 Regnault indicates that this saying is also found at I 505, but it does not appear there.
9 Soul: *anjn*. Two words are used for 'soul': *anjn*, lit. 'person', and *hogi*, lit. 'spirit'.
10 Souls: *hogik*; see n. 9 above.
11 Lk 21:26.

[A5] 1 521: They said concerning Father Arsēn, that brothers from Scete came to him and he was unable to receive them from the great grief and sadness that he had. And when the brothers saw it, they were frightened and departed.
Leloir 1974–1976, I 119

[A6] 1 560–1: 'And have always in you the fear of God, for that will preserve you and expel from you all your sins and iniquities. For who has the fear of God in himself, he has a treasure-house filled with myriad blessings, because the fear of God saves the soul[12] from sin.'
Leloir 1974–1976, I 167

[A7] 1 562–3: A certain brigand, repenting, came to a great and wonderful elder, who was a father of a monastery.[13] He commanded him to remain quiet for seven days only with a view to the confirmation[14] of the place. After the seven days, the pastor summoned him alone and asked him whether it pleased him to make his habitation with him. Now he so wished with an upright heart. Once more he asked him about his transgressions; and immediately he eagerly confessed. Again he tested him by saying: 'I wish to present you to all the brethren' and he agreed willingly. Then the father summoned all the brethren, 250, bringing that innocent condemned one. Some of the brothers dragged him about and some afflicted him with moderate blows. They put a sack on him and filled it with ashes on top of his head,[15] so that from the sight of him they were all terrified and cried out with tears. But he, trembling, confessed all his sins one by one, whereby he astonished the ears of all, because he had committed very many transgressions. Then the father of the monastery reported to the brethren: 'I saw a certain fearsome [person] who was holding a letter written by hand and a reed. And as soon as he declared his sins very precisely, it obliterated them all, because it is written: "I shall myself relate my iniquities, and you will forgive the transgressions of my sins, my Lord and my God."'[16]
Leloir 1974–1976, I 169

[A8] 1 575: The elder said: 'Gluttony is the root of fornication. Who controls his stomach can control fornication and his tongue.'

[12] Soul: *anjn*; see n. 9 above.
[13] Father of a monastery, *hayr vanic'*. *Vank'* implies a coenobitic monastery.
[14] Confirmation: *hastatut'iwn*, [his] approbation?
[15] This recalls one of the 12 torments inflicted on St Gregory the Illuminator according to the *History* of Agathangelos, §107.
[16] Ps 31:5. The Armenian Bible follows the numbering of the LXX.

[Variant in footnote 1:] The elder said: 'Gluttony is the mother of fornication. Whoever is able to control his stomach, he is also able to hold his tongue.'
Leloir 1974–1976, I 185

[A9] I 575: The elder said: 'Sobriety[17] is the wealth of the soul.[18] Let us practice this with humility and flee from impiety, which is the mother of all evils.'

[Variant in footnote 2:] The elder said: 'Fasting is the wealth of the soul. Let us acquire this with humble mind and flee from haughtiness, which is the mother of all evils.'
Leloir 1974–1976, I 185

[A10] I 580: Abba Eligius said to his disciple: 'My son, gradually accustom yourself to afflicting your stomach with fasting. For just as a [wine-] skin becomes thinner when stretched out, likewise also the stomach when receiving much food. But if it receives little, it is constrained and requests little.'
Leloir 1974–1976, I 192

[A11] I 580: The 40-day fast was once proclaimed at Scete, and someone came to a great elder and said: 'Abba, the fast has arrived.' The elder said: 'What fast?' The brother said: 'The 40-day one, father.' Then the elder replied: 'Truly, my son, behold for 53 years I do not know when it begins or when it ends, but all my time is a fast.'
Leloir 1974–1976, I 192

[A12] I 583: Father Esayias [Isaiah] said: 'Love silence more than speaking, because silence concentrates[19] the mind, but speaking scatters and destroys.'
Leloir 1974–1976, I 196

[A13] I 622: There was a solitary[20] who fell into fornication for three years, and the father of the monastery was spiritually discerning[21] but could not realize it. One day the father realized his evil deed, summoned him, and said: 'Tell me where you were this evening, and why you angered God.' He fell at his feet and said: 'I have sinned before God, and

---

[17] Sobriety: *žužkalut'iwn*, which can also mean 'endurance'.
[18] Soul: *hogi*; see n. 9 above.
[19] Concentrates: *žołovē*, lit. 'gathers'.
[20] Solitary: *miaynakeac'*, lit. 'one who lives alone'.
[21] Spiritually discerning: *hogetes*, lit. 'seeing in the spirit'.

for three years these actions by which I have been seduced have soiled
[me].' The father said: 'And what deed did you perform, that God hid
from me the evils in which you were caught?' He said: 'It was my habit
that every night I would go to the act of impurity. Weeping, I said eight
kanons of the Psalms and hymns of repentance in going and in returning.
This evening the evil demon made me lazy and caused [me] to despair,
and he said my prayers were useless. And I did not remember God at all,
nor did I sing psalms.' The father said: 'Blessed is the mercy of God and
his gentleness, who does not wish the loss of a man. Now, since God did
not remember your other deeds of the three years, likewise I forgive you
that of this evening by the mercy of God.' And he returned to God and
became a man perfect in repentance and good works.
Leloir 1974–1976, II 31

[A14] I 623: There was a monastery on the Euphrates river whose name
was *surrounded*,[22] in which there were many monks. The father summoned five of the brethren to sell their handiwork in the city and to
bring [back] necessities. When they had departed, one of them separated
for some need. When he had gone a little way, a prostitute found him,
and deceived him and persuaded him, and he lay with her. The brothers
came up but were unable to bring him to the monastery because he had
lost hope. When they had gone on their way, great mourning took hold
of the brethren. In a vision the father saw that men with swords had
come and pierced the father's ankles, had bound him with iron bonds,
and were tormenting him cruelly, saying: 'Bring the image of Christ
which you received in a pledge.' The father said: 'I do not know what
you request.' The men said: 'The image of Christ, the monk whom you
cut from the body of Christ.' And for many days they tormented him
thus. He was half-dead and begged the brethren to help with their
prayers. They fasted for a week with zealous effort, and supplicated God.
He had mercy on him, and he was freed from the torments. From then
on, he did not remain as superior, but lived humbly with the brethren.
Leloir 1974–1976, II 32

[A15] I 682: A certain brother asked Father Poemen about thoughts of
fornication and he said: 'The mercy of God that surrounds man is infinite,
although we do not see it. Unless it were so, all flesh would not escape it.'
Leloir 1974–1976, II 98

---

[22] Surrounded: *šrjapateal*, or 'enclosed', i.e. with a wall.

[A16] I 692: The elder said: 'It is totally alien for a monk who is among coenobitic[23] brothers to have for himself anyone of the community[24] and to love him more, because it is a harm to them and to many through passion and defamation and judgment.'
Leloir 1974–1976, II 108

[A17] I 713: A certain elder at the time of prayer used to see great grace. A general came, gave him *dahekan*s,[25] and the elder accepted [them]. But when he had accepted, he was unable to see his accustomed vision and was astonished. Having examined his thoughts, he found no reason. Then he begged God to reveal the matter to him. The angel said to him: 'As long as your *dahekan*s remain with you, you are unworthy to see grace, because you have a share of the evils of the general proportionally with the *dahekan*s. So, if you wish, return them to the general, or if you wish, give them to the needy. To keep them is not for monks, nor is it pleasing to God.' The elder, after gathering the brethren, told them. And from then on, they did not accept anything from the laity, but said: 'Give it to the needy, and we shall pray for you.'
Leloir 1974–1976, II 132

[A18] II 8: A certain brother asked an elder and said: 'If I should wish to accomplish something, and there occurs some admonition[26] and it prevents me from the task, is it better to persevere until I shall have accomplished it, or should I abandon it?' The elder said to him: 'If you persevere while praying without being troubled, it is better to persevere; but if exasperation come upon [you], abandon it.'
Leloir 1974–1976, II 147

[A19] II 9: Once Father Moyi built a small house because of the heat; but he did not know how to build, and he destroyed it again. Tayis observed, but he did not speak to him. Then afterwards Tayis said to him: 'Do you wish to do it in this way, father?' And he struck him and said: 'I did not know how to do it thus.'
Leloir 1974–1976, II 148

---

[23] Coenobitic: *miaban*, lit. 'united, in agreement'.
[24] Anyone of the community: *ṙamik zok'*, lit. 'anyone common'.
[25] *Dahekan*: a coin, often rendering the Greek *dēnarion* or *drachma*.
[26] Admonition: *azdumn*, or 'influence'.

[A20] II 11: Gregory the Theologian said: 'If anyone comes to monasticism[27] and does not prepare himself for tribulations, the path of salvation is untested.'

[Footnote 2:] Father Gregory the Theologian said: 'If you come to learn wisdom, and you do not watch out for evil events, that is a thoughtless beginning. But if you expect tribulations and it does not come, it is good. However, if you do not expect and it comes and you are unprepared, it will be a double shame. For you will give up through the tribulations, being impatient, and your unpreparedness in that you did not expect tribulations, against which you must prepare patience.'
Leloir 1974–1976, II 151

[A21] II 17: An elder was asked: 'Why am I fearful on going into the desert?' He said: 'Because you think yourself alone, and you do not see God with you.'
Leloir 1974–1976, II 160

[A22] II 19: The nun[28] Sara said to her sisters: 'The male monks have three advantages over us.' The sisters said: 'What are they?' She said to them: 'One, that they go around with uncovered faces; and another that their thought is male and valiant; and the other that Satan wages war with them more than with us. And it is clear that they will receive rewards for their labours.'
Leloir 1974–1976, II 162

[A23] II 20: Father Makar [Macarius] said to the young brother Zak'arē [Zacharaeus]: 'What is the task of the solitary?' And Zak'arē said: 'To give thanks for temptations and to be silent.' [in *hêsychia*]
Leloir 1974–1976, II 163

[A24] II 67: One of the elders said: 'One man keeps silence, not by virtue but in order to give praise to himself.[29] But who keeps himself silent in accordance with God, that is virtue, because he has grace from God.'
Leloir 1974–1976, II 215

[A25] II 67: [They said about the (monks) of Scete...] They also said that when they went up to Egypt and wished to receive the payment for their harvests or the price of their handiwork, each one of them limited his

[27] Monasticism: *krōnaworut'iwn*, lit. 'the religious state'. Cf. n. 1.
[28] Nun: *hawatuhi*, lit. 'female believer'.
[29] The sentence is incomplete.

provisions according to their needs, and they gave everything else to widows and orphans.
Leloir 1974–1976, II 215

[A26] II 68: There was one of the fathers by the name of Onofrios, a great and virtuous ascetic, who from his great asceticism had become like a log. A certain king heard of his fame and summoned him, but he did not wish to go to him, saying the following: 'If he asks me for property and possessions, I do not have them to give him. If he wishes to kill [me], I am ready to die for the name of the Lord. Cut off my head and give it to him. And if he seeks advice, it is not necessary for the one giving advice to run to the one being advised, but let the latter come himself and receive the blessing.'
Leloir 1974–1976, II 216

[A27] II 76: One of the fathers spoke about two brothers, and the words were spoken about a brother who kept purity. The other one said in addition: 'I heard.' When he went to his house, he did not find peace for himself or pure contemplation, until he went and said to his brother: 'I heard nothing.' Likewise the other one also said: 'Neither was I at peace.' And when they had repented of saying the words, they had respite from those thoughts.
Leloir 1974–1976, II 225

[A28] II 83: Once his disciples said to Father Makar [Macarius]: 'What is the great and what is the small?'[30] He said: 'What someone sees in his thoughts as small, that is great; and what he understands as great is small.' They said to him: 'Explain to us your saying, father.' And he said to them: 'Purify your hearts and you will find [the meaning of] this saying.'
Leloir 1974–1976, II 234

[A29] II 98: Two villages had a dispute with each other in Egypt. Father Poemen went and begged the larger and more powerful village to make peace with the smaller village, but they did not wish to heed him. So he shook the dust of his feet over them and they went to war with each other. The men of the large village were routed and defeated, because the Lord provides justice to the deprived.[31]
Leloir 1974–1976, III 3

---

[30] Armenian has no superlative form: perhaps here 'greatest, smallest'?
[31] Ps 145:7.

[A30] II 105: [Footnote 1, in a saying attributed to Father Poemen:] '...
For the power of God does not dwell in a man who is a slave to passions.
And if anyone pursues tranquillity, it escapes him.'
Leloir 1974–1976, III 13

[A31] II 112: Once two brothers went to Father Poemen while Father
Anoub was also staying there. They asked him and said: 'Father, we have
life in common[32] with someone, and we have neither profit nor harm
from him.' When the elder heard [them] he remained silent, because he
did not speak when Father Anoub was there, because he was older[33] than
him. Father Anoub said to him: 'It is a great trouble. What need is there
for a man to have familiarity[34] with someone when he gains no profit?'
Leloir 1974–1976, III 22

[A32] II 114: They said that the fathers spoke according to their thoughts
and according to the man.
Leloir 1974–1976, III 25

[A33] II 121: The elder said: 'Take care that reflection of mind comes to
you in order to make judgment, and to abhor evil thoughts and to
arrange a crown from shipwrecks.'
Leloir 1974–1976, III 34

[A34] II 131: The elder was asked: 'Is it good to go to brothers?' He said:
'No. But to acquire the love of God and tribulation, that is good.'
    [Footnote 1:] A certain brother asked the elder and said: 'Is it a good
habit to go to one's companion?' The elder said: 'Such a habit is unneces-
sary, but you should acquire love and a desire for God.'
Leloir 1974–1976, III 47

[A35] II 137: The monk who strips at the bath is stripped of God's grace.
Leloir 1974–1976, III 56

[A36] II 141: An Alexandrian priest went into the desert, to the archbishop who was living as a monk,[35] residing in *hêsychia* and said to him:

---

[32] Life in common: *miabanut'iwn*, the abstract noun from *miaban*, referring to coenobitic life; see n.
    23 above.
[33] Older: *mecagoyn*, lit. 'greater', of age or status.
[34] Familiarity: *merjaworut'iwn*, lit. 'closeness', of place or relationship.
[35] To live as a monk: *krōnaworil*. For *krōnawor* see n. 1 above. The infinitive could imply purpose, as
    of the priest just below.

'Father, I wish to become a monk here, but I have a wife and children.' And he said: 'Instead of purity do you wish to sin, my son?' The priest said: 'You teach others, but yourself you do not teach. You have left as a widow your wife the holy church and as orphans the sons of the Spirit, and you say such words to me! The Lord's saying has been fulfilled in you: "Having a beam in your eyes, you try to remove the mote in mine."'[36]
Leloir 1974–1976, III 58

[A37] II 142: If you wish to live in tranquillity, this is it: not to bring the week to completion, nor two,[37] but on every day at the ninth hour to drink moderately, and to eat in measure, and in moderation to speak, to pray, to sing psalms, to keep a vigil, and to fast strictly, and reside in the world and have women,[38] to be merciful regarding orphans and widows. These three virtues are greater than all others: compassion and prayer and fasting. Compassion is greater than prayer, and prayer is greater than fasting. Prayer emaciates the body, and fasting dries up the bile, and keeping vigil reduces the bone.
Leloir 1974–1976, III 63

[A38] II 143: Father Job said: 'A man who falls into doubt about scripture and does not come to the wise ones and learn, resembles a wall broken down by the shock of floods; for in that way he is oppressed and torn in schisms by his distorted view.'
Leloir 1974–1976, III 64

[A39] II 143: When Evagrius went to Egypt and saw the way of life of the fathers who were there, he was astonished and said to a certain great elder: 'Why is there not such asceticism and discretion in the nation of the Greeks?' And the elder said: 'Because of pride, for that vice has removed labour[39] from them and placed disputation among them.'
Leloir 1974–1976, III 65

[A40] II 143: A certain brother asked an elder who was a seer: 'What is that saying that speaks about Moses: "He looked this way and that way

---

[36] Mt 7:3, but divergent from the Armenian biblical text.
[37] The phrase *oč̣' šabat' hanel i glux, ew oč̣' erkus* is obscure. The context seems to refer to fasting, so it may imply that one should not fast continuously for a week or two, but eat and drink moderately every day.
[38] To have women, or wives: *kanays unel*. Regnault renders as 'to keep [yourself from] women'.
[39] Labour: *vastak*, or 'work, merit, service'.

and saw no one, then he killed the Egyptian?"'⁴⁰ The seer said: 'Moses looked into the depths of God [to see] whether it would be pleasing or not. He looked to the left [to see] whether Satan would be there and provoke him, and he did not see him. He looked to the right [to see] whether there was one of the angels preventing him, and he saw none. Then, knowing that the deed was without sin, he killed him.'
Leloir 1974–1976, III.65, cf. *APanon* 674, *APsys* 10.145

[**A41**] II 143: One of the brethren asked an elder and said: 'What is this, that my thought does not assist my actions?' And the elder said: 'Because you do not have perfect action; for if you did have, it would assist you.'
Leloir 1974–1976, III.65

[**A42**] II 148: Once a certain great elder came to see those dwelling in cells. There was there a youth who easily had learned the holy scriptures by heart. The fathers asked him about him: 'How does he absorb in himself so easily the holy scriptures? There are others who even if they labour, yet are able to recite only a little.' The elder replied and said: 'Waters below heaven are in one place. But there are parts in the world that are lower, in which if any water wishes it immediately goes. There are again in the world higher places, in which if any water wishes only with effort is it able to go. Likewise with persons.⁴¹ Because there are persons that have little association with evil, when they wish to seek knowledge they immediately find it. And again there are persons that participate in evil; these receive knowledge with an effort.'
Leloir 1974–1976, III.71

[**A43**] II 149: A certain brother asked Father Sisin [Sisoes?] and said: 'I am tormented, father, to comprehend any example of the holy Trinity, and I am unable [to find one].' And he said: 'Understand the sun as a sign of the Father, and the Son as the ray, and the Spirit as the manifestation. Just as you do not attain the height of the sun, nor touch the ray nor examine the manifestation, even more are you unable to comprehend the Trinity. For this example is a servant and a small thing for [the Trinity.]' When the brother heard this, he praised God and was at peace.
Leloir 1974–1976, III.73

---

⁴⁰ Ex 2:12.
⁴¹ Person: *anjn*, sometimes used for 'soul'; see n. 9 above.

[A44] II 152: Do not leave the fold or the sheep-pen, lest on leaving you be eaten by a wolf. Stay in your dwelling,[42] monk, and nourish your soul with divinely inspired words, and you will find for yourself pious thoughts of God as a teacher.
Leloir 1974–1976, III.76

[A45] II 152: God said to me: 'Do you love me, monk?'[43] 'Yes, I love you.' 'You love me; do what I wish, do not do what I do not wish.'
Leloir 1974–1976, III.76

[A46] II 152: Wealth and lineage and wisdom without someone conducting himself are of no profit at all.
Leloir 1974–1976, III.76

[A47] II 181: The brother asked and said: 'What does the saying teach that says: "He has no salvation with his God"?'[44] The elder said: 'It says that about evil thoughts that alienate the soul from God, when a man falls into some tribulations.'
Leloir 1974–1976, III.110

[A48] II 186: He said again: 'Just as silver, although it blackens, again becomes white; likewise too the believer, although he becomes black through sin, is cleansed again by repentance. And thereby faith resembles silver.'
Leloir 1974–1976, III.116, cf. *APanon* 717

[A49] II 194: Father Theodore of Pherme[45] said about Father Ak'ełeay [Achilles] that he was like a lion in Scete, inspiring fear in his time.
Leloir 1974–1976, III.127

[A50] II 197: An elder said: '[Acquire] the silence of monks without being concerned, but look to your discipline[46] in the fear of God. On sleeping and rising praise God, and you will not fear the onslaught of the impious.'
  [Footnote 2:] The elder said: 'Acquire silence and do not be concerned with anything [else], and ponder the fear of God. And whether you stand or sleep, you will never fear.'
Leloir 1974–1976, III.131

---

[42] Dwelling: *tun*, lit. 'house'.
[43] Monk: *abełay*; the Syriac term for 'monk', *abila*, lit. 'weeper'.
[44] Ps 3:3.
[45] A monastic settlement of 500 monks in a mountain on the way to Scete, *HL* 20.
[46] Discipline: *krt'ut'iwn*, or 'practice, exercise'.

[A51] II 203: Father Moses said: 'A man cannot enter the army of Christ unless he become totally fire, and despise honour and repose, and cut off the desires of the body, and keep all the commandments of God.'
Leloir 1974–1976, III.138

[A52] II 209: The elder said: 'Reflect always on death so that you may reap its profit, because none of the thoughts of mankind are hidden from God, and your mind will become vigilant and pure of all evils.'
Leloir 1974–1976, III.146

[A53] II 209: The elder said: 'Let us take care, brethren, and let us be vigilant at the time of our battle, and let us abandon transitory things and care for those that pass not away. Let us not allow our minds to think evil thoughts, lest we allow some wickedness and impiety to dwell in our souls.'[47]
Leloir 1974–1976, III.146

[A54] II 210: The elders said: 'Always consider the good, so that you may do it. Let us labour, brethren, and have an eye for the future blessings, and prepare ourselves regarding our departure hence. Let us not spend in vain the few days of our lives, but always pray for the bountiful mercy of God.'
Leloir 1974–1976, III.146

[A55] II 250: An elder said: 'If you wish to be known to God, be unknown to mankind.'
Leloir 1974–1976, III.196

[A56] II 269: Father Moses said to a certain brother: 'Come, let us acquire submission, because from it is born humility and patience and long suffering and brotherly love, and in addition love. And these are the shields of our souls.'
Leloir 1974–1976, III.219

[A57] II 279: Abba Macarius the Great said: 'As much as a soul loves the glory of mankind, it is that far from the glory of God, because it does not have humility. Otherwise, it would not seek praise, which is perishable. Now where there is no humility, neither is there God.'
Leloir 1974–1976, III.231

[47] Souls: *anjins*, or 'selves'; see n. 9 above.

[A58] II 306: The elder was asked: 'Is kneeling good?' He said: 'Joshua [son] of Nun when he knelt, then he saw God.'
Leloir 1974–1976, III.265

[A59] II 310–11: A certain child had been given to a monastery by his parents and after some time they came to see him. So the elder told one of the brethren to summon the little one. When he approached the abbot,[48] he said to him: 'Who called you?' And giving him a blow, he said: 'Go to your cell.' His parents were distressed. And after a little they said to him: 'Command that the little one come so we can see him.' And the abbot summoned a brother and said to him: 'Call the child.' When he approached the elder, he struck him and said: 'Who called you? Go to your cell.' Again his parents were distressed and said: 'Alas, we should not have come here.' Then after a little, moved by nature, they said to the abbot: 'Command that the little one come.' He said to a brother: 'Summon him.' But when he approached the elder, he struck him and said: 'Who called you? Go to your cell.' And when he had gone off a little, the abbot summoned him, and holding him by the hand gave him to his parents and said to them: 'Behold your son has become a solitary.' Then the parents, much profited, thanked God for the child's progress on the testimony of the abbot. So let us pray to attain such humility with the help of God.
Leloir 1974–1976, III.271

[A60] II 315–16: Father Gelas[ius] said: 'We cannot descend to life-working humility unless first we pluck out the heavy weight of pride that destroys souls. For if we struggle against that, we shall find humility. Let us not say that this will not harm us, because everything that helps us will harm its opponent, as the Lord said: "Who does not gather with me, scatters."[49] For just as a seal marks whatever it is stamped upon where it seals it, likewise too actions are stamped and marked on souls. So let your appearance and clothing and walking and sitting, and food and way of life and bed and shoes and all [your] provisions and house and all its vessels be simple and despicable. In this way too let your prayers and psalm-singing and life in common[50] all be humble and modest. Do not speak arrogantly, or affectedly[51] or with an insolent

---

[48] Abbot: *abas*.
[49] Mt 12:30.
[50] In common: lit. 'with your companion'.
[51] Affectedly: lit. 'rhetorically'.

voice. Do not speak or do anything at an inappropriate time, and do not pray by singing or respond proudly. But in everything, in words and deeds, accept the great and give the little. Be kind to friends and gentle with those subject to you; bear no malice towards the haughty and be benevolent to the humble. Be the consoler of those afflicted and a visitor of the ill. Do not despise anyone of mankind, and be affable in speaking, joyful and mild in responding, and a mediator in everything and pleasant with everyone.'
Leloir 1974–1976, III.277

[A61] II 318: He[52] said also: 'Let not your tongue speak, but your deeds; and let your words be humbler than your deeds. Do not think at all without sense, and do not teach without humility, so that the land may be able to receive your seed.'
Leloir 1974–1976, III.279

[A62] II 318: He said also: 'To speak is not wisdom, but wisdom is to recognize the time for speaking, when it may be appropriate to speak. Hear the word with wisdom and you will speak with wisdom. And be attentive before you speak, and give an appropriate response. In knowledge, be ignorant so that you may escape many tribulations; for he accumulates troubles who shows himself wise. Therefore, you will not boast about your knowledge. For no one knows how it is at all, and the end of everything is shame. But humbling yourself below your companion unites you with God.'
Leloir 1974–1976, III.279

[A63] II 318: Father Esayias [Isaiah] also said about humility: 'Remember, brethren, the one who had nowhere to place his head.[53] And consider, brother, and do not be presumptuous. See who he was and what he became for your sake: he was a king and became a stranger and an exile[54] for you. O, your ineffable benevolence, Lord! Why did you thus humble yourself for your sinful servants so that, although creator of everything, you had nowhere to place your head? Yet we, ungrateful and totally mean and worthy of abject humility, desire this transitory splendour and honour. So why are you troubled, O miserable man, and why do you gather

---

[52] He: This is from a long section on father Esayias [Isaiah].
[53] Mt 8:20.
[54] Exile: *panduxt*, 'foreigner or pilgrim'.

possessions? And why are you blind in promiscuity? And why do you pursue the deceits of this life, and why do you not acquire the future blessings? So examine all this, and you will choose the better.'
Leloir 1974–1976, III.279

[A64] II 319: 'So if you are able to act thus, you must still say: "I was unable to carry out the commandments of God." For to carry out the commandments is humility, in which God reposes on the meek and humble.[55] Who accomplishes humility, also accomplishes all the commandments; and who does not have humility, does not perform any other commandment. For all the virtues without humility are unacceptable to Christ the recipient.' So that brother humbled and prostrated himself, and went away joyfully with profit.
Leloir 1974–1976, III.280

[A65] II 348–9: They said about Father Longinus that they had denounced his own disciple to him so that he might expel him. For the disciples of Father Theodore had come to him and said to him: 'Father, we hear about your disciple some deed that is not good. And if you wish, we shall take him from you and bring another, good brother.' The elder said to them: 'I shall not dismiss him, because he provides me with much calm.' And when the elder heard the brothers' reasons, he said: 'Woe to me, for we come here in order to become angels, yet we become beasts, debauched and impure.' Then the brothers were ashamed; they came to their senses and realized that it is necessary to be forgetful of evil.
Leloir 1974–1976, IV.9

[A66] II 355: There was one of the great fathers in Scete who did not taste bread or drink wine. Gathering the elders, he came to the church of Isidore. When he did not find the priest there, trusting in the openness that he had with him and knowing that the fathers lived in such piety[56] and labour, he entered inside and took what he needed and a little wine. And he himself was the first to begin to eat and drink. And they were astonished how, for the sake of God, he denied his own wishes in order that he might provide refreshment for the elders.
Leloir 1974–1976, IV.17

---

[55] Cf. Is. 66:2.
[56] Piety: *krōnaworut'iwn*, 'religious life', the abstract noun from *krōnawor*, 'monk'; see n. 1 above.

[A67] II 357: An elder said: 'If a man seeks something from someone, and immediately his mind is opened so that he gives him more than the request, this is grace from God because of the action of the one who asked. There is furthermore another who asks and receives the gift, but he does not give it to him willingly, and this is reckoned a payment for him, because he gave under constraint.'
Leloir 1974–1976, IV.20

[A68] II 365: Father Esayias [Isaiah] said: 'Love is preoccupation with the Lord in unremitting thanksgiving, and God accepts our thanks. And this is the sign of quiet and impassibility.' [*hêsychia* and *apatheia*]
Leloir 1974–1976, IV.30

[A69] II 372–3: A certain brother asked the elder and said: 'Why, father, when I carry out my prayers, is it that sometimes I have the inclination and compunction in my mind, and sometimes I do not?' The elder said: 'Whence does it appear that a man might have the love of God? For the love of God brings compunction.'
Leloir 1974–1976, IV.39

[A70] II 373: A certain actor [*mimos*] was going on his way, and he found a certain monk sitting in a cell. The actor began to pray for the elder and said: 'God, have mercy on this poor and humble one', for he did not know who he might be. And when he returned to the same place, he did the same again, and the elder immediately greeted him. Now the elder told this to those who came to him: 'Those who come to elders and pray for them and say: "May the Lord preserve you for the sake of us sinners", they will receive great rewards.'
Leloir 1974–1976, IV.39

[A71] II 410–11: A ship's captain brought a gold piece to Father Eligius. And he said to him: 'Up, sit on your horse and go on the road to Petros, and you will find a child gaily dressed. Ask him and give him this gold piece.' And he went and found [him], and behold, taking a rope he was going to hang himself because of his father's debts. And he gave him the gold piece and returned to the city.

[Footnote 2:] They said about Father Longinus that a certain ship's captain brought him a gold piece from the profit of his ship. However, he did not accept it, but said to him: 'I have no need of it here, but you will

do a kindness and mount your horse and hasten to go on the road of saint Petros. And you will find there a youth dressed in gay garments, and you will ask what he is doing. And give to him your gold piece, and you will gain much reward.' The captain mounted his horse and rapidly went and found the youth in the place that the elder had said. And he said to him: 'Where are you going, my son, and what is the reason that Father Longinus sent me to search you out?' The youth said: 'I have lost many possessions, and now, being oppressed by debtors, I am going to hang myself and be freed from their wickedness. For I have no means of compensating [them]. And behold this cord for my hanging myself.' He took out from his bosom and showed him the rope for his hanging. Then the captain drew out the gold piece and gave it to him, and made the youth return to the city, while he himself went to Father Longinus and reported this. The latter said: 'Believe me, brother, unless you had arrived, I would not have been innocent of his blood.'
Leloir 1974–1976, iv.84, cf. *APanon* 709

[A72] II 430: A certain one of the brethren, Simon by name, went to Antony and said to him: 'Father, I saw a dream that said to me: "Dwell with a man who is twice as industrious as you."' Antony said: 'It is a demon that appeared to you, because he praised you and called you industrious.' And the brother said to him: 'He was robed in light.' And Father Antony said: 'He is able to transform himself into an angel of light.' And the brother said in his mind: 'Antony does not know things hidden.' And Antony understood and said to him: 'Foolish one, I knew when the evil one came to you and did not greet you. Did you not recognize him, at least by the fact that a greeting was not in his mouth?'
Leloir 1974–1976, iv.108

[A73] II 430: Father Proutos and his disciple saw a bear hitting the sand with its paw and crying out loudly. The disciple was afraid and said: 'What is that, father?' And Proutos said: 'My son, it is Belial, prince of the air.' And the disciple said: 'Did then Christ not slay him?' And the father said: 'For the perfect he has been slain, my son, but for the imperfect he is alive and cries out, which signifies the sand.'
Leloir 1974–1976, iv.109

[A74] II 430: Father Awtaw [Avita?] saw a dragon going into the desert, and a black [man?] sitting on it, and he heard a voice saying: 'The darkness has come into the desert, and the sun of righteousness has departed.' And he understood that choice works[57] would be lacking in the desert.

Leloir 1974–1976, IV.109

[A75] II 432: Father Poemen was continually saying to his disciples: 'Go out.' Once they begged him and said: 'What do you see, father?' And he said to them: 'The demons are fighting visibly against me, but not in my thoughts. For when I was like you, they struggled in my thoughts; but now that I am deprived of strength they fight openly. They do the same also with everyone.'

Leloir 1974–1976, IV.111

[A76] II 434: A certain elder saw a layman whose body burning nails had wounded. He summoned him and asked: 'What are your deeds?' And when he began to speak the nails leaped out, and when he stopped speaking the nails had been consumed. The elder told him the vision and said to him: 'Desist from your evil deeds, otherwise unquenchable fire will test you.'

Leloir 1974–1976, IV.113

[A77] II 434: At Terenuthis on Sunday the brethren came to the church and communicated in the holy mystery. Now a certain elder saw angels coming and serving some with respect, but others they did not allow to communicate and took the holy communion for themselves. On seeing this, the elder was astonished. On investigating them he found nothing save only thought and word, and he said: 'Beware of thoughts and words that do not please God.'

Leloir 1974–1976, IV.113

[A78] II 438–9: Father Longinus sat in his cell, and some fathers had come to him. He did not speak to anyone, but suddenly stood up and came to the seashore. When he arrived there, behold a ship was coming from Egypt and it arrived there. In it was a certain holy elder who saw in the spirit,[58] who was coming to see him. They greeted each other with a holy kiss and prayed. The elder from Egypt began to say to God: 'Lord, I begged you not to reveal to the elder about me, lest he take the trouble to

---

[57] Choice works: *ěntrut'iwn gorcoy*, the abstract noun for the adjective.
[58] Saw in the spirit: *hogetes*; see nn. 21 and 63.

come to meet me.' And they came to the cell of Father Longinus, and on the next day the elder from Egypt died there.
Leloir 1974–1976, IV.118, cf. *APanon* 710, *APsys* 18.12

[A79] II 447: Another time they brought to Father Longinus a woman who had an incurable wound in her right hand. She stood silently outside the elder's cell by the window and another woman was with her. The elder looked through the window while he wove the mat.[59] When he saw her, the elder scolded her and said: 'Be on your way to your house, woman.' The woman arose and went to her house cured.
Leloir 1974–1976, IV.127

[A80] II 447: Again at another time a certain elder brought the hood of father Longinus to the house of a demon-possessed person. When he opened the door to enter, the demon began to cry out and said: 'Why have you brought Father Longinus here to torment me?' Immediately the demon left the man and fled, and the man was cured.
Leloir 1974–1976, IV.127

[A81] II 498: An elder was dwelling at Kellia, and he had the following rule:[60] at night he slept for four hours, he prayed for four hours, he worked for four hours and prayed orally; during the day he worked for six hours, and read the scriptures for three hours, and after the ninth hour he took food. In this way, he completed all his days, and was always glorifying God.
Leloir 1974–1976, IV.181

[A82] II 498–9: A certain elder who was spiritually discerning[61] had a disciple, and he made him dwell far from him, about three miles. He had commanded him to know and recognize the deceit and multifaceted falseness of Satan, just as he had seen and learned from the elder all the forms of the evil one's fraud. Now one day Satan took on the appearance of a bishop; he came to the elder's disciple and sat down opposite him at a distance as if he were weary from the journey. Now when the brother saw him, he did not realize that it was an apparition of the evil one, but he ran to meet him and made him reverence as to a bishop. Satan said:

[59] Mat: *siray*, lit. 'rush'.
[60] Rule: *kanon*.
[61] Spiritually discerning: *hogetes*; see nn. 21, 58, and 63.

'Brother and son, welcome. But do me a kindness and receive me, because I am worn out by the city and its crowd and the disobedient people who obey Satan rather than God. I have fled from them and have come to live quietly in the desert, which I desired from my youth. But this I request of you, that no one may know about me, not even your father the great elder, lest the citizens learn and come to importune me.' The brother believed the evil one like a bishop and carried out all his wishes: he built for him a habitation in a cave near himself, and once a day he visited the bishop and heard from him instruction mixed with relaxation.[62] The brother was filled with confusion and anger and did not understand, because knowledge had been closed to him since he was without the command of his father. And in this fashion all self-willed zeal is bad for children and youths. God revealed this to the great elder, and he prayed with requests for the brother's salvation lest he totally perish. Now the bishop, Satan, that is, was unable to hide his scheming, but said to the brother: 'My son, whose is this axe?' And the brother said: 'It is my father's, lord.' The bishop said: 'See, my son, your father's love that he did not make you worthy of an axe, for which reason you did not say: "It is mine."' The brother said: 'What is his is mine, lord, and there is nothing that he does not wish for me.' The bishop said: 'Not so, my son, but if you wish to know the true intention of your father, go to him and say with authority: "That axe is mine and not yours", and thereby test his sincerity towards you.' The evil one did not understand that by this he would reproach his own trickery. But the brother again did not recognize the bishop's disturbing advice in his foolish ignorance, but was confused and disturbed in his soul with anger against the elder who saw God.[63] That night agitation possessed his mind, yet not even by that did he understand. On the next day, he went to his elder in confusion; he paid him reverence and said: 'I have come, father, that you may know and recognize that the axe is mine and not yours, and I shall not give it back to you again.' The holy elder said: 'Yes, my son, it is yours and not mine, and not only that, but everything that is with me you may take with you, and not bring it back again to me, because I am obedient to you under your authority.' When he heard this, the erring brother awoke at the prayers of the holy elder, and repenting, fell at the feet of his father and said: 'Forgive me, the erring one, because I do not know what I said.' The holy elder said: 'Blessed is the Lord God, because he gave me back my

[62] Relaxation: *t'ulut'iwn*, i.e. a weakening of discipline.
[63] Who saw God: *astuacates*; or 'who saw through God', parallel to *hogetes*, 'who saw in the spirit'; see nn. 21, 58, and 61.

lost son.' And he said to the brother: 'My son, did you not see a bishop and keep him with you, so that you spoke in that fashion?' And the brother said: 'Yes, father, I saw a bishop and I have him with me without your permission, for which reason this error has befallen me.' And the elder said: 'My son, how much did I labour in teaching you all the trickery of the evil one, but you did not understand! So was it not sufficient for you to recognize the wicked Satan that he did not greet you? For that reason, he did not come to you, but he sat down there so that you would come to him, and he is Satan himself. And did you not recognize [him] in his teaching that filled you with confusion?' When the brother saw that he related the events one by one and he knew the spiritual discernment[64] of his father, he cried out to his father and fell before him saying: 'Have mercy on me, the erring one, and pray to the Lord God lest I fall into another temptation of the deceiver.' For until his father had explained, the brother did not know that that bishop was Satan. And when the father had prayed, they went together to the brother's hut, but in the cave they did not find that bishop who had appeared, for his deceit was revealed and he was expelled from the region by the prayers of the holy elder. And the brother was saved and came to his senses.
Leloir 1974–1976, IV.181

---

[64] Spiritual discernment: *hogetesut'iwn*; see the previous note.

CHAPTER 6

Sayings Preserved in Coptic

Translated by Tim Vivian

Sources:

Marius Chaîne, *Le manuscrit de la version copte en dialecte sahidique des Apophthegmata patrum*, texte copte et traduction française, Bibliothèque d'études coptes 6, Cairo: L'Institut Français d'Archéologie Orientale, 1970.

Emile Amélineau, ed. and trans., *Histoire des monasteres de la Basse-Égypte*. Monuments pour server a l'Histoire de l'Égypte chrétienne, Annales du Musée Guimet 25 (Paris: Lernoux, 1894). Available online: http://archive.org/details/annales25mus

---

[C1] *A Dead Man Reveals the Truth*[1]

It has been said of an elder at Scete that he set out to go work at the harvest. Some brothers set out too and while walking came upon a man who had been murdered. They stopped beside him. Some others came and seized them because they thought the brothers had killed the man. While they were saying to each other 'You are the ones who killed this man', the elder arrived, walking along, staff in hand. When the brothers saw him, they ran to him, weeping and saying, 'Help us, our father!' and they explained the situation to him. The elder prodded the dead man with his staff and said, 'Did these brothers kill you?'

'No', the dead man replied. The elder said to him, 'What did you do?'

---

[1] The translator wishes to thank Maged S. A. Mikhail for his suggestions.

'We were thieves', he replied. 'We fought among ourselves and I was killed; the others took off.' The men were completely amazed but the elder hurried away [. . .] on account of the mighty work they had seen the elder do.[2]

Chaîne 1970, #227

[C2] *Abba Agathon and a Serpent Eat Figs Together*

It was said of Abba Agathon that at one time he lived in a cave in the desert in which there was a large dragon. The serpent decided to go away and leave him. Abba Agathon said to it, 'If you leave, I am not staying here', so the serpent decided not to leave. Now there was a sycamore-fig in that desert.[3] It was their custom to go out together. Abba Agathon marked a line in the sycamore and divided the tree with the serpent: the serpent would eat the fruit from one side of the sycamore while the elder ate from the other. When they had finished eating, they went back into the cave, both of them together.

Chaîne 1970, #235

[C3] *An Angel Bears Witness to Saint Simeon Stylites*[4]

It was said of Abba Simeon the Syrian that he spent more than 60 years standing on a column without eating any human food at all. Nobody knew how he stayed alive. Those around him didn't know what to think about this. Thinking that he might be a spirit, they gathered together 12 bishops who prayed to God to help them understand this. While those around Abba Simeon were fasting and praying, Saint Abba Simeon would say to them, 'I too am a human being, like everybody else.' But they would not believe him and inflicted on themselves even greater spiritual discipline. One of them, a man whose life was without stain, saw Abba Simeon from where he had seated himself so he could see the holy man at the top of the column. Suddenly an angel came from the east with food in his hand such as the angels eat. When he had given some to Saint Abba Simeon, he then gave some of this same food to the other person who was with him. This person bore witness: 'Until I die I could

---

[2] The ellipses indicate where the text is corrupted; Chaîne notes, 67 n. 1, that the Coptic text is the result of an error by the translator or copyist.

[3] *Ficus sycomorus*, the sycamore fig or the fig-mulberry, extensively grown in the Middle East.

[4] Ca. 390 – 2 September 459.

forswear human food because of the efficacy of that heavenly food.'[5]
When everyone was convinced and they understood that Abba Simeon
was a person of God, they believed in him on the word of the 12 bishops.[6] They continued to pray without ceasing [see 1 Th 5:17] at his column until he had completed his witness to Christ.[7] To everyone who
came to him he bore witness to repent and to turn to God with good
works. When he had finished his course [see 2 Tim 4:7] numerous miracles occurred on account of his holy body, just as in the days when he was
alive. Many are they who have been healed by him and still more numerous are those among the infidels and heretics who have turned to God.
Chaîne 1970, #243

[C4] *Stones Afloat*

This story was told of someone in Egypt whose name was Bane, who
lived in the mountain of Houōr:[8] he spent 18 years standing up. He lived
enclosed in a cell where there was no light at all. There was a small courtyard in front of the door of the cell. He did [not] eat human food, nor
did he sleep at all until he had finished his course [see 2 Tim 4:7]. This
was his life before: he was a devout monk and severe ascetic. The govern-
ment officials of his district feared him because of the way he lived, in
such great nobility and holiness; it made them very fearful. They would
force him to take money from them and distribute it to the poor. So, he
went traveling from city to city and village to village distributing money
to those in need. He adopted this procedure: when he was away from his
monastery, occupied with helping the poor, if it took ten days for him to
complete his ministry, he would not eat or drink until he returned to the
monastery – as a spiritual discipline. He continued to practice this way of
life until the approach of old age. Afterwards, he shut himself up alone
and adopted the way of life we have described. He stood until the bones
of his foot were so hard they resembled deer-hooves. One day his disciple
insisted on telling his fortune. 'Go to the mountain', the elder told him,
'and bring back three small stones.' So, the disciple brought them,

[5] Coptic has a play on words here. 'I could' is literally 'it is possible for me, I'm able', which uses
čom, 'power, strength', while 'efficacy' also translates *čom*. Thus the power, strength, efficacy of the
heavenly food gives the monk the ability to forswear human food.
[6] Coptic often has pronoun referents that aren't clear. The masculine singular pronouns could indicate either the monk or Abba Simeon.
[7] 'Witness' – *marturos*, also means 'martyrdom'.
[8] 'Mountain' in Coptic often designates a monastery or monastic community, e.g. 'Mount of Nitria'.

thinking they were for telling the elder's fortune. Now the elder showed him what to do with them. There was a large bowl filled with water in his courtyard. 'Throw them in', he said. The Lord demonstrated that each of the stones floated, just as the prophet made the iron float in the water [see 2 Kgs 6:6].
Chaîne 1970, #244

[C5] *His Dwelling Place is not in the Flesh*

When the brothers used to question the elder Abba Abraham about Abba Bane's way of life, he would say to them: 'Bane, well, his dwelling place is not in the flesh at all.' People have testified that he would extend the 40 days of fasting by three days and the three days were not at all onerous for him.[9] No, he would humble himself for not being the equal of the saints.
Chaîne 1970, #245

[C6] *If Adam Had Sought Out the Angels for Counsel*

One day Abba Bane asked Abba Abraham: 'If a person were in paradise like Adam, would he still need to seek counsel for himself?' 'Yes, Bane', he said to him, 'because if Adam had sought out the angels for counsel, saying: "Shall I eat of the tree?" they would have told him: "No."'
Chaîne 1970, #246

[C7] *Abba Bane's Prescience*

The priest who brought Bane[10] the Eucharist found him downhearted and forced him to explain. 'Why are you so troubled?' he asked. He said to him: 'The earth has lost its foundation today.' The priest said to him: 'What has happened, my father?' Bane told him: 'The emperor Theodosius[11] died today.' When he left him, the priest wrote down that day's date and, when letters were brought south, it turned out that the date Bane had told him agreed with what was said in the letters that had been brought.
Chaîne 1970, #247

---

[9] The '40 days of fasting' is Lent. According to Maged S. A. Mikhail, who is preparing a study of Lent in the Coptic Church, from roughly the 330s to the 650s the fast was 40 days, and Lent included Passion Week; it was a six-week observance ending with Easter, introduced by Athanasius based on the Roman model.

[10] Text: him.

[11] Is this Theodosius I [*ob* 395] or his grandson, Theodosius II [*ob* 450]?

[C8] *An Abomination in My Sight*

When Bane[12] was going to eat he would stand in front of a wall and eat
his bread; and he used to work standing up. Moreover, when he was
going to sleep, he would lean his chest against the wall which he had
built for this purpose. Each Sunday the fathers among the brothers used
to come and see how he was doing. Once they had arrived and gathered
around him, they would ask him: 'Our father, are you more satisfied now
than when you were feeding so many poor people?' Blessed Abba Bane
for his part would testify to them, saying, 'Everything about the life I
lived before secluding myself for quiet solitude,[13] whether spiritual discipline or helping those in need, they are all an abomination[14] in my sight
now, in comparison with the person I have become.'
Chaîne 1970, #248

[C9] *The Power of Abba Bane*

One day, moreover, the elders went to Abba Abraham, the prophet of the
region, and asked him about Abba Bane, saying: 'We talked with Abba
Bane[15] about the seclusion he has imposed on himself. He spoke to us
with words of great import; he said he considered all the spiritual discipline he used to observe and all the help he gave those in need to be an
abomination.' Abraham the holy elder replied to them saying: 'What he
said was right.' The elders were deeply disturbed because their own lives
were like that, but Abba Abraham the elder said to them: 'Why are you
upset? When Abba Bane was helping the poor, didn't he feed a village, a
town, a region? But now Abba Bane has the power to raise his two hands
for barley to be supplied to the whole world in abundance. He has the
power, furthermore, to ask God to forgive the sins of this entire generation for them.' When they heard these things, the elders rejoiced that
they had such an intercessor to pray for them.
Chaîne 1970, #249

[C10] *'I am Sleeping but my Heart is Awake'*

There was also another monk in the same place, whose name was Daniel,
a person accomplished in living ethically, who had great powers of

---

[12] Text: he.
[13] Coptic *sĕraht* often translates Greek *hēsychía*, which in monastic usage suggests solitude, quiet,
tranquillity, contemplative silence.
[14] Strong language. 'Abomination' translates Coptic/Greek *porn(e)ía*, 'fornication', 'sexual impurity'.
[15] Text: Abba Abraham; clearly a mistake.

discernment.[16] He had learned all of scripture by heart, both the New and the Old Testaments, as well as all the canons and episcopal treatises. This man was a watchman with regard to what he said, and did not speak at all except when the matter was important and necessary. Moreover, his memory and the way he used it were a wonder to behold; he was very sweet-tempered, patiently weighing each of the words he spoke with great scrupulousness. It has been testified about him that, while meditating on the prophet Jeremiah, he was uncertain about a verse and continued to struggle with it, wanting to know its meaning so it would not remain inexplicable. Suddenly the Prophet replied to him: 'This is the meaning of what I said.' They also testify about him that he recites 10,000 verses[17] by heart each day. Moreover, when he steals a little sleep in order to stay up, he finds himself lingering over the recitation of a verse. It has become second nature for him to increase the number of verses he meditates on, as it is said in the *Song of Songs*, 'I am sleeping but my heart is awake.'[18]

Chaîne 1970, #250

[C11] *Neither Joists, nor Capitals, nor Columns*

It was said of Abba Niran that he was extremely conscientious about what he said and very spiritual in his excellent way of life. He spent 60 years leading services at a church.[19] He never saw the joists, nor the capitals or columns. He held a service[20] twice a day. We have learned this about him since he died; his colleague in God told us this.

Chaîne 1970, #251

[C12] *Putting Down Arrogance and Self-importance*

It was said of Abba Dioscorus that he was a scribe who earlier in his life had recorded the wheat output. When he became a monk, if people said to him, 'You're an important person', he would reply to them: 'Look, from this person I stealthily and wickedly took his sack and from

---

[16] The Coptic uses Greek here for two traits that the monks valued highly: 'a person accomplished in living ethically' translates *praktikós* and 'powers of discernment', *diakritikós*.

[17] Gk *stíchos* usually indicates a verse of the Psalms.

[18] Song 5:2. Gk *meletáō*, used twice in this saying, does not mean 'meditate' in the modern sense but rather slowly to say the verses of scripture *sotto voce* or out loud.

[19] *-sunage*: hold a service, esp. of celebrating the Eucharist (Lampe 1295A2).

[20] *Synaxis*.

somebody else I took his basket.' He said this right out, like that, to put down arrogance and self-importance.
Chaîne 1970, #252

[C13] *Three Blessings*

It was also said that he said: 'Three blessings God has granted me: an eye to discern good,[21] a place in a cell, and physical suffering.'
Chaîne 1970, #253

[C14] *Dioscorus' Ascetic Discipline*

With regard to his clothing, he wears a coarse linen robe with a coarse linen hood and he has another linen robe, as the rule requires. If somebody asks him, he gives away one and keeps the other. Furthermore, with regard to food, his practice is to eat nothing but bread, salt, and water. Furthermore, as for sleeping, he never puts a reed mat or a fleece or anything like it beneath him but sleeps on the earth itself (as we have heard) and it is impossible to put any oil in his cell at all.
Chaîne 1970, #254

[C15] *Dioscorus' Severe Ascetic Discipline*

Here is another amazing thing that happened to him when he first approached God to serve him. His intestines hemorrhaged blood because of the way he ascetically disciplined his body and his feet were gangrened. He didn't treat them at all, nor did he let anyone know about them; instead, he just covered his feet with scraps of rag until God gave him relief. His disciple once said to him: 'Apply a little cooked safflower to them', but he refused to listen.
Chaîne 1970, #255

[C16] *Dioscorus Teaches what he Practices*

When he was a scribe he had one cushion to put under him when he sat down; but he was not attached to it nor did he give much thought to something like that. But when he copied a book for somebody, he would

---

[21] Literally: a good (-*agathos*) eye.

give it to him, and the other person would give him some bread[22] or something else he needed. If no one looked after him, he was not sad; nor would he bother anyone. If a brother came to the mountain, he would take him in and show him the basket of bread, saying: 'Do not fret about our possessions at all, brother, for God himself provides.'
Chaîne 1970, #256

[C17] *Dioscorus' Hospitality*

A person living in the world[23] once put on the monastic habit and came to him, saying, 'Give me some loaves of bread.' He got some bread from his pantry and brought it to him. The brother did not say: 'That is enough.' The elder had decided in his heart: 'Unless he says "That is enough", I will not stop.' When all the loaves of bread were gone (except for one little one), the person finally said: 'That is enough', and the elder stopped.[24]
Chaîne 1970, #257

[C18] *The Door of Hospitality*

A brother once came to him saying: 'I have not found a door for my dwelling.' He said to him: 'Pull this one off for yourself.' The brother pulled off the door that led to the street, took it, and went his way. The elder hung a mat there until he made a door of palm to put in its place.
Chaîne 1970, #258

[C19] *Abba Dioscorus Sees What is True*

Here is another marvellous thing that happened through him. The monastery priest used to come to give him Communion and in addition would go to see him often. Abba Dioscorus[25] would say to him: 'Do not let a woman enter the monastery.' The priest said: 'No woman has ever entered the monastery.'

'There is one there now', the elder said to him. The priest went to find out and discovered it was true.
Chaîne 1970, #259

---

[22] Chaîne notes, 79 n. 1, 'The conjunction that follows this verb indicates one or more words are missing here after the verb.'
[23] *Kosmikós* indicates someone living 'in the world' rather than the monastic life.
[24] 'Enough' and 'stop' translate the same word, *sō*.
[25] Text: He.

[C20] *Which Would You Give to Jesus?*

At one time he had two tunics: the one that was good he set aside; the one that was in poor shape he wore. A stranger asked him for it. He gave him the good one and kept the one that was worn out. The priest asked him: 'Why did you not give him the worn out one and keep the one you wear to go to church in?'

He said to him: 'Would you give the worn-out one to Jesus?'
Chaîne 1970, #260

[C21] *Kill Me First*

It was said of him in addition that one time when the barbarians invaded the east, he was living in the desert and they came to his cell. There was also a brother there, whom the elder hid. They asked him: 'Is there someone here?'

'No', he said. But then they searched and found him. They took them away to their leader who said to them, 'If you two knew we were coming, why didn't you run away?' Abba Dioscorus raised his head and said, 'If you're going to kill him, then kill me first.' The barbarians said to him: 'We're not going to kill you; nor are we going to kill him. Get out of here! Next time, if you two hear that we're coming, run away!' and they let them go. When it was night, they left and someone came and brought Abba Dioscorus his knife (they had taken it with the rest of his possessions) and gave it back.
Chaîne 1970, #261

[C22] *The Mat of Covetousness*

One time he laid out a nice mat for himself. A brother came to visit him. The brother lay down to sleep in the cell and Abba Dioscorus threw the mat over him. The brother coveted the mat so he said to the abba, 'Where did you find this? I would like to get one like it for myself.' Abba Dioscorus remained silent until morning. The elder then gave the sheepskin mat to the brother who was leaving and the brother said to Abba Dioscorus: 'This sheepskin you've given me is burdensome.'[26] Abba

---

[26] There is a play on words here: *shaar* is a homonym meaning both 'sheepskin' and 'price', and *horsh* means both 'heavy' and 'a burden, burdensome'. Thus, the covetous monk is unknowingly saying that he's paying a heavy price for his covetousness. See the next two notes.

Dioscorus said: 'The mat I've given you is the light one;[27] as far as I am concerned, I can find another one.' So he let him take it.[28]
Chaîne 1970, #262

[C23] *Goodbye to this World*

He was now sick and near death. He had been sick for a number of days and wouldn't let anyone prepare the least little thing for him, nor would he take anything. Rather, when he was about to die someone brought two mats and put one on top of the other for him until he completed his life, but for him they were chains binding him. He threw them off and said goodbye to this world.
Chaîne 1970, #263

[C24] *The Hand and the Fire*

Abba Elijah of Scete recounted: 'When I fled to Scete I importuned Abba Hierax: "Allow me to be your son so I may be your disciple and sit at your feet." To test me he said to me: "Will you obey me and do everything I tell you?" "Yes, I will", I said. "Absolutely." He lit a fire and, to put me to the test, said to me: "If you want me to have you at my side and if you will obey me, stick your hand in this fire." So I put my hand in the fire. I left it there until it was black and, if he hadn't taken my hand and lifted it off, I would no longer have it.' It was us to whom he told the miracle of his hand.
Chaîne 1970, #270

[C25] *How Will We be Saved?*

Abba Elijah was asked: 'How will we be saved these days?' He replied: 'We will be saved through each of us having no regard for himself.'
Chaîne 1970, #271

[C26] *Stay Put*

It is said of a brother that he went to an elder and said to him: 'I want a small dwelling of my own.' The elder said to him: 'Stay where you are

---

[27] *Koui* also means 'small, insignificant', thus not worth taking.
[28] *Afkaaf ebol* (*kō ebol*) also means 'He forgave him'.

now and I will go look for a place.' The brother stayed there where the elder had left him, alone. The elder left and was gone three years. He came back after three years and found the brother there where he had left him; the brother had not even gone into another part of the dwelling. The elder marvelled in amazement at the brother's [patient endurance. . .][29]
Chaîne 1970, #272

[C27] *Giving Birth*

Abba Antony said, 'There is someone who regularly gives birth to death but if he did what is good for him he would give birth to life.'
Amélineau 1894, 15.7–9

[C28] *Precepts from Abba Antony*

Abba Antony said: 'If you are living a life of spiritual practice[30] with Christ, let your cell be a prison for you. Always keep in mind that you will be leaving the body. Never forget the eternal judgment that will come and no sin at all will ever overtake your soul. Share in the Holy Spirit in order to live with the Lord for ever. If you persevere in the presence of God, you will obtain eternal life and God will do away with your sins and restore you once more to his Kingdom.'
Amélineau 1894, 17.4–10

[C29] *The Whole Thing*

It was said of a brother that he had defeated anger. One day he went to visit Abba Antony after the *synaxis* was finished. Abba Antony wanted to put him to the test to see whether he had really defeated this passion. 'Get up and recite something from memory', he said to him. When the brother stood up, he said to the elder: 'What do you want me to recite? Should I recite something for us from the Old or from the New Testament?' When he heard this, Abba Antony said to him: 'Sit down! Your arrogance is off-putting; it knows no bounds.' When the brother sat down again, the elder once again spoke to him: 'I just told you to get up

---

[29] The conclusion is missing, but this seems like a reasonable conjecture, among many. The possessive *tef-*, 'his' requires a feminine noun, so Gk *hupomonē*, 'patient endurance', and Coptic *metrefôou nhêt*, 'patience', and *metrefcôtem*, 'obedience', are possibilities.
[30] Gk *politeúesthai* (noun: *politeía*); Lampe 1114a–b: 'conduct oneself', 'live as a member of a community', 'share a particular mode of life, esp. of Christian life', 'perform ascetic exercises'.

and recite something from memory.' When the brother got up, he said to the elder: 'Do you want me to do it from the New Testament or from the Old?' 'Sit down! Your arrogance is amazing', the elder said to him once again and, once again, the brother sat down. Now the elder said to him: 'Get up and recite something from memory.' Again, the brother said to him: 'Should I do it from the Old or should I do it from the New Testament?' The elder said to him: 'Truly, my son, you have mastered all of the Old and the New Testaments; do whichever one you want.'
Amélineau 1894, 21.4–22.4

[C30] *The Discerning Crocodiles*

The story is told of two brothers who met each other in a monastery. One had mastered spiritual practices[31] while the other was obedient and humble. They asked themselves: Which activity is the greater? When they came to the Nile there were numerous crocodiles there. The obedient brother went right through them to the other side: they respected him. He said to the spiritually disciplined brother: 'You come over to the other side too', but that one said: 'Forgive me, my brother, I have not reached your spiritual maturity.'[32] When they got back to the monastery, a voice spoke to Abba Antony on the mountain: 'The obedient one has surpassed the spiritually disciplined one.'
Amélineau 1894, 22.5–13, cf. *APanon* 294 / 14.27 / *BHG* 1438m, *de crocodrillis*

[C31] *Abba Antony Teaches about Thoughts*[33]

A brother's thoughts were making him feel claustrophobic; so he left home and spoke to Abba Antony. The elder said to him: 'Go, stay in your cell; pledge yourself[34] to the walls of your cell and do not come out of them. Let your thoughts go wherever they want; only, do not let your body come out of the cell. It will suffer and will not be able to work at all. Finally, it will get hungry and at meal time it will come back, looking for you to feed it. If, as the time approaches, it says to you: "Eat a little

---

[31] *-askētēs* (Gk *askēsis*); or: ascetic disciplines.

[32] Literally: I haven't reached this measure/weight (*shi*). Scetis, the Wadi Natrun, the site of some of Egypt's earliest monastic communities, in Coptic is *shi hēt*, 'measure/weigh the heart'.

[33] The scriptural exchange in this apophthegm is modeled on the temptation of Jesus (Mt 4:1–11 // Lk 4:1–13), with the body playing the Devil's part.

[34] Literally: 'Give your body.'

bread for yourself", arm yourself [see Eph 6:14], stand guard, and say: "One does not live by bread alone, but by every word that comes from the mouth of God" [Dt 8:3, Mt 4:4]. Now it will say to you: "Drink a little wine for yourself like the blessed Timothy" [1 Tim 5:3]. For your part, do you say in turn to it: "Remember the children of Amminadab who kept the commandments of their father."[35] If it tries to make you sleepy, do not let it, for it is written in the Holy Gospels: "Watch and pray" [Mt 26:41], and again it is written: "They have gone to sleep and have found nothing at all that benefits them" [Ps 75:6]. Nourish your soul with the words of God, with vigils and prayers, and above all with the constant remembrance of the name of our Lord Jesus Christ.[36] With these disciplines, you will teach yourself how to claim victory over your evil thoughts. If the hunter who hunts for evil lures you out of your cell, after he does so he will cut you down and devour you because of your lack of judgement,[37] whether you came out for a good reason or not. He will assault you in all sorts of ways: in the feet, in the hands, the heart; through sight, hearing, and actions; by the tongue and the mouth and as you walk. If you stay in your cell, you will be free from everything I have told you.'
Amélineau 1894, 22.14–24.7

[C32] Stoning our Thoughts

Abba Antony said to the brothers: 'One day when I was walking in the mountain I came across an ostrich with her young. When they saw me, they ran off and I heard the mother saying to her little ones: "Throw rocks at him so he does not catch you." We should do likewise. When the demons throw thoughts at us, let us throw rocks at them, rocks from the stone hewn from the undefiled womb of the holy Virgin Mary, the cornerstone [Ps 117/118:22; Acts 4:11; Mk 12:10 etc.], who fights mightily on our behalf and delivers us from their evil snares.'
Amélineau 1894, 24.8–15

---

[35] By having Antony tell the monk to respond 'Remember' (ari phmeui), the narrative is teaching how to respond to the 'thoughts' (phmeui) that are troubling the monk at the beginning of the saying. The Septuagint has 'Aminadab', not the Masoretic 'Abinadab' at LXX 1 Sam [1 Kgs] 7:1–2; 2 Sam [2 Kgs] 6:3. Aminadab's sons guarded the Ark for 20 years while it was in their home.

[36] 'Constant remembrance': Coptic athmounk, 'unceasing, imperishable', can translate Gk adialeíptōs, as in 1 Th 1:2: 'Pray without ceasing.' 'Remembrance': see the previous note.

[37] Gk diákrisis, 'judgement, discernment, discrimination', a key concept and practice in early monastic spirituality.

[C33] *Precepts from Abba Antony*

Abba Antony said: 'Rid yourself of evil; put on simplicity. Rid yourself of the evil eye;[38] put on transparency and compassion.[39] Hate no one, and do not walk with someone more humble than you, but rather with someone more advanced than you and who shows it by the way he lives.[40] Do not fear people's disdain; hate everything that hurts your soul. Do not abandon the will of God. Do not do the will of people; by doing this God will be with you.' Amélineau 1894, 24.16–25.6

[C34] *Three Gifts of the Spirit*

Abba Antony said, 'In this world I have seen the Spirit of God descending on these three persons: the Spirit descended upon Athanasius, and he was given the archbishopric; on Abba Macarius and he was given the gift[41] of [healing] the sick; and on Abba Pambo: he was given the diaconate.' Amélineau 1894, 27.15–28.2

[C35] *What Makes Me Notable*

It is said about an elder who was a grower that he once went to see Abba Antony. When the latter elder was told about his visitor, he came out to see him. They went into the cell, prayed, and sat down. Abba Antony said to him: 'Give me spiritual instruction, my father.'[42] The faithful elder and grower said to him, 'There are three different tribes among these people called monks. The first burn like fire; the second are like lions;[43] and the third are like foxes.' Abba Antony said to him: 'Who do you see yourself as, my father?' The elder said to him: 'I see myself as Adam before he transgressed.' Abba Antony said to him: 'You are also a promise, father.'[44] 'Not so', the elder said; 'what makes me notable is my love for God.'

---

[38] See Marvin Meyer and Richard Smith, eds., *Ancient Christian Magic: Coptic Texts of Ritual Power* (San Francisco: HarperSanFrancisco, 1994) and David Frankfurter, *Religion in Roman Egypt: Assimilation and Resistance* (Princeton: Princeton University Press, 1998).

[39] In Coptic, 'evil eye' and 'transparency' both use *bal*, 'eye', and 'transparency' and 'compassion' both use *hēt*, 'heart/mind'.

[40] 'The way he lives': *praktikon*; see n. 16 above.

[41] In Coptic, *hmot* also means 'grace', and often translates Gk *cháris*.

[42] 'Give me spiritual instruction': literally 'Teach me a word/saying.' 'Give me a word' is a common request by one monk of another, usually an elder, asking for spiritual instruction and insight.

[43] We have omitted what looks like an erroneously repeated 'fire' after 'lions'.

[44] It is difficult to decide what Antony means here. Gk *epangelía* can indicate God's promise to humankind, a promise or reward, as in 'the promised land'. *Epangelía* can also mean a 'profession, declaration'. Since the term applies especially to monastic profession, perhaps Antony is saying that the elder is a sign of monastic vows, profession. See Lampe 505a.

Amélineau 1894, 28.3–13

[C36] *Abba Antony Teaches about the Signs of the End*

When Abba Antony was near death, the brothers asked him about the
end of the world. The holy one said to them, 'The prophets already
prophesied, Christ spoke about this in his own words, and, after him,
the apostles preached about the end. So who am I to say anything
about it?' The brothers said to him: 'You, too, are a prophet, an apostle,
and a father for these times; please do us a kindness and teach us.' He
said to them: 'You know about the first world, the one that God
destroyed on account of the sexual immorality and violence and evil-
doing to which people had come. The same thing for Sodom and
Gomorrah: because of the sexual immorality and heartlessness, God
obliterated them back then [Gen 19:24–25]. So the end of the world
will come about as a result of these three things.[45] If violence and evil-
doing multiply among people and if sexual immorality multiplies
among monks, this signals the fulfilment of the end. If you see monks
who are elders renouncing the desert and [those in] the monasteries
using any excuse whatever to go into the towns and villages, mimicking
withdrawal into the desert [only in reverse], living with their wives in
homes as people in the world do; if you see young monks living in the
monasteries of virgins, their cells adjacent to each other, their windows
facing one another; if you see those who live in the desert more in love
with eating and drinking than with labour and suffering, self-restraint
and privation; if you see monks acting like merchants, buying and selling like those in the world, this signals the fulfilment of the end. There
will be no more relief for the world, only suffering and misery until the
consummation of the age.'[46]
Amélineau 1894, 28.14–29.13

---

[45] Three things: (1) sexual immorality, (2) violence and evil-doing (one word in Coptic), and (3)
heartlessness.
[46] 'The consummation of the age': see Mt 13:39, 40, 49; 24:3; 28:20; and He 9:26.

[C37] *Living Continually with God*

Abba Antony said, 'If you want to have a way of life[47] that is with Christ, make your cell a prison for yourself. Remember at all times your departure from your body and never forget the judgment that is coming; then no sin of any kind will ever come to your soul. Partner with the Holy Spirit in order to live with the Lord forever. If your practice is to live continually with God, you will obtain life eternal and God will wipe away your sins and will establish you anew in his kingdom.'
Amélineau 1894, 17.4–11

[C38] *Bringing to Completion Both Testaments*

It was said about a brother that he had defeated anger. He once paid a visit to Abba Antony. When they had finished the *synaxis*,[48] Abba Antony wanted to test the brother to see whether or not he had defeated this passion.[49] He said to him, 'Get up; say something about a piece of scripture you have learned by heart.' Standing up, the brother said to the elder, 'What do you want me to offer a reflection on? Do you want me to offer something for you on the Old Testament or the New Testament?' When Abba Antony heard these words, he said to him 'Sit down, you! You're arrogant and rash!' After the brother had sat down again, the elder again spoke to him: 'I just finished telling you "Stand up!" and "Reflect on a bit of scripture you have learned by heart"!' After the brother stood, he said to the elder, 'Do you want me to offer something for you on the New Testament or do you want something on the Old Testament?' Once again the elder said to him, 'Sit down! You're being even more arrogant than before!' Once again the brother sat down. The elder said to him again, 'Get up and reflect a bit on some scripture you have learned by heart.' The brother said to him again, 'Should I offer something on the Old Testament or the New Testament?' The elder said to him, 'In all

[47] 'Have a way of life': GK *politeúesthai*, from *politeía*, way of life, especially a monastic way of life.
[48] The monastic office. On *synaxis*, see Robert Taft, S.J., 'Praise in the Desert: The Coptic Monastic Office Yesterday and Today', *Worship* 56 (1982), pp. 513–36.
[49] To use an old Anglican phrase, the 'passions' are 'the devices and desires of our own hearts' that draw us away from God and neighbour.

truth, my son, you have brought to completion all of the Old Testament and New Testament. Whatever you wish to say, say.'
Amélineau 1894, 21.3–22.4

[C39] *Measuring Up*

It was said about two brothers who lived together successfully in a monastic community that one was an accomplished ascetic while the other was humble and obedient. They inquired of each other, saying, 'What is the greatest work?' When they came to the Nile there was a large group of crocodiles there. The one who was obedient went to the other side through their midst and they did obeisance to him. He said to the ascetic, 'You too, come on over to the other side.' The ascetic said to him, 'Forgive me, my brother, I don't measure up to where you are.' They returned to the monastery. Word reached Abba Antony at his monastic community[50] informing him that the one who was obedient was someone who surpassed the ascetic.
Amélineau 1894, 22.5–13

[C40] *Sit in Your Cell!*

A brother who was so distressed by his thoughts that he wanted to leave his monastic dwelling spoke with Abba Antony. The elder said to him, 'Hurry! Go! Sit in your cell! Give your body as a pledge to the walls of your cell and do not leave your cell; let your thoughts go where they please, only do not take your body outside your cell and they will not trouble you or be able to do anything to you. Later, your body is going to get hungry and will be sure you know when it is time to eat. If it says to you before it is time to eat "Eat a little bread; it will do you good", be careful and say to it, "A person will not live by bread alone but by every word that comes from the mouth of God" [Dt 8:3; Mt 4:4]. Again it will say to you, "Drink a little wine, like blessed Timothy. That will do you good" [see 1 Tim 5:23]. For your part, respond to it by saying "Keep in mind the children of Aminadab, who did what their father commanded" [Jer 35:6]. If your body causes you to be hungry while you are sleeping, do not welcome that, for it is written in the holy Gospel: "Be vigilant and pray" [Mt 26:41]. It is also written: "Those who sleep gain nothing" [Ps

---

[50] *Tōou* indicates a mountain and came to indicate a monastery. In Antony's day the word most likely meant a (remote) monastic community.

75:6]. Do you rather nourish your soul with the words of God, with vigils, and with prayer; especially with constantly keeping in mind the name of our Lord Jesus Christ. By these means you will find instruction: knowledge of how to be victorious over evil thoughts. If your body hauls you out of your cell, the one who hunts for evil will cut you into pieces and swallow you, leaving you without the ability properly to discern[51] whether what you are doing is to your advantage or not. Your body will, like an army arrayed for battle, fight against you in a wide variety of ways, whether through your feet or your hands or your heart or sight or hearing or actions or tongue and mouth [see Jas 3:1–12] or the way you walk.[52] If you stay in your cell, you will be someone who is free from all these things I have told you about.'
Amélineau 1894, 22.14–24.7

[C41] *Stones from the Cornerstone*

Abba Antony spoke to the brothers: 'While I was walking one time on the mountain, I encountered an ostrich and its young. When they saw me, they ran away. I heard the mother saying to her offspring, "Throw stones at him so you do not get captured!" It is the same with us, too: if the demons throw thoughts at us, we need to throw stones at them from the stone cut [Dan 2:34, 45] from the immaculate womb of Saint Virgin Mary; she is the cornerstone [Ps 117/118:22; Acts 4:11; Mk 12:10 etc.] who fights so well on our behalf and delivers us from evil snares.'
Amélineau 1894, 24.8–15

[C42] *God Will be with You*

Abba Antony said, 'Strip yourself of evil; clothe yourself with singlemindedness. Strip yourself of the evil eye; clothe yourself with openheartedness and a compassionate heart. Hate no one; do not walk with anyone who is your inferior but rather with one who is superior to you; and practice a life of asceticism.[53] Do not fear people's contempt. Hate

---

[51] Discern/discernment: Gk *diákrisis*. Discernment (of spirits) is very important in early monastic literature. See Anthony D. Rich, *Discernment in the Desert Fathers: Diákrisis in the Life and Thought of Early Egyptian Monasticism*, Studies in Early Christian History and Thought (Bletchley, Milton Keynes, UK; and Waynesboro, GA: Wipf & Stock, 2007) and John Wortley, 'Discretion: Greater than All the Virtues', *Greek, Roman, and Byzantine Studies* 51 (2011), pp. 634–52.

[52] 'Walk', as in English, can indicate 'walk of life'.

[53] Or: practice a life of contemplation. 'Practice': *-praktikon*. For Evagrius, *pratikē* is contemplation of the physical world and of God; see his *Praktikos*.

everything that damages your soul. Do not abandon what God wills for you in order to follow human will.[54] If you do this, God will be with you.'
Amélineau 1894, 24.16–25.6

[C43] *Athanasius, Macarius, and Pambo*

Abba Antony said, 'I saw the Spirit of God descending on three persons in this world: upon Athanasius, for to him was given the archiepiscopacy; upon Abba Macarius, for to him was given the grace to heal the sick;[55] and upon Abba Pambo, for to him was given the diaconate.'[56]
Amélineau 1894, 27.15–28.2

[C44] *My Great Love is for God*

It was said about an elder, one who cultivated the land, that he once paid a visit to Abba Antony. The elder [Antony] had been informed of his visit so he went outside to greet him. After they had gone inside the cell, they prayed and sat down. Abba Antony said to him, 'Offer me a word, my father.' The faithful elder who was a cultivator said to him, 'There are three kinds of people among the tribe called monks: the first is those who are a flaming fire; the second is those who are like lions; the third is those who are like foxes.' Abba Antony said to him, 'In which of these do you see yourself, my father?' The elder said to him, 'I see myself like Adam before he transgressed' [Gen 3]. Abba Antony said to him, 'You yourself are a promise, my father.' The elder said to him, 'No, but my great love is for God.'
Amélineau 1894, 28.3–13

[C45] *The Consummation of This Age*

The brothers asked Abba Antony, who was going to die soon, about the end of the world. The holy man said to them, 'The prophets already prophesied and Christ in his own words spoke about this [Mt 24:14, 28:20]. Afterwards, the apostles preached about the end. As for me, what can I say about it?' The brothers said to him, 'You too are a prophet and

---

54 'Wills' and 'will' translate *ouōsh*, which also means 'desire, love'. Thus: Do not abandon what God desires for you so you can follow human desires.

55 Athanasius (ca. 296–373) was archbishop of Alexandria, a defender of Nicene theology against the Arians and of Church unity against the Melitians. Macarius the Great (ca. 300–390) was an imminent monk at the Wadi Natrun; numerous sayings and works are by him or were attributed to him. See the Bohairic *Life of Pachomius* 43–6.

56 *APalph* Macarius of Egypt 2 suggests that Pambo was a priest; the *Life of Pambo* does not say he was ordained. There were probably several Pambos.

an apostle and a father at the end of this present age. Have compassion for us. Tell us about it.' He said to them, 'You have seen the first world that God destroyed on account of the sexual sin and violence taking place among them [Gen 6:11]. In the same way, moreover, God destroyed Sodom and Gomorrah at that time on account of their sexual sins and pitilessness [Gen 18:16–19:29]. So too now: the end of this world will take place because of these three [*sic*] things: if violence increases among people and sexual sin increases among the monks. This will bring about the consummation of the age. If you see certain monks, spiritual elders, abandoning the desert and monasteries, leaving them behind, and finding any pretext whatsoever to go into towns and villages, imitating the anchoritic life while living in the homes of those living in the world with their women; if you see young male monks living in the monasteries of virgins, their cells adjoining one another, their windows accessible to each other; if you see even the inhabitants of the desert loving to eat and drink more than labouring to practice continence and circumspection; if you see monks acting like merchants, buying and selling like those in the world; all these things signal the consummation of the end. There will be no relief for the world, only suffering and hardship, until the consummation of this age.'
Amélineau 1894, 28.14–30.2

[C46] *Keep Watch over Everything*

Abba Antony said, 'It is not the person who is victorious in one thing only, namely abstinence, nor the person who masters only one of the things that oppose[57] virtue who is better.[58] If abstinence boasts that it is virtuous, a multitude of evils are enemies of it. But the person who is saved must watch over everything because of his enemies and pray that God's goodness will save him.'
Amélineau 1894, 30.3–9

[C47] *Slavery*

Again Abba Antony said, 'The person who hastens to be perfect in abstinence is not a slave of any passion. The person who is a slave of a single evil is far from the path of God.'
Amélineau 1894, 30.10–13

[57] Oppose: *ti ekhoun ehren* has a number of nuances: 'defy', 'fight against', 'set against', 'resist'; also 'to be annoyed or disturbed by'.
[58] Coptic *sōtp* also means 'chosen'.

[C48] *Each and Every Day*

Abba Antony also said, 'Every labour that the angry person takes on will
be destroyed and taken away from him, each and every day.'
Amélineau 1894, 30.14–15

[C49] *Sheep and Goats*

Abba Antony also said, 'I spent an entire year beseeching God to reveal
to me the path of the righteous and the path of those who sin. I saw
someone as large as a giant standing there reaching up to the clouds. His
hands stretched as far as the heavens; beneath him was a lake as large and
broad as the ocean. I also saw souls flying like birds and all those who
were flying high above his hands and high above his head were saved and
all those whom he had caught in his hands and whom he had beaten
plummeted into the lake filled with fire. Then a voice came to me from
heaven, saying, "Antony, these souls that you have seen flying high above
his hands are the very souls of the righteous who will be in paradise. And
those whom you have seen falling into his hands are the souls of sinners
being drawn down into Amente[59] because their desires were for the
things of the flesh and their pleasures that last but a short time and they
were people whose thoughts were so evil that, truly, their evil desires
threw them into the fire."[60]
Amélineau 1894, 31.11–32.8

[C50] *The Spiritual Body Giving Birth*

Abba Antony said, 'In everything you do, think nothing of yourself:
thinking nothing of yourself is the body of humility. Humility gives birth
to a person willing to learn, and the willingness to learn gives birth to
faith. Faith brings forth obedience to God; obedience to God brings
forth love for your brother.'
Amélineau 1894, 32.9–13

---

[59] The *Life of Paphnutius* 22 speaks of 'the punishments in Amente' and 128 speaks of being thrown
'into the pit of Amente'.
[60] Amélineau's text towards the end here is corrupt; my reconstruction is based on that of Regnault's
translation, 145.

[C51] *Stop Worrying*

A brother asked the elder Abba Antony concerning what is written in the Gospel: 'Do not worry about tomorrow; tomorrow will worry about itself. Each day has enough wickedness of its own' [see Mt 6:34]. The elder said to him, 'I think this verse is telling you to stop worrying yourself for one year about what the body needs so you won't be excessively concerned about life's needs beyond its basic necessities. In this way you can be saved.' Amélineau 1894, 32.14–33.3

[C52] *Antony Learns about Compassion and Forgiveness*

It was said about Abba Antony that the matter of a virgin who had fallen into a transgression was revealed to him one time. He got up, took in his hand his staff made from a palm branch and set out on the road, walking to the monastery so he could, because of the purity of his ascetic practice, severely rebuke them and condemn them. While he was still walking, getting near the monastery, there suddenly appeared to him Christ, the King of glory, he alone who is compassionate, who has numerous treasuries of compassion, who forgives and takes away human sins and transgressions. The Saviour, with a face of gentleness and a smile full of grace, said to him, 'Antony! What is the reason for this great suffering of yours?' When the elder heard these words of the Saviour, he threw himself to the ground face down on the earth and said to him, 'My Lord, since you have made me worthy to see your presence,[61] you already know the cause of the outrageous behaviour that is causing my suffering.' The good lover of humankind said to him, 'You have taken on this suffering and this immense hardship because of the transgression of this young virgin.' Abba Antony, still face down on the ground, said to him, 'You, Lord, know everything before it happens!' The Lord said to him, 'Get up, follow me.' When Antony went into the wilderness with him and was drawing near the monastery, the gates were shut where the virgin was and he heard the virgin weeping, saying, 'My Lord Jesus Christ, when you consider all our sin, who can stand before you? [Ps 129/130:3–4] When we stand in your presence, forgiveness truly lies solely in your hands. Jesus Christ, you who are my Lord, take vengeance on the jealous person who has acted out of spite against me and destroyed me! Jesus, you who are my Lord, I beseech you, do not turn your face from me [Ps 26:9]: I am a weak and fragile vessel [1 Pet 3:7]!' She spoke these words with numerous

---

[61] Gk *paroúsia*.

tears. The merciful and compassionate God, our Lord Jesus Christ, said, 'Antony, are you not moved with compassion now? Do your eyes not weep when you hear how frail and weak she is and how she cries out to me with many tears of grief? Truly, she has summoned my mercy, like the adulterous woman who washed my feet with her tears and wiped them with the hair of her head; because of her repentance, she has received forgiveness of her sins from me on account of her faith. But I will not let your suffering be in vain. Offer them some respect, in deference to them, and go.'[62] After the Saviour said this, he disappeared from Antony's sight. Abba Antony returned; while on the road he glorified God. His tears flowed down to the ground as he marvelled greatly at the goodness of God and the numerous mercies he has for every creature of his hands that he has made and the way he quickly takes to himself every person who sins and turns to him with an upright heart.
Amélineau 1894, 33.4–35.10

[C53] *A Breath of Fresh Air*

Abba Antony said, 'When you are moved by thoughts that distress you and that you cannot chase away sufficiently, go outside into the fresh air and they will leave you.'
Amélineau 1894, 35.11–13

[C54] *Very Good Practices*

Abba Antony again said, 'There are very good practices that we can take refuge in in our cells and intensely use to reflect on ourselves throughout our lives so we may know what kind of person we are. When you [*sic*] remain in your dwelling, then you become someone who has anticipated the time of his death; when you persevere in praying night and day, then you have anticipated the time of your death; when you remain in the desert without any kind of friendship according to the flesh, then you are ready to die to the world. I say this to you (pl.): I have passed all my time eating one measure of barley bread,[63] while drinking one measure of cloudy water, and when I wish to go somewhere I am careful while walking not to place my foot anywhere where there is the slightest trace of a woman.'
Amélineau 1894, 35.14–36.8

[62] The translation of this sentence is uncertain. The Coptic is *ma nkouji nhexis* (Gk *héxis*). Perhaps it suggests 'reverence' or 'homage', implying a customary act or gesture of respect.
[63] That is, as opposed to higher quality wheat bread.

[C55] *The Purified Heart*

Abba Antony also said, 'It is not what is written in the letter of the law that makes for righteousness; rather, it is the purified heart: this is what makes for human righteousness.'
Amélineau 1894, 36.9–10

[C56] *The Heart Alone*

Abba Antony said, 'I wanted to go to Upper Egypt, but I was held back: "Do not go; go to the monastery instead." There are three things that belong to the world and do not belong to the monastery: the eye fights with each person; so do the tongue [Jas 3:5] and the ear. But in the monastery, it is the heart[64] alone that fights with a person. Is that one not more valuable than [the other three]?'[65]
Amélineau 1894, 36.11–15

[C57] *Flesh and Spirit*

Abba Antony said, 'If I come out of my cell to meet with people, I strip myself of my clothing and am naked. When I go back inside, I put it back on. That is to say, when I go outside to be with people, I become flesh, and when I return to my dwelling I become spirit again. I become mortal with mortals and I become spirit with God. Truly, the body houses the heart: the heart has a door and windows. If I leave to be with people, they – all of them – open their homes and squalls and waves come in. That is, they hear and see and speak and smell. If I remain in my cell, the door and windows stay shut and I become unperturbed. My heart is by itself; my concerns are with it and I become someone who is free from the four.[66] The person who speaks with understanding edifies himself, edifying also his fellow monks; the one who remains silent is not in danger. This is what Mary first practiced before arriving at the true knowledge of God' [Lk 1:28–29].
Amélineau 1894, 36.16–37.12

---

[64] See n. 49.
[65] Three: the text has 'four' (delta).
[66] It's not clear what 'the four' refers to. [Senses? – Ed.]

[C58] *The Consummation of Everything Good*

A brother once asked Abba Antony, 'How do you sit in your cell, my father?' The elder said to him, 'What appears to human beings is this: [fasting]⁶⁷ until evening every day, keeping vigil, and meditation. But on the other hand, this is what is hidden from people: having no regard for yourself, the struggle against evil thoughts, being without anger, keeping the approach of your death in front of you, and maintaining a humble heart. These are the consummation of everything good.'
Amélineau 1894, 37.13–38.3

[C59] *The Wise Person Knows the Path*

Abba Antony said, 'Do not walk with someone who is self-important and haughty and arrogant, nor with someone who is angry, but walk with those who are always humble. Let your words be measured in a balance so they are profitable for those who will hear them. Be zealous; let your heart feel grief for your brother, showing compassion for him. May your speech always be sweet. It is poverty that you should especially love. Love toil; take refuge in it. Welcome suffering in your flesh [see 2 Cor 2:7] so that you may be victorious over the passions of the body; do battle in order to be victorious in the war being waged against it. The wise person knows the path he walks in order to meet the heavenly stars in the heavens above' [see Is 40:26; Dt 4:19].
Amélineau 1894, 39.1–10

[C60] *Be Like the Camel, not the Horse*

Abba Antony also said, 'The camel needs just a little food; it conserves it within until it goes to where it lives. The camel regurgitates and ruminates it until it enters its bones and flesh. The horse, on the other hand, needs a great amount of food; eating all the time, it consumes everything it eats all at once. Now, therefore, don't be like the horse. That is, we recite the words of God all the time and we keep not a single one of them. No, let us be like the camel, reciting one by one the words of holy scripture, safeguarding it within us, until it accomplishes its purpose.

---

⁶⁷ Amélineau, 137 n. 4, says that a word is missing. Regnault, 148, has 'le jeûne' without brackets or comment.

Those who have brought to completion the words of scripture were themselves people like us: the passions clung to them, too.'
Amélineau 1894, 39.11–40.5

[**C61**] *The Monastic Habit Gives Us All This Trouble!*

While the brothers were sitting around him, Abba Antony said, 'Let us fight. Truly, the very habit of the monk is worthy of being hated in the presence of the demons. One time I wanted to test them concerning this matter: I brought a short garment, dalmatic, and scapular and hood. I threw them on a dummy; I dressed it; I set it up; I saw the demons standing around it in the distance. They were shooting arrows at it. I said to them, "You, you evil spirits – what is this you are doing to it? It is not a person! It is a dummy!" They said to me, "We know that. We are not shooting arrows at *it*. No, we are shooting at the clothing it is wearing and the monastic habit." I said to them, "What evils are these you're doing to it?" They said to me, "These are the implements of war of those who afflict us and beat us all the time. It is this clothing that gives us all this trouble!" When I heard what they were saying, I gave glory to God who saves those who have faith in him, that he will rescue them from the evil spirits of the Devil, these who fight against the saints day and night as God brings their counsels to nothing.'
Amélineau 1894, 40.6–41.4

[**C62**] *The Three Loaves of Bread*

Abba Antony said, 'A person went to his neighbour in the Gospel in the middle of the night and said to him, "Loan me three loaves of bread because a friend of mine on a journey has come to visit me" [Lk 11:5]. The three loaves of bread that the man gave his neighbour are the three practices of hospitality, hunger, and need. Repentance has knocked, seeking compassionate giving, as though it knew that these things guide the person who does the will of God.'
Amélineau 1894, 41.5–10

[**C63**] *The Habit of the Heart*

Abba Antony said, 'Let the monk not go to a womancs monastery and speak freely with them unless it be with women who possess the power of

God: truly, when he sees them, they will not allow him any rest when he sits in his cell.'

One of the monks said to him, 'Is it not permissible to visit them so we can encourage them?' The elder said to him, 'If you have received the Spirit, go. Otherwise, I do not want you to go. What assaults you until you fall is what encourages them to fall, too. The nature of the heart and the law within it are one: truly, the human heart is inclined towards what is evil.' The brother said to him, 'What do I do concerning the steward-ship of the women's monastery with which I am entrusted?' (His service was at the women's monastery.) The elder said to him, 'If you have received the Spirit, then go. Otherwise, I do not want you to go. The one who flatters you until you fall is the one who entices them until they fall, too. If, however, the person gives the power to God, that person will become fire upon the earth' [Lk 12:49–53; Mt 10:34–39]. The brother said to him, 'What I meant, my father, is that the person who is faithful will take precautions everywhere he goes.' The elder said, 'No. Watch out. If a herd of pigs rises up from the Nile smeared with mud and you walk through their midst, even if they don't knock you down, they will, never-theless, make you black and blue.'
Amélineau 1894, 41.11–42.13

[C64] *Athanasius the Great, the Foundation of the Apostolic Faith*

Our holy father Abba Antony said, 'It happened that I went to Alexandria in order to receive the blessing of the luminous pillar [Ex 13:21], the crown and strong tower [Prv 18:10; Ps 61:3], the foundation of the apostolic faith; he who made a dwelling place for the Holy Spirit [1 Cor 6:19], the Paraclete [Jn 14:16, 26; 15:26; 16:7]; he whose heart became a holy throne of the Pantocrator; he who was made protector of the faith of the consubstantial[68] Trinity and sole beloved of our Lord Jesus Christ: Athanasius the Great, the son of the apostles, he who, on account of the emperors, bore witness[69] many times for the truth faith of orthodoxy. I stayed with him two days and it came about that he spoke with me about some scriptural matters and, as a result of the sweetness of his sweet and living words, I slept a little. When I woke up, he said to me, "Antony, get up! Stop sleeping like this! Truly, the Holy Spirit has said, 'Those who slumber deep asleep find no profit in it [perhaps Is

[68] (H)omoousios.
[69] Martyros.

56:10] and the person who keeps watch and is vigilant [1 Th 5:6; 1 Pt 5:8] is the person who rejoices and is filled with joy in eternal life.' Truly, the rejoicing here is not rejoicing and the sweetness of this world is not sweetness." These are the things he said to me. I prostrated myself; I venerated him; I returned home, glorifying God.'
Amélineau 1894, 42.14–43.15

[C65] *What Great Help God Has Appointed!*

Abba Antony again said, 'I beseeched God one time to tell me about the help that surrounds each monk. While I was praying, I saw fiery lamps and a chorus of angels surrounding each monk, protecting each as the apple of his eye [Dt 32:10]. A voice came down from heaven saying, "Do not let them perish while you are in the body." And as I saw such great help surrounding each person, I groaned, saying, "Woe to you, Antony! What great help God has appointed for you – and yet you are negligent all the time!"'
Amélineau 1894, 44.4–11

[C66] *Individual Responsibility*

Abba Antony said, 'I beseeched God, saying, "My Lord, what help you have so readily given to each monk! How does Satan just as readily trip them up?" I heard a voice saying, "No, the one who is violent has no power to do violence. He has no power to do violence because I am the one who has rebuked him with complete power [see Mt 4:11; Lk 4:1–13] and I have crushed him. No, each person is tempted by his own desires; truly, he is negligent about his well-being and is responsible for the hardening of his own heart.[70] Truly, such a person does not seek his own heart." I asked him, "Lord, have you ordained help such as this for each monk?" and he showed me a multitude of monks who have such help surrounding each and every one of them in the same way I had seen earlier. I said, "How blessed is the human race that this good Saviour, the lover of humankind, has done this for them!"'
Amélineau 1894, 44.12–45.7

---

[70] Hardening of the heart: *pithōm nte pefhēt*; 'crushed' renders *themthōm*, both from *thōm*. The imagery behind *–thōm* is the shutting of a door, mouth, or eyes; here, the door of the heart. As a noun, *thōm* means 'fence, barrier'.

CHAPTER 7

Sayings Preserved in Ethiopic (Ge'ez)

Translated by Witold Witakowski

Source: the following volumes edited by Victor Arras with Latin translation and published by the Secrétariat of the Corpus Scriptorum Christianorum Orientalium:

Collectio monastica, CSCO 238–9, Scriptores Aethiopici 45–6, Louvain, 1963;

Patericon Aethiopice, CSCO 277–8, Scriptores Aethiopici 53–4, Louvain, 1967.[1]

In this section the original numbering of the items has been retained, as most of these were not known elsewhere. Some items were however known elsewhere, and no attempt has been made to include them here (nor was there in Dom Lucien's French translation). Hence, there are inevitably some irregularities in the numeration of the items in this section.

Collectio Monastica Chapter 13, Part 1

The saying[s] of the Fathers; how they lived

[E1] A brother asked Abba Poemen saying: 'I want to study[2] the Scriptures a little.' The elder answered: 'Yes, my son, it will profit you.' The brother said to him: 'If I were to study the Scriptures a great deal, that would hinder my handiwork.' Said Abba Poemen: '[One's handiwork] is both teaching and learning.'

---

[1] See also idem, *Asceticon*, CSCO 458–9, Scriptores Aethiopici 77–8, Louvain, 1984; *Geronticon*, CSCO 476–7, Scriptores Aethiopici 79–80, Louvain, 1986; and *Quadraginta historiae monachorum*, CSCO 505–6, Scriptores Aethiopici 85–6, Louvain, 1988.
[2] Eth. *'ap.angala* [< ἀπαγγέλλειν] – lit. 'expound, interpret, comment'.

146

[E2] A brother asked Abba Poemen saying: 'My father, why do you not show your virtues and the works that you have been performing since your youth?' Looking at me with fear and trembling, he said to me as many as three times: 'Take care that, from now on, you do not dare to tell me that I might speak to the brothers with [the words of] Scripture, even though you would talk to them with the sayings of the elders, or I will destroy my dwelling place in order to build a dwelling place for my brother.'[3]

[E3] I have heard from a brother living at Scete what he said to Abba Moses who was bent over: 'Father, I am sad because I am poor.' Abba Moses said to him: 'Ought you not to be poor for the Lord's sake? Yet the Lord will not permit you to lack in any respect, [ensuring] that you may eat as much as you wish and have yet more to enable you to give to other[s], so that the Lord may give [you] repose when he judges you.'

[E4] An elder said to me: 'If you go away and live patiently with anybody and everybody, you will not gain any profit in the eyes of the Lord. You will be like sweepings, full of impurity. But if you go away with discretion, you will quickly prevail and you will be a workman for the Lord.'

[E5] A brother spoke to Abba Poemen: 'I have heard of an elder who for a long time fasted every second day and [only] ate unleavened barley bread.' Said Abba Poemen to him: 'We, on the other hand, [would] have kept on working with our two hands all our days without satiating ourselves, except for the hand of God which satiated our flesh and our spirit.'

[E6] A brother told me: 'I kept visiting an elder for many days. A brother became jealous of me and said to me: "How much you visit that elder! Don't you have work to do too?" I said to the elder: "Do you see that brother who admonished me not to come to you?" The elder said to me: "I asked Abba Poemen many times about this matter and he told me: 'Do you see that field? Numerous are those who watch over it because it is full of crops. But if you come to the farthest [part] of the field, you will not find fruits in it, except for a few. The owners of the field and their workmen will, therefore, take sticks and guard [the field] lest animals and birds come and eat [the crop.] Thus, now, these last days are that field: you will find few elders [to be your] companions. So, do not be angry at people who visit the elders in order to live according to [the rules of] God.'"'

---

[3] The text of this saying is probably corrupt.

[E7] A brother told me: 'For many days I went to Abba Cronios of Mount Panahon.⁴ He bound me with a great oath and ordered me saying: "Do not open your door except on Saturdays and Sundays." Then I went to Abba Poemen, and he released me from every oath, ordering me to open my door. He said to me: "They say that when an ostrich gives birth in the desert, the hunters follow the traces of its claws to find its egg and take it. Therefore, guard [pl.] the works that you have done on God's account; guard them that your labour be not in vain, because God loves everything that a man does in secret. What [comes] from man's labour is clean, because by it man prevails. Man's soul desires glory, and that is the soul's death: the fear of God and discretion prevail over every stain."'

[E8] A brother asked an elder saying: 'Do you see those written words saying: "Woe to him that fell, who has nobody to lift him up?"'⁵ The elder said to him: '[They are about] the man who only listens to his own wishes and says: "This is good" – and does not even listen to the good teaching of his brother.'

[E9] I asked an elder saying: 'What is the meaning of what is written in the Prophet: "May the one who trusts in man be cursed"⁶?' The elder said to me: '[This refers to] a man who has brothers and his heart relies on them, saying: "Great is the work of their hands; it is they who feed me and, if they pass away, I will die of starvation", yet he is doubtful [of God's existence]. [It also refers to] a man who uses force against his neighbour to take what is his [and also to one] who has confidence in a rich man and says: "He is mighty and loves me very much; he will come to my aid", but he does not fear God with whom the power resides.'

[E10] Abba Poemen said: 'A dog alive is worth more than a dead lion.' A brother asked him: 'My father, "a living dog and a dead lion", what does this mean?' He answered him saying: 'A living dog is a brother who has a bad reputation and the brothers who see him say of him: "He is bad." Yet his work is beautiful in the eyes of God and is very good. And a dead lion is a brother who has a good reputation among all the brothers, but so far as it concerns him and God, his work is dead and he is quite useless.'⁷

---

⁴ Possibly the monastic community [mountain] of Pamaho, Arabic Bamhâ, in the Province of Gîzeh.
⁵ Qoh / Eccl 4:10.
⁶ Jer 17:5.
⁷ According to Dom Lucien, the continuation of this section does not belong with this apophthegm, but is a fragment of an ascetic treatise of Stephen of Thebes; J.M. Sauget, 'Une nouvelle collection éthiopienne d'*Apophthegmata Patrum*', *Orientalia Christiana Periodica* 31 (1965), p. 182.

[E11] An elder said: 'If a man fulfils the will of God, a shouting voice will always be within him.'

[E13] A brother asked an elder and said to him: 'Do you wish me to meditate on what people read in the Scriptures when I go to church?' The elder said to him: 'You are going to the source of life.'

[E14] A brother said that when the elders of Scete found a young brother who had succumbed to a corporal sin, they sent him to the land of Egypt, saying: 'Go and stay there.' But there was one elder among them, a man of God who, seeing that they were exiling the boy to Egypt, took the young brother, saying: 'I will not let him go to the land of Egypt, but I will bring him back to Scete.' The elders said to him: 'If God asks you about this boy, what will you say?' The elder said to them: 'I will say: "I raised him up because of you, since you are compassionate and merciful and you absolve sins."' Indeed, the elder let him have a small cell and [the young brother] served God with all his heart and was reformed.

[E15] A brother asked Abba Theodore of Phermê[8] saying: 'How are we now, my Father?' He said to him: 'We are as a city outside which there is an evil tyrant [for] king, but inside which there is a righteous king, and all the inhabitants of the city beseech the righteous king, saying: "Save us from that evil tyrant of a king!"'

[E16] An elder said: 'I recall the brothers in those [bygone] days who followed God while burning in spirit with their mouths full of God's words. But when I consider the coldness [of the brothers] nowadays and the strange speech in their mouths, I feel like a man who was carried away to another country, one he does not know.'

[E17] An elder said: 'I paid a visit to another elder, and a brother said to me: "If you go to [that] elder, tell him about the struggle that assails me; [ask him] what I should do." And when I came, I told the elder [about him] and he said to me: "Tell him: the patience of God purifies every evil that is in man's heart."'

---

[8] 'There is a mountain called Phermê in Egypt, on the way to the great desert of Scete. About 500 men are living on that mountain, practicing spiritual discipline.' *HL* 20.1.

[E18] An elder in Scete said: 'It is either [the fear of] God or discretion; but fear of God and discretion are really brothers.'[9]

[E19] An elder said: 'When a war breaks out upon people, help also descends upon them; for it is written: "Another king arose over Egypt who knew not Joseph"[10] and in those days Moses was born. They describe that king as an enemy, Joseph as a man of God and Moses who, by his hand, was the helper of God for the people.'

[E20] Abba Poemen said: 'Quarrels trouble every man; but when God's judgment approaches, it causes the great and the small to speak.'[11]

[E21] A brother asked Abba Dioscorus of the Mount Yotarem[12] saying: 'What do you wish me to do, my Father?' Abba Dioscorus said to him: 'Go and find a small bone for yourself, and clean your mouth with it.' Said the brother: 'What is this "little bone"?' And Abba Dioscorus said to him: 'The "little bone" is mortification, or fasting until evening, or a short vigil, that it might be [for you] a sweet fragrance before God.'

[E22] Said a brother: 'Abba Mios of Beleos said: "We have stayed until the last hour in order to see the affliction of the monks,[13] [their] penury, and grief." He spoke thus about the love that had cooled among the brothers and the penury in this generation. And so they do not find wisdom in peace, nor limited understanding that they might be without sorrow. An idle man does not find wisdom through insight, the spirit does not dwell in idle people.

> May he who loves wisdom toil in search of it.
> May he who desires understanding dwell in innocence.
> May he who wishes to be clothed in glory eradicate desire.
> May he who loves toil rejoice in the fruit of wisdom.

May he who is diligent, seek in toil and he will eat the good things of the spirit and will inhabit the land of the living. His name will be reckoned among the saints. Ask God for fear and humbleness of spirit that he may teach you to overcome yourself in everything.'

---

[9] Presumably, this is an answer to a question such as: 'What is the greatest virtue?'

[10] Ex 1:8.

[11] Cf. Dom Lucien's version: 'Abba Poemen said: "Quarrelling creates consternation in everybody and when one treads the judgment of the Lord underfoot one creates consternation in great and small, so to speak."'

[12] An unidentified monastic settlement.

[13] Three sayings are attributed to Mios of Beleos in *APalph*. Beleos remains unidentified.

[E23] Abba Misyani of the Tamerias community said: 'One day, I and many others gathered at the place of Abba Nadbay of Persia when he was dying. We said to him: "Abba, give us a word that we may remember and live by it." And he said to us: "What should I say to you? The generations that will come after you will be voracious and talkative, they will not work but will seek to teach their predecessors."'

[E24] Abba Isaac [the disciple] of Abba Bis said: 'A brother told me that Abba Poemen had said: "You will find many [brothers] who greatly mortify themselves. They fast every Friday, every Wednesday, and every Monday; they give many alms and they love [fellow] brothers, but you will not find many among them who are inwardly penitent." A brother asked: "What is it, this penitent heart?" And Abba Poemen said: "It is a man who abandons his thought[s] of everything on account of God."'

[E25] Abba Nisteros [the disciple] of Abba Paul said: 'Never has an [evil] thought ever entered my heart.' Said a brother to him: 'Why, Abba?' And he answered him: 'Believe me, my brother, because I have relied on mortification for the Lord.'

[E26] A brother said to me: 'God's patient expectation [towards a worshipper][14] is this: ...[15] also his heart is [directed] to the Lord, while he shouts, saying: "Jesus, have mercy on me! Jesus, help me! I bless you, my living Godhead, all the time!", and little by little he raises his eyes while uttering these three phrases to God in his heart.'

[E27] A brother said: 'Abba Poemen said: "Formerly, these two things were customary, while people were doing them; but nowadays, they have disappeared." The brother asked him: "What are these things, my father?" And the elder answered him: "They are poverty and affliction; in olden times people loved them, but not now."'

[E28] An elder said to me: 'It is good that people find your name written in the house of widows, orphans, the poor, and those who have no strength, rather than find it among wine sellers. It is also good that they will find your mouth smelling of fasting and mortification, rather than smelling of wine.'

---

[14] The text of this saying seems to be corrupt; the suggested additions are tentative.
[15] A few words must have been lost here.

[**E31**] An elder said: 'Does it appear to you that Satan wants to impose all [evil] thoughts upon us? Not so! But by one [sinful] thought he captures the soul and hopes that he will lead it into condemnation. He would impose this thought on the [soul]: this alone is enough, because he wishes to take the soul to condemnation. So, let us protect ourselves that we might not find pleasure in [that] evil thought, [but] that we [rather] may be rescued from him.'

[**E32**] Abba John [the disciple] of Abba Jacob said: 'My brother Macarius, when he was dying, told me: "I regret two things that I did in this world. I bought a tunic from a brother and then I paid him the price. And I drew two pairs of scarves from a weaver's workshop, but I left the shorter because of the threads that were lacking."'

[**E33**] A brother said to me: 'Demons once brought unchastity upon me. I became troubled by it and thought to return to the world and take off my *askema*.[16] [Then] an elder told me: "Listen to me and God will give you peace." I said to him: "What do you wish me to do? Show me!" And he said to me: "Go, eat less than usual. If you ate two slices of bread, [now] eat one, and if you ate one, half of it will be enough for you for the whole day. Do not drink water until you are sated, but only a little once [a day] to moisten your tongue. Beseech God [for forgiveness], bow your head before Him, and God will give you peace." I obeyed and did that for a few days. God gave me relief and turned the impurity away from me completely.'

[**E34**] A brother told me what Abba Joseph of Kellia said: 'When he was dying, I was staying with him, and I said to him: "My father, tell me a word by which I will live." He answered me: "Go, do not flatter people at all." And he said to me as many as three times: "Go, and do not flatter people, because those who want to flatter people, kill them. Escape from them and you shall be saved."'

[**E35**] Abba Cronios of Mount Panahon said: 'I know two brothers who left Scete because enemies chased them away. They arrived at a river but did not find any craft with which to cross. They rested a while, and one said to the other: "Rise up, let us cross the river on foot." The other brother said: "Do you not care? If people see us crossing, they will come

---

[16] From Greek σχῆμα – 'monastic dress', habit.

to us and bother us!" The [first] brother said: "If you are not coming, I will go [alone]." And he rose and entered the water on foot. There were people on the other shore of the river who saw him entering the water. They rose and entered the water to welcome him. When he saw them coming to meet him, he turned back and came to his brother. The two ran along the western bank of the river,[17] and when they were far from those people, both of them crossed the river together on foot and went to the east, arriving at Mount Panahon. As to myself, I confirm: It was Abba Cronios and his brother, but he did not want to say: "We were the ones who saw those great things of God in which there is power." God listens to those who fear Him with their whole hearts.'

[E36] A brother said to me: 'Abba Paphnutios,[18] the copyist of Scete, told me that Abba Ammoes who dwelled in the western quarter when in Scete had stated: "Taking sides among people removes a man from God, like a gourd when it is rotting."[19]

[E37] And again that brother said to me: 'Abba Paphnutius said to me: "I said to Abba Ammoes: 'There were two brothers: one became a monk and did not save anything for himself. He impoverished himself greatly on account of God, whereas the other put [aside] goods necessary for the body, in case his poor brother would come to him to receive alms, for he [just] worked in order to eat bread. Which of them is then better?'" Then Abba Paphnutius said to me: "My Father, Abba Ammoes, said to me: 'The one who had made himself poor on account of God is greater, because [being] poor on account of God is a great [thing]. There is in [being poor] great affliction and hardships, [well known] to those who experience it.'"'

[E38] That brother also said to me: 'Abba Paphnutius said to me that our fathers who lived before us guarded their hearts, [but] if indeed anybody of this generation of yours guards his body against unchastity and his hands against stealing and fights a little with his belly [to stave off] gluttony, he is blessed. Gluttony alone engenders unchastity, stealing, and numerous other evils.'

---

[17] Lit.: *...ran towards the west.*
[18] The successor of Macarius the Egyptian at Scete.
[19] A parallel difficult to understand. The known meaning of Eth. *tasāḥsǝḥa* is 'to be moved back and forth, be rubbed'. The meaning of 'rotting' or 'putrefying' is suggested by V. Arras, in his Latin translation, p. 68.

[E39] And again that brother told me that Abba Serapion the copyist said to him: 'An elder said to me that Abba Alonios of Tamerias turned himself into somebody in his father's possession,[20] until his death. At the end of [Alonios'] life, God revealed mysteries to Abba Alonios. God showed him very great signs,[21] but he did not understand what he saw. He related what he thought [about it] to his father, who did not understand the meaning[22] of this matter. He told his father the story again, but the father did not understand the meaning. [Then] he told his father the story again, for the third time, but he could not clarify it. Then Abba Alonios[23] left to go to Abba Poemen and tell him about this matter. Abba Poemen said to him: "Go to Abba Semyas[24] and he will tell you the significance of your vision." Said Abba Alonios to Abba Poemen: "Why don't you reveal it to me?" Abba Poemen answered Abba Alonios: "Now, I would wish to reveal[25] [it] to you but my place is far away,[26] and probably you will have to come to me many [times] and your father would not accept this conduct. But go to Abba Semias and he will show you the significance of this matter." Then Abba Alonios set out to Abba Semias, and having walked, arrived in the region of Aksewitis. God revealed the matter of Abba Alonios to Bishop Abba Menas. *Papas*[27] Abba Menas stepped aboard a small boat to cross to the opposite bank. When he was approaching [the other side of] the river, he did not know that Abba Alonios was there, and [although] he did not know the man, he cried out: "Abba Alonios of Tamerias!" Hearing his voice, Abba Alonios arose and, after Abba Menas and the boat were moored, [the latter] said to him: "Are you Abba Alonios of Tamerias?" He answered: "Yes." Then Abba Menas said to him: "Do you go to Semias?" He answered: "Yes." And [Abba Menas] said: "Right, you are going there because of the mysteries that God revealed to you, because you told your father about that matter and he was unable to explain [its meaning] to you. You told him again, and he could not answer you. And you told him a third time, and he was [still] unable to tell you. Then you went to Abba Poemen but he did not want to reveal it to you, so that you would not come to him

---

[20] Reading of Ms B [*lectio difficilior*]. 'Alonios de Tameryas vécut en compagnie de son père jusqu'à la mort de celui-ci; et à la fin le Seigneur révéla des secrets à l'abbé Alonios', *sic* Dom Lucien [Ed.].
[21] Or: *power*.
[22] Lit.: *power*.
[23] The Alonios of *APalph* was well known to Poemen.
[24] Eth. *Məsyā*, but it seems to be a scribal error [metathesis], as the name is spelled below as *Səmyā*.
[25] According to V. Arras's correction, Eth. text, p. 93, n. 1.
[26] Corrected; Eth. has *qərub - near*, which does not make sense.
[27] The title of bishops, metropolitans, and even patriarchs.

many times; and he sent you to Abba Semyas. Now then I will show you what God revealed to you about your problem and its resolution." And he revealed to him the mystery that God had shown him and its implication. When Abba Alonios realized that he had told him everything he had asked about, he said: "Then I will not go to Abba Semias, because you have shown me everything that I was looking for." Abba Menas said to him: "Go, come to the Elder, because if you see him, it will profit you." And Abba Alonios went to Abba Semias and stayed with him for some time. [One day] Abba Semias said to Abba Alonios: "Rise and go to see your father, and if you wish, come [to me] again." Abba Semias [said this] because, thanks to God, he had seen that Abba Alonios' father was mortally ill. Abba Alonios obeyed Abba Semias: he rose and went to his father. He found him mortally ill, and [then] Abba Alonios' father died.' See these signs and mysteries of God that he reveals to his servants and to those who listen to him and fear him. Blessed then is the man who fears God and those who tremble at his voice.

[E40] An elder said: 'If you wish to become a monk and delight God, purify your heart towards all people, dismiss your [evil] thought[s] about everybody, do not reproach anybody; place your death before you. If you see somebody that has sinned, pray to God, saying: "Forgive me, for I have sinned." May the words "There is no greater love"[28] be fulfilled in you.'

[E41] Abba Angelos said: 'My Father Cronios from Mount Panahon said to me: "If you see two brothers walking by, and you know that one is faithful and the other a sinner, then which of them would you love and which would you hate?" I answered: "I would love the faithful one more." He said to me: "And if you were the sinner, would you not weep over God's goodness that he might send grace to you? Do you [pl.] see God's grace that the elders have in their likeness to God?"'

[E42] Abba Paul the Coenobite said: 'When you live in a community, work, learn, and, little by little, raise your eyes towards heaven, saying to God in your heart: "Jesus, show grace and have mercy on me. Jesus, help me. I bless you, my Lord!"'

[E43] Abba Jacob said: 'I went to Balihaw, to Abba Isidore of Nesare, and found him sitting in his dwelling place and writing. I stayed with him a

---

[28] Cf. Jn 15:13.

short while and watched him. And every now and then I saw him raising his eyes heavenwards, but his lips did not move and his voice was inaudible. I asked him: "What are you doing, my father?" He said: "Don't you know what I'm doing?" I said: "No, Abba." [Then] he said: "If you do not know this thing, Jacob, then you haven't been a monk, not even for a day. What I am saying is: Jesus, have mercy on me. Jesus, help me. I bless you, my Lord!"'

[E44] A brother asked Abba Poemen saying: 'Does man understand whether he has gained some profit from [his pious efforts]?' 'Yes, [answered Poemen,] the man would understand. He would know that, if there were temptation, there was [also] fruit in it. [If] the man be prepared for his temptation, this man may know that there is fruit in it. But if there were a temptation that man did not find [himself] prepared [to face], he should know that there would be no fruit for him.'

[E45] Abba Poemen said: 'If a man has died because of his sins, he is then dead for the entire world,[29] [then] in order that he not torment himself for all the days of his [new] life, he should not forget the good things between him and his brother.'

[E46] Abba Poemen said: 'There are three mysteries before me when I meditate: that I should pray to God all the time, without respite; that I should place [the vision of] my death before me all the time; and that I should [bear in mind] that, when I am dead, they will throw me into the fire on account of my sins.'

[E47] A brother said: 'Abba Joseph, the disciple of Abba Lot, said to me: "We, the brothers of these days, eat and drink[30] [for] the pleasure of the body. Therefore, we do not gain victory like our fathers. For our fathers loved all the mortifications on account of God and, therefore, they came to the Living God."'

[E48] I heard a brother asking Abba Poemen about some matter, and Abba Poemen said: 'If a man who is alive is willing to do so, he may die rather than blame his brother.'

---

[29] This saying probably refers to a person who became a monk, having sinned 'in the world', i.e., in his former period of life.

[30] The Ethiopic text has here *ṣalaʾna* – 'we hate', instead of *ṣalaṭna* – 'we drink [to the last drop]', as in the Arabic version, quoted by J.-M. Sauget, 'Une nouvelle collection éthiopienne d'*Apophthegmata Patrum*', *Orientalia Christiana Periodica* 31 (1965), p. 181.

[E49] I heard that one brother was passing near Scete and he asked Abba Macarius, saying: 'Can a man die being alive?' He said: 'Yes.' The brother again asked Abba Macarius: 'Can a man die because of his brother?' And he answered: 'Yes.' [Then] Abba Macarius said: 'Are these, perhaps, the words of Abba Poemen?' The brother answered: 'Yes.' Abba Macarius [then] said to him: 'I thought that these seemed to be the words of Abba Poemen.'

[E51] A brother asked Abba Serapion saying: 'My father, I was so overcome by sadness that I [thought I] would go into the world and work [there].' Said Abba Serapion: 'What work are you doing that you wish to leave your dwelling place and go into the world to work?' The brother answered: 'I make these curtains.' Said the Elder: 'Do you not have a mat under you, when you are weaving?' I answered him: 'Yes, I have.' He said to me again: 'Do you not have another mat at your doorway?' I answered: 'I have.' He said to me: 'Do you not have a window of glass where you sleep? Do you not keep yourself warm in the winter?' I answered him: 'Yes, I do.' He said to me: 'Believe me, my son; if a man could see beyond [this world to] the inheritance, glory, and rest that God has prepared for those who loved him all the days they had in this world, then, [even] if he lived in a cell full of worms up to his knees, it would not sadden him.'

[E52] I heard that Abba Semias and Abba Aaron lived together in the desert. Abba Semias went out one night from his cell and went to the cell of Abba Aaron and called upon him saying: 'Aaron my son, What are you doing?' Aaron said to him: 'I am becoming insane, my father.' Abba Semias said to him: 'Say to God "I am becoming insane".' Another night he again called upon him and said: 'How are you, Aaron my son?' He said to him: 'I do not know what I am doing.' Said Abba Semias to Abba Aaron: 'Carry your sins on your head, my son, and go to God.'

[E53] A brother asked Abba Poemen saying: 'My father, when a brother lives in my dwelling place, what do you wish me to watch?' He answered him: '[Put] your sins on your head and observe them.'[31]

[E54] A brother said to me 'When I came to Abba Cronios of Mount Panahon, he said to me: "Take heed, my son, wherever you go and stay, do not let your heart stay there forever, but be as a stranger there."'

[31] Eth.: 'him'.

[E55] A brother said: 'I went to Abba Achilles and I stayed there over-
night for one night. He lay in the inner chamber which is small and I
slept outside it. When he had slept a little, he rose in the middle of the
night and shouted: "Woe to the day on which the man was born!"[32]
Thereafter he stayed [silent] a long while, and then said three times: "Do
not be afraid, Jacob, to go down to the land of Egypt. Do not be afraid,
Israel, I will go down with you to the land of Egypt."'[33]

[E56] I went one day to Abba Dioscorus and enquired of him concerning a certain matter. 'Take some wagon for example', he said, 'or some
other heavy object [and consider] how much time it would take if you
wished to bring it up a high mountain. But if you wish to bring it down,
you let it roll down from the height and it will quickly come down to
where you lifted it in the first place.'

[E57] I heard Abba Poemen saying to me: 'This you cannot do: to rest
here and also go into the Kingdom.' I said to him: 'What is it you are
saying my father? That I do not care?'[34]

[E58] I heard of one elder who said: 'One who has humility of the spirit
has a crown in his dwelling place and a cover for his cauldron.'

[E59] A brother said to me: 'A disciple of Abba Paphnutius said to me: "I
heard my father, Abba Paphnutius, saying: 'I saw our Lord Jesus three
times, and he said to me these three words: "Guard [these] and you will
be saved: poverty, mortification, and patience."'"'

[E60] A brother said to me: 'Abba Kamis told me these words: "My
father, Abba Anter, said to me: '[No matter] how many sins I have committed, if I repent, God will forgive me, but if my brother asks forgiveness and I will not forgive him, then God will not forgive me.'"'

[E61] I heard about Abba Ammoes of Tamerias that [some brothers]
came to him to ask for a word. He called upon John, his disciple, and
said to him: 'Show the brothers how they [may] become monk[s].' John
said to him: 'Are you making fun of me, Abba?' Said Abba Ammoes to
him: 'No.' Said John to Abba Ammoes, his father: 'Do you want me to

---

[32] Cf. Jer 20:14.
[33] Cf. Gen 46:3-4.
[34] 'Que je n'ai pas de zèle,' *sic* Dom Lucien [Ed.].

speak, while you would be silent?' Abba Ammoes said: 'Yes.' Then John took off his clothes and stood naked, and Abba Ammoes said to him: 'What is this, John?' John answered him: 'If a man does not strip off from himself his glory and praise of this world like that, he cannot become a monk at all.'

[E62] A brother told me the story about the parable of wealth: 'The riches of man are the redemption of his soul. That is, if a man be rich in [obeying] God's commandments, he will save his soul from sins. The poor, however, simply cannot bear mockery. That is, if he be poor in [observing] God's commandments, he cannot prevail against those who throw stones at him; and he falls into many evils on account of [his search for] the repose of [his] body and [the satisfaction of] all his wishes.'

[E63] An elder said: '[There is] a city full of blessing and the only way that leads to it is narrow. On the right side, there is a road of fire and, on the left, a sea. Man comes to that city by tribulation; so that [to get there] you should impose all [manner of hardships] on yourself, on account of God.'

[E64] That brother also said: 'An elder said: "Fleeing [from the world?] changes [a man's] heart that it may gain peace, whereas voluntary exile[35] makes that man attain that which is above: the free Jerusalem.[36] Man's soul is the heavenly bread. The soul eats it until it gains for her [i.e., the soul] lamentation on account of God. Humility of the spirit is the fear of God, and [the consciousness] that you should not reckon on yourself in anything."'

[E65] Abba Achilles said: 'Make yourself like an animal, that you may not let [people] recognize you at all.'

[E66] Abba Paul the Galatian[37] said: 'I will always remember these three things: silence, humility of the spirit, and that you[38] may say "I have no worry".'

---

[35] Probably = Gr. ξενιτεία [Lat. *perigrinatio*], living among strangers rather than going on a journey [Ed.].
[36] Cf. Gal 4:26.
[37] Or: Paul of Galatia.
[38] Perhaps a mistake for '…that I may say…'.

[E67] Concerning the words of Scripture: 'Be [pl.] gentle and warriors'
Abba Isaiah of Qalabo said: 'Combat is [in order] that you [sg.] should
counter your [evil] thoughts and that you should impose hardships upon
yourself on account of God.'

[E68] Abba Nedbew said: 'Where, indeed, would the man go who has
caused scandal, strengthened its path, and done wrong? The flight from
mortification is the flight from God.'

[E69] Abba Peter [the disciple] of Abba Ammonas said: 'Persuade yourself not to eat much food, just as you would in order not to eat the flesh
of humans.'

[E70] I asked my father, Abba Joseph, [the disciple] of Abba Alonios,
saying to him: 'In those days, were bad thoughts indeed, found in your
heart?' He answered me: 'I also asked my father, Abba Alonios, about the
same thing and he said to me: "Not at all, my son; no evil thought was
found in our hearts, because there was no bad odour among the brethren
at that time, but a sweet fragrance. Indeed, the heart may draw unto itself
the abundance of beautiful fragrance. So then the purity of the heart [is]
the beauty of the fragrance. Now, however, the bad odour has increased
and, from the abundance of it, the heart draws bad odour unto itself.
And bad thought[s] are bad odour. In those days, a villain would not be
found among the monks, except one or two, and those two would have
no friends among the monks. They would not be able to endure the
places [where there were other monks], and they would flee. But now
there can be found among the monks barely one or two men of God, and
the two of them would have no friends. Therefore, the servants of God
flee [as] they cannot survive in a place."'

[E71] A brother told me: 'Abba Jacob said to me: "Make your heart [so]
that you may come to God." The brother said: "How, my father?" and
the elder said to him: "As Jesus made his disciples step aboard a boat, so
also can you so make your heart so that you may come to God."'

[E72] A brother who was an elder said to Abba Poemen: 'When I am
staying with you there [my] thoughts assail me, my father, [telling me]
that I should not have come to you.' Abba Poemen said to him: 'Why?'
and the brother said to Abba Poemen: 'Because I come to you and listen
to your words, but I do not do [as you say]. May your words not pass

judgment on me on that [last] day.' [Then] Abba Poemen said to him: 'One day I was talking about this matter to Abba Macarius in Scete. He said to me: "But do not neglect visiting the elders, because the days will come [when], if you wish to serve [God], you will prevail due to the words of the elders. And then, if [evil] thoughts should throw themselves upon you, remember the words of the elders, and you will find their help and you will be saved."'

[E73] I asked my father Abba Sisoes of Petra, [the disciple] of Abba Antony, saying to him: 'My father, what is appropriate for a monk?' He put his finger in his mouth and said to me: '[Just] watch your mouth, my son.'

[E74] Abba Nisteros, [the disciple] of Abba Paul, said to me about the words of the Gospel: '"Blessed are peacemakers, for they will become sons of God."[39] May a man always be peaceful within himself in everything together with the Holy Spirit.'

[E75] A brother said to me: 'Abba Ammoes of Tamerias told me: "These things elevate the monk: poverty, mortification, voluntary exile, and a solitary life."'

[E76] A brother said to me: 'Abba Cronios of the Mount Panahon told me: "If a monk does not have in him humbleness, estrangement [from the world], and love of hard work, he works for his death."'

[E77] A brother said to me: 'My father Abba Soy of the Mount Diolcus[40] told me: "If [bad] thoughts come into the heart of a brother, he will not be able to hold [them] back completely from his heart, unless he invoke words from the Scripture or from the sayings of the elders. If the lord of the house enter his house, the strangers who have been in the house flee."'

[E78] Abba Poemen said: 'The stones that Moses placed in[41] his two hands, until Joshua prevailed over the Amalekites and exterminated them, [symbolize] the fear of God and the humility of spirit, [whereas]

[39] Cf. Mt 5:9.
[40] 'There is another desert in Egypt, lying along the shore, extremely difficult to access. Many great anchorites are living there; it is adjacent to Diolcopolis.' *HME* 25.1. Cassian refers to it as Diolcus [Ed.].
[41] Eth. *wəsṭa*, instead of the expected *tāḥta* – 'under'; cf. the story in Ex 17:11–13, where it is told of Moses sitting on a stone with his hands raised.

the flight from sins and not serving them is the fear of God, just as your carrying all the sins would be humility of spirit. When Karam, son of Kerem,[42] stole the tongued wedge of gold and the robe of Shinear from Jericho and when the Israelites were fighting the Philistines, and the Philistines were winning, Joshua was distressed and cried out to God saying: "Why, O God, did you deliver us into the hands of our enemy? That we might be exterminated?" Said God to Joshua "Why are you crying before me? Go, remove from yourself what is cursed and I will give your enemy back into your hands." And when the Israelites removed from themselves that which was cursed, God delivered their enemies into their hands. Also we, [may] we remove what is cursed from among us now and whenever we have evil thoughts. [For] evil thoughts are cursed. Evil thoughts are [what] we are subjected to and whose will we do. Therefore, God does not dwell with us, and our enemies defeat us. But if we remove [evil thoughts] from us, we will defeat [our enemies] and eradicate them because God is with us.'

[E79] Abba Poemen said to me: 'I saw two elders in Scete, namely Abba Paesios and Abba Isaiah. When they were traveling Abba Paesios went first. In the place where Abba Paesios raised his feet from the sand, Abba Isaiah stepped in his footprints, saying "I imitate my father." Both of them mortified themselves. When they went to church, they left their dwelling places open, and when they returned from praying, Abba Isaiah went [first] to his dwelling place, left his book and his tunic,[43] [then] came to Abba Paesios and they stayed together for two days, Saturday and Sunday. One such day, [Isaiah], as he usually did, went [home] to leave [his things] in order to come [then] to the elder and he found a brother in his dwelling place who was taking some of his household goods. Abba Isaiah did not wish the [brother] to see him so he hid in the sand until that brother took some of his goods and went away. When the brother left, Abba Isaiah, rejoicing, ran [to Abba Paesios] and said "My father, do you know [what]?" Abba Paesios said "What has happened to you?" Abba Isaiah said: "I went back, as usual, to my dwelling place to leave my book and clothes and to come here, and I found a brother taking [something]. I was afraid he would see me and flee, so I hid in the sand until he had taken [a vessel] and left." Said Abba Paesios: "You did not act well, Abba Isaiah, in not wanting to show yourself to him and to

[42] Cf. Josh 7:1 [Eth.], where his name is *'Akān son of Karmi*.
[43] Eth. *labiṭos*, cf. Gr. λεβίτων, λεβητονάριον, the dress of a Levite.

beg him on your knees that he might take [that vessel] because now, when he eats therefrom and prays to God, his heart might condemn him as one who stole it."'[44]

[E80] Abba Ares of Arwe said: 'I know a brother whose talk revealed that he came from Scete. He made mats and every day he went to sell them. When he returned he [used to] take a container to bring water. When he went to fetch water, a brother who was his neighbour, came, equipped with a key, opened [the door,] stole the money gained from selling the mats and left. He kept doing so for six months. Then the maker of the mats divided his money into two parts and, leaving it on his window, wrote a note saying: "I beg you, for God's sake, do me a favour; take one part of this money and leave the other part for me, so that I may keep the rest to live on." But [the robber] had not complied with the note; he took all the money. When the mat maker saw that [his neighbour] did not comply with the note, he tore it up and returned to putting his money in one place. The mat maker had a miserable life; yet, when he went to fill a vessel with water, he always left his dwelling place open and did not lock it, saying: "May the brother have no trouble in opening the door: he will find the door open." [That one] continued to take [the money] every day for three years; then he became mortally ill. Then he called for the mat maker and said to him: "Intercede with God! I am asking you, do me a favour, and pray for me on account of the mats, because today it is three years that I have been stealing, and therefore I am afraid, because here, before my eyes, there will be punishment for me." And the mat maker said: "You have not talked to me in time, 'when the sun is in the sky', as they say; only when the sun is setting for you. Now you are telling me, but what can I do for you? Nevertheless, for what it is worth, I will pray to God for you." And the mat maker raised the hands and legs of the sick man, kissed him and said: "God, bless these hands and legs because they taught me how to be a monk." Then that brother died. The brother, the maker of mats, tore asunder his book and buried him.'

[E81] I heard that my father, Abba Paphnutius, said: 'If a man do not change the skin of his face [to be] as the sole of his foot, he cannot be a monk at all.'

[44] Cf. *APanon* 7 for a shorter version of more or less the same tale.

[E82] When Abba Paphnutius the *sindonite*[45] was dying, the brothers who stayed with him said: 'Blessed are you, our father, as you go to the Kingdom.' Abba Paphnutius said to them: 'I have made my life here a mockery.'

[E83] I heard that brothers visited my father, Abba Joseph, and when they were to return to their dwelling places, Abba Joseph said to them: 'When you go to your homes, pay a visit to Abba Semias and request him that he may tell you the words by which you will be able to live.' They went to his place and stayed with him night and day, but he said nothing to them, except this: 'My sins have become the wall of darkness between me and God.' On another day, they visited Abba Joseph again and said to him: 'When we came here previously, you said to us: "When you go to your dwelling places, pay a visit to Abba Semias, and ask him for a word", and we went to him, but he said nothing but this: "My sins have become the wall between me and God."' When Abba Joseph heard this, he shouted and wept saying: 'Behold, he has found the way, and I have still not found the way!'

[E84] A brother told me: 'Abba Poemen said to me: "Look at this empty vessel. If somebody fill [it] with snakes, lizards, and scorpions and, having filled the vessel, leave it covered; would not all those creeping animals die there? But if you would uncover the opening of the vessel, would all those creatures not escape and bite people? Likewise, if a man guard his mouth and keep it closed, all those animals die therein, but if he compel his mouth to talk, the animals get out and bite his brother – and God will be angry with him."'[46]

[E85] A brother said to me: 'When Abba John of Cilicia was dying, I said to him "Abba, my father, will you not tell me a word by which I can live?" And he said to me: "Yes, I will tell you the word, and when I have said [it] to you, you will be able to live by it." I said: "What is it, my father?" He said to me: "Go and love your neighbour as yourself[47] and all your enemies will fall beneath your feet."'

---

[45] Gr. σινδών = 'sheet', cf. Serapion Sindonites, 'the sheet-wearer', *HL* 37.1, *APanon* 565 and 566, *APsys* 116 and 117.

[46] Cf. Poemen 21 [328A], *APsys* 10.60.

[47] Cf. Lev 19:18; Jas 2:8.

[E86] I heard my father, Abba Jacob from Per,[48] as he was saying to Abba Dioscorus from the Mount of Yotar: 'How should one love somebody?' Abba Dioscorus said to him: 'If a man put not both of his hands upon his head and say "I have sinned", he cannot love his neighbour as himself.'

[E87] I also heard Abba Dioscorus saying: 'God does not give man sins[49] and afflictions, but the man himself starts it, bringing upon himself sins and afflictions.'

[E88] I heard Abba Serapion saying: 'Before I was consecrated a cleric, when I was [still] young and living in a *coenobion*,[50] I had been living for 25 years, going to the refectory and eating [only] one piece of bread.'

[E90] A brother asked Abba Poemen by saying to him: 'My father, is it really possible for the heart of a man to be totally clean?' He said to him: 'Yes, it is possible. If a man makes right what is [wrong] in his body, his heart will be clean.' The brother asked [again]: 'Is it not possible for his heart to be clean while he does the wishes of his body?' And he answered: 'Yes, but if a man make right what is [wrong] in his body, [then even if] he wish to defile his heart, he will not be able to, but [the heart] will stay pure all the time.'

[E91] A brother told me: 'I heard Abba Sisoes saying: "Is it not strange that people come over here these days and ask us: 'How can we purify our body more than our heart?'" Then I asked him too: "How then, my father, can a man keep his heart [pure]?" The elder answered me: "Go, take care of yourself, set right what is [wrong] in your body, and as for your heart, it will not be necessary for you [to take care of it]."'

[E92] I heard that an elder said: 'If a man want, he can be like Christ from dawn until evening. And then again, if he want, he can be from dawn until evening like the Devil.'

[E93] I heard about Abba Agathon, who originated among aristocrats, that he said: 'I allow no evil thought at all to arise in my heart, until I pull up my yarn[51] [on the spindle] from the den.'[52]

---

[48] Or: *of Emper* [*za-'əmper*]; Eth. *'əm* means 'from'.
[49] Or: 'losses'.
[50] Eth. *Qinobəyon*.
[51] Eth. *maftal* [from *fatala* – 'to spin'], an otherwise unknown word.
[52] Not clear; perhaps a box with yarn [?].

[E94] He also said 'If all the work of a monk were like cutting trees and staying away from bodily things, Agathon would enter the Kingdom right away.'

[E95] My father, Abba Aaron of Awran, said to me: 'Do you see those words that David uttered: "Those who have been tested like silver[53] are not excluded?"' I said to him: 'Explain [them] to me, my father.' The elder said to me: 'Do you see those who hold silver in contempt, and renounce the things of this world that are desired? Indeed, it is for them that the gates of life will be opened so that they may enter in joy.'

[E96] Abba Jacob told me: 'I asked Abba Poemen saying to him: "What do those words that David uttered mean: 'You have given your grace to people, [but] they, indeed, renounce [it] that they may dwell.'"[54] He said: "The Son of God is the Gospel [saying]: 'If someone slaps you on your cheek, turn to him the other.'[55] Indeed, the Jews spat on the face of our Lord and he allowed them, although he could destroy them. And he showed to us that if someone slaps our right cheek, we should turn the other cheek to him too, and [then] we will become the sons of God. Therefore, let us, indeed, do that.[56] That is why [David] said: 'They renounce [it] that they may dwell.'"'[57]

[E97] I heard that Abba Poemen also said: 'It is a great glory that man should know his measure.'

[E98] I heard that the great Abba Agathon used to say: 'All the time God was showing me the way that I was to take.'

[E99] He said again: 'God neither wishes that I please people nor that I accept the error of the demons.'

Collectio Monastica Chapter 14, Part 1

[E101][58] An elder said: 'If a man eat once a day, he is a monk; if he eat twice a day, he is carnal; but if he eat three times a day, he is an animal.'

---

[53] Cf. Ps 66:10.
[54] The text of the alleged Psalm [67.19] seems corrupt.
[55] Cf. Mt 5:39.
[56] The text is nonsensical: *Therefore, let us, indeed, not* [sic!] *do that.*
[57] So in Ms B, in agreement with the beginning of this saying. Ms A [printed by V. Arras as the main text] has '...*that they may worship*'.
[58] E101 = No 1 etc. in the numbering of the items in ch. 14.

[E102] A brother asked Abba Poemen, saying to him: 'How can a man be at peace with a brother who lives with him?' Abba Poemen said to him: 'If a man can bear his [brother's] insolence, then he can live with beasts, not only people.'

[E103] I heard that a brother asked Abba Poemen about the words of the Apostle: 'One who wants to become wise should become a fool so that he may become wise.'[59] The brother said to Abba Poemen: 'My father, how is it possible for a man to become both wise and foolish?' Abba Poemen answered the brother: 'If two brothers live [together] and if one of them says a word that is true, while the other responds: "It is not true, it is not like this, but like that"; if the one who opined first force himself to kill his truth, thus allowing the error of the other, you would rightly declare the one who forced himself to kill his truth on account of God to have become a fool. Yet he also became wise in the eyes of the living God.'

[E104] I heard that some elders went to a community and found there a young brother, an anchorite, who stayed in his dwelling place and did not go out from it except on Saturday and Sunday. The elders who arrived there asked the priest of the congregation: 'We have heard about one young brother who stays at home and does not go out; we wish to see him.' The priest said: 'Nobody can meet him except on Saturday or Sunday.' One of the elders said to the priest: 'Allow me to go alone; perhaps he will open to me.' The priest said: 'Go.' The elder went to him and called upon him and the brother responded. The elder said: 'Open for me, that I may tell you something that will be very beneficial for you' and he let the elder in. When they had prayed, they sat down and the elder said to the young brother: 'I will ask you one question and I want you to tell me the truth. Do you live in this house now because of God or because of people?' I heard that the young brother answered the elder: 'I came into this house because of people, in order that they might be proud of me and that they would praise me, for I desire fame. And when I had waited patiently in the house, I saw glory and pride entering my house and coming upon me. But I saw a vision of God spreading himself out and not allowing pride to come upon me in my dwelling place. Because of that I found rest.'

---

[59] Cf. 1 Cor 3:18.

[E105] A brother said: 'I asked Abba Theodore of Pherme saying: "How can a man expel Satan from himself, so that his heart might be pure from all of these thoughts?" Said Abba Theodore to him: "If a man allow a stranger to bring his possessions into his home, will he be able to expel him, while his possessions are still in his home? But if he remove the stranger's possessions from his home, the stranger will leave at the same time himself. In this way also we cannot put Satan from us unless we first remove his possessions. And these possessions are all the evil[s] that the Scriptures forbid us to do."'

[E106] Abba Isaac, [disciple] of Abba Bis,[60] said: 'If a man gives himself to God with all his heart, I believe God will open his heart and he will know the story of everything.'

[E107] A brother asked an elder saying: 'My father, what do you wish me to do that I might find salvation?' The elder said to him: 'Forgive me, my son; what pains you have been to in order to oblige me [to answer]. I do not know how many tunics I have cut and destroyed. Only one thing I was unable to destroy: my nature.'

[E108] That brother also said: 'I asked an elder about the body and he said to me: "If you treat [all the wild animals, the beasts, and even wolves][61] well, they will respect you, but if you treat man's body well, it will repay your goodness with evil."'

[E109] Again that brother said: 'I asked another elder who was severely mortifying himself, saying: "My Father, if you come among people, do you not lose your mortification?" He said: "Yes, but what do you want me to do to that animal of mine to which I am saddled, my body? When it finds much food it exults, throws me to my enemy, and abandons me."'

[E110] Abba John said to me: 'Is it not strange that we abandoned what was written and listened to what was not in the Scripture? God wrote for us the holy books, but we do not listen to them. The Devil does not have any books, but we listen to him. God said: "Love your brothers" and we hate them; Satan says: "Hate" and we hate them. Woe to the man to whom the Scriptures indicate the right way and he ignores it! Our

---

[60] Pis? Cf. [E144] below.
[61] Completed and supplemented on the basis of the Arabic version published by J. M. Sauget, 'Une nouvelle collection éthiopienne', *Orientalia Christiana Periodica* 31 (1965), p. 182.

fathers, who did listen to God, gave us the right way; but our disobedience has destroyed it for us.'

[E111] Abba Poemen said: 'There are people who keep chopping a tree but are unable to fell it; and there are those who only strike three times and fell it. These [three] are humility of spirit, fear of God, and mourning. The man who has these fells the tree.'

[E112] Abba Pishoy said: 'Man cannot pray with fear of God but without mortification; and man cannot purify his heart except by mortification. If however a man persevere in his mortification, God will grant him fear and purity of heart and he will become the beneficiary of all God's glories.'

[E113] A brother asked an elder saying: 'My father, what do these words in the Gospel mean about one scribe who approached Jesus saying to him: "Shall I follow you?" and Jesus said to him: "Foxes have holes, and the birds of the sky have nests, but the Son of Man has no place to lay his head"?'[62] Said the elder: 'Jesus found the place where the birds of the sky take shelter and [where there were] foxes' holes in that man. Therefore, Jesus did not find a place where he himself could rest. If, then, a man make holes for the foxes and nests for the birds of the sky [in himself] the Son of God cannot live in him. But if a man expel from him[self] both the foxes and the birds of the sky, then the Son of God will make a shelter in that man. If a man sow seed in his field and do not guard it, the birds of the sky will eat it up and the field will become a desert. But if he guard his field until [the seed] take root, then it will grow and will yield much.[63] There is a place in the Scriptures which says: "Catch for us the little foxes that ruin the vineyards."[64] Now, the foxes and the birds of the sky are the bad thoughts [planted by] the devil.'

[E114] An elder said: 'Riches are a trap of the devil. As people set traps in the reeds to catch birds, so also riches are a trap of the devil.'

[E115] I asked an elder saying to him: 'My father, if a little of the Spirit of God did, indeed, exist in a man, would he be saved these days?' He said to me: 'Yes; have you not heard what the prophet said: "If you find juice

---

[62] Cf. Lk 9:57–8.
[63] Cf. Mt 13:1–9.
[64] Cf. Song 2:15.

in a cluster of grapes, do not throw it away, because God's blessing is in it"?[65] These days that are now upon us are days of scarcity.'

[E116] Abba John said: 'If Moses had not entered the darkness, he would not have seen God.[66] People interpret darkness as the dwelling place of a monk. If you stay in a dwelling place you will see God's full glory.'

[E117] I heard that Abba Ammon of Kellia said: 'I underwent all the mortifications my ear heard of, but I did not find among them a hardship [more difficult than] these two: raising from the table while you are still hungry, and forcing yourself not to say a bad word to your brother.'

[E118] Abba Abraham of the eastern region said: 'If a man patiently endure his mortifications, he will be victorious and shall see the power and glory of God.'

[E119] Abba Achilles said: 'Guard the true faith and guard your body from impurity and theft, and you shall be saved according to the account [of your conduct] during these days.'

[E120] A brother said: 'Abba John of Kellia said to me: "Look at the plants in the field: before they bring forth ears of corn they stand upright, but as soon as they bring them forth, the ears of corn make them bend. And also, so far as man is concerned, in times when there is no fruit for God, one cannot find humbleness of spirit in him; but when fruit appears in a man, he lowers his head in everything on account of God."'

[E121] An elder said: 'Three brothers went to Abba Ammoes and one of them said to him: "My father, if I have been very diligent[67] and have learned much; shall I find salvation?" But Abba Ammoes did not answer him. The second brother said: "My father, if I have been doing much manual work and have been giving many alms; shall I find salvation?" But Abba Ammoes did not answer him either. And then the third [brother] said: "My father, if I have been fasting much and have shown love to brothers; shall I find salvation?" But no answer did Abba Ammoes give to him either. When they realized he would not answer them, they

---

[65] Cf. Is 65:8.
[66] Cf. Ex 20:21.
[67] Or: 'have kept much vigil'.

said: "Pray for us, father; we shall leave." However, Abba Ammoes did not wish to send them away in sadness and he began talking to himself, but so that the brothers might hear. He said to himself: "If I have been very diligent, and have been learning much, shall I be saved?" And he answered: "No." "And if I have been working much and giving alms, shall I be saved?" And he answered: "No." "And if I have been fasting much and loving brothers, shall I be saved?" And he answered only to himself: "And if I have done all those things but will not find salvation, how can I find it?" And he answered only to himself saying: "Verily,[68] if you have a good heart, you will be saved."[69]

[E122] A brother asked Abba John of Kellia saying to him: 'My father, how can a man give alms with his own hands without being able to give as little as possible to his brother?' The elder answered him: 'Such a man is still estranged,[70] and our Lord Jesus has not yet touched him with his hands that he might be healed.'

[E123] An elder uttered these words that were written in the Gospel: 'A broad and wide road leads to death.' And again: 'Narrow and confined is the road that leads to life.'[71] 'This is man's choice: if man listen to his wish he will enter death, but if the man compel himself and not listen to his wish, he will enter life.'

[E124] A brother asked Abba Poemen saying to him: 'My father, did impurity beset you, the elders, too, as it does us now?' Said Abba Poemen to him: 'Yes, my son, but hunger and thirst would not allow us to think about impurity. We watched the sun until it set so that we could eat a little of our bread and [drink] some of our water. In our day we used to eat honey instead of bread and [drink] mead instead of water [because] mortification turned the bread in our mouths into honey and the water into mead. But we did not kill our bodies: we disciplined them until it was sufficient for us. We did not expose them to excess, only in the measure that was acceptable to God.'

---

[68] Here the name of the elder, as V. Arras assumes [trans. p. 84], and the French translators after him [p. 318], is given as *'Am[m]on*, not *'Am[m]oy*, and therefore, following the Polish translation by S. Kur [p. 108], this name variant should be taken as erroneously spelled *'aman* – 'verily, truly'.

[69] Cf. *APalph* Pambo 2, *APsys* 10.94, ending: 'Works are good, but if you keep your conscience [clear] with respect to your neighbour, in that way you are being saved.'

[70] The Ethiopic text seems to be corrupt here by negating the verb.

[71] Cf. Mt 7:13–14.

[E125] An elder said that Abba Isaac lived in Scete in Karawer inside …[72]

[E126] Abba Moses said: 'One day when I was young [thoughts of] impurity beset me. I went deeper into the desert, and stayed there for 42 days. I did not eat bread and did not drink water, nor did I lie or sit, but I prayed to God and God gave me relief from this [temptation]. Thereafter, for all the days of my life [such thoughts] never plagued me again.'

[E127] Abba Joseph of Aframet said: 'One day [thoughts of] impurity beset me while I was at my father's [dwelling] and my father was good [to me]. I said to him: "My father, I see that impurity plagues me very much. I will go into the world and marry a woman, like all men." My father said to me: "No, my son, do not commit that sin! Listen to me and God will give you peace." I said to him: "What do you wish me to do?" He said to me: "Take these 40 pieces of bread and go and stay at Scete. Take with you some palm branches, stay there 40 days, and make plaited mats of them, but do not moisten them with water. Fast every second day and on the other days eat [only] two pieces of bread." As he had instructed me, I went [to Scete] and worked, staying for 20 days. After 20 days, during which I plaited mats of dry palm branches and fasted every second day, a small black girl came to me, [entered] where I was sitting, and said to me: "Do you recognize me?" I said "No." She said: "You are in all this trouble because of me." I said to her: "Then you are impurity!" and she said "Yes." I said to her: "Since you are impurity and your face is so repellent, it is easy to treat you with contempt." And she told me: "I wanted to appear to you in this way, since you are the man of God, [one of] those who say: 'We are columns', whom I made fall down." When she had said these words to me, she disappeared and I did not see her [again]. I rose up and went to the land of Egypt, to my father, and stayed with him for three days, but he did not want me to speak; he continued to do what he had been doing. I did not understand [why]. Then he said to me: "Tell me what you saw, and do not hide anything from me because everything you have seen has been revealed to me." He kissed my mouth and my head many times, and said: "Behold, today you have become a son to me!" And he said that from that day on I would not be troubled by impurity.'

[72] The saying is damaged. A place called *Karawer* is unknown. 'Dans les collines intérieurs', Dom Lucien.

[E128] Abba Sisoes of Petra, [a disciple] of Abba Antony, said: 'If a man does good, he will moor his boat in a good port.'

[E129] Abba John, [a disciple] of Abba Jacob, said: 'My brother Macarius said to me when he was alive: "I have lived for 40 years without sleeping on either my side or on my back."'

[E130] I also heard Abba Macarius say: 'If, in these days of scarcity, a monk guard his body against impurity and his hands against theft and curb a little his [sinful] will, he will not be condemned.'

[E131] I heard that Abba Theodore said: 'Our fathers guarded their hearts, and I say that in these days of scarcity, if [a monk] keeps his body from impurity and theft, and curbs a little his lust, he will not go into condemnation.'

[E132] Abba John, [a disciple] of Abba Jacob, said to me: 'I heard Abba Moses of Scete often say: "If a monk fulfills God's wish, yet lives with his family, then when he dies he will also be buried together with them."'

[E133] Abba Jacob said: 'I knew two brothers who lived in Scete and they were very good [monks.] One of them fell ill and was unable to come to church for prayer on Saturday.[73] We found the other in prayer and asked him about his brother. He said to us that [his brother] was sick with fever. When he finished praying we went to his dwelling place to pay a visit to [his brother] and we found him very ill. On Sunday we went again for prayer and, when the prayer was over, we went to pay a visit to him and found him dying. His brother said to him: "Are you dying, my brother, and leaving me?" And he answered him: "Yes." Said again his brother: "Forgive me, I cannot let you to die and abandon me," and he said: "Bring us here a mat and a coverlet." And when they brought them, he lay down and grew hot, shivering with fever, and died before his brother. Afterwards, his brother also died. We took both of them and buried them together. Do you see how God heard these people who did [his] will with all their hearts?'

---

[73] The Ethiopic text has *sanbat*, which is not clear: it is either *sanbat qadamit* – lit., 'the first Sabbath', *sanbata 'Ayhud* – lit., 'the Sabbath of the Jews', i.e., 'Saturday', or *sanbata Krəsṭiyān* – 'Sunday'.

[E134] Abba Jacob said: 'Abba Moses, Zachariah, and I met where the water sprang up at Scete. Abba Moses said to Zachariah: "Show me how I should become a monk." Zachariah fell down with his face to the ground, touching the earth with his face. He sprinkled sand on his head and wept, saying to him: "I am but a child and you are my father; it is I who should ask you how I should become a monk." Abba Moses said: "I have seen your [pious] work[s]", and Zachariah asked him: "What have you seen, except for my sins?" Said Abba Moses: "Do you not believe me that I am not lying to you?" Zachariah said to him: "Yes, I believe you." [Then] Abba Moses said to him: "I have seen the Spirit of God descending from heaven and settling upon you. Show me then how my monastic behaviour should be." And Zachariah said to him: "Since you do not cease [asking] me about it, [I say:] Compel yourself in everything on account of God. This is entire perfection for a monk."'

[E135] A brother said that Zachariah had told Abba Moses: 'Show me the abstinence you have observed since your youth, that I might observe it [too].' Abba Moses answered him: 'My abstinence since my youth until today [is this]: I eat one piece of bread a day; if I have fasted two days I will eat two, if I have fasted until evening I will eat one.' Zachariah, having seen and heard this, [did] likewise. Thereafter Zachariah fell mortally ill. Abba Moses said to him: 'Was something revealed to you?' And he said: 'Yes.' Abba Moses said to him: 'What have you seen?' Said Zachariah 'Is it proper for me to tell [you]?' Abba Moses answered: 'No,' and Zachariah died.

[E136] I heard about one elder, a man of God: it happened that he was to go on a journey. He was clothed in an old and wretched garment, carrying an old basket and he looked like a poor beggar. On his way he encountered some brothers but they did not greet him. He accosted them saying: 'Bless me, brothers, I would like to ask you something.' They looked at him and he said: 'Is it neglect that eats clothes or moths?' They stood astounded, and he said to them: 'I asked you about [this] matter that you might explain it to me.' And they told him: '[It is] man's neglect of [his] clothes: [for if] he do not air [them] moths will eat them and they will be destroyed.' [Then] the elder cried out and wept, saying: 'I myself have been so neglectful that I will perish!' Then they fell down on the ground before him, having understood that he was a great vessel of God.

[E137] A brother asked Abba Sisoes of Petra, [a disciple] of Abba Antony, saying to him: 'My father, what would you advise me to do? Brothers make fun of me, saying: "You go, you circulate, you make a habit of moving from one place to another, and you do not choose to stay [in one place] and you do not work with your hands."' Said Abba Sisoes to him: 'If the brothers of those times had met us, the elders, wearing sheep-skins[74] in our own time and moving here and there, they would have mocked us, saying: "These people are possessed by demons."'

[E138] An elder said: 'I saw Abba Isidore of Scete as he touched a blind man's eyes and he recovered his sight.' The elder continued: 'I caught hold of Abba Isidore and said to him: "I will not let you go until you tell me how you touched the eyes of the blind man so that he could see", and Isidore said to the elder: "Since you won't let me go [you shall hear]. From the time I began to wear this *askema*,[75] I have not allowed anger to rise in my throat."'

[E139] Abba Poemen said: 'I went one day to Abba Ammonas to ask him: "Tell me a word." And he told me: "Only goodness brings [a man] out of Sheol.[76] Goodness does not allow man to be damned. Look at Tabitha, how her goodness raised her from the dead.[77] Look at the woman who did good to the Prophet Elisha who brought her son back from the dead.[78] Look at King Hezekiah to whom, because of his right-eousness and the beauty of his deeds, God granted another 15 years."'[79]

[E140] Abba John of Cilicia said: 'Do you see that word that is written: "Remember the days of old"?[80] The Scriptures of our Lord awaken us because they remind us of our previous days when you [pl.] left the world and began to put on the likeness of God and when you burned with the love of God with all of your heart. But then you reverted to the pleasures of the world.'

---

[74] Eth. *məloṭər*, usually *maleḷiṭo* [< Gr. μηλωτή, cf. 1/3 Kgs 19:19, 2/4 Kgs 2:8, 13, and 14] – 'sheep-skin', or 'headcloth', 'turban' worn by Ethiopian priests.
[75] Monk's attire [< Gr. σχῆμα], habit.
[76] Hades.
[77] Cf. Acts 9:36–42.
[78] Cf. 2 Kgs 4.
[79] Cf. 2 Kgs 20:5–6.
[80] Cf. Dt 32:7.

[E141] Again the same Abba John said: 'Do you know about the five porches of Solomon where the sick, the lame, the blind, and the crippled were lying? One of them had been there, sick on his bed, for 38 years [when] Jesus said to him: "Do you want to get well?"[81] Jesus granted the man his wish. Now, the lame, the blind, and the crippled are evil thoughts that live in a man. In fact, Jesus granted [that] man his wish, so that when one is willing, Jesus will listen to him, save him, and drive evil thoughts out of him.'

[E142] Again the same Abba John said: '[There is] the passage written in the Gospel where Jesus called upon Lazarus [to come out] from his tomb with his hands and legs bound and his face wrapped in a cloth. Jesus untied him and sent him away.[82] Our hands and legs are indeed bound, and a cloth laid over our faces by the Enemy. If, however, we listen to Jesus, he will release us from all that and will set us free from the bondage of all evil thoughts. We shall become God's children, and inherit His commandments, becoming children of the eternal Kingdom.'

[E143] An elder said: 'Toil brings about mortification and watchfulness, because toil changes a man's mind so that he might explore the Scriptures. It also brings forth [awareness of] the full extent of the glory of God. Mortification also teaches a man to continue the labours he performs on account of God. But what is merely external, involvement in numerous affairs and thinking too much about things of this earthly dwelling, these plunge a man into darkness and he knows not where he is going, since darkness blinds the eyes of his heart. Joy and bodily rest change a man as if all his toil on account of God were lost. Joy alone strengthens the beast that is within a man because, when a man is glad, he is not able to fight the beast inside him. But suffering on account of God will kill the beast that is within; then he will be able to overcome his enemy.'

[E144] A brother said: 'One day I went to Abba Poemen, and while I was staying with him a brother came and said: "My father, help me, because I went to Abba Pis and said to him: 'Help me, because impurity besets me.' He laughed at me and said: 'Why do you let impurity defeat you?'" Abba Poemen said to the brother: "It seems Abba Pis, as he has reached the level as God, believes that all people are like him. He does not know

---

[81] Cf. Jn 5:2–5.
[82] Cf. Jn 11:43–4.

that you and I are the dwelling places of impurity." Do you see how the elders strengthened the brothers?'

[E145] A brother said to me: 'When Abba Agathon the Great saw a brother committing a sin, he was overcome by a wish to upbraid him, but rebuked himself and said: "Agathon, do not commit this sin!" And after he had said that to himself, he would not rebuke the brother.'

[E146] Abba Poemen said: 'The elders of Scete said that a beautiful boy of Alexandria had cut off his genitals and become like a harlot, sitting in the doorway of a house as a prostitute. After a long time, he entreated Pope Athanasios[83] saying: "Baptize me, that I may become a believer." Athanasios said to him: "Go, beseech people that they may pray for you." After he had been beseeching people for a long time, they entreated Abba Athanasios saying: "Baptize him!" And we heard that he took him into the baptistery and baptized him: [then] his genitals returned to him, and all the people were amazed.' A brother said to me: 'After Abba Poemen had told me this story, [he said]: "Come back to me." [Then] he said these words three times to me: "What is sin beside penitence? And the penance for sins is that henceforward you should not sin again. Do you see God's goodness?"'

[E147] A brother asked an elder, saying to him: 'What would you advise me to do against those evil thoughts that penetrate the heart?' The elder said: 'Look at your clothes: when you put them in a chest, you forget them there and you do not take them out or shake them, they perish and become fit for nothing. But if you shake your clothes and wear them often, they do not decay, but remain [sound]. It is also like that with evil thoughts: if you entertain them and find pleasure in them, they will always take root in the heart, move upwards, and never leave your heart. But if you do not entertain them, nor find pleasure in them, but fight them, they will die and leave the heart.'[84]

[E148] Abba Theodore of Pherme recounted how when [demons] brought uncleanliness upon him, for six years he ate [only] two small pieces of bread [a day]. When he arose at dawn, he moistened his two pieces of bread with water and added a small pinch of salt; and every

[83] Patriarch of Alexandria 328–73.
[84] Cf. *APalph* Poemen 20, *APsys* 10.42.

evening, he ate it with a spoon like porridge. After he had completed six years [on this diet], he rose to say his evening prayer and eat again in this way, and a voice came to him saying 'I say to you, this mortification is enough.' 'When I heard this voice, [God] removed impurity from me.'

[E149] An elder said: 'Eating and sleeping are the servants of unchastity. All three of them have the same function. When impurity sets in, it brings hunger to a man. Then a man says: "I will give thanks to God as I have stayed without food until now." And then he says: "I will get up to eat a little that I may gain strength and be able to say a little prayer." Then sleep comes and, having slept, when he gets up, unchastity embraces him and, at that moment, prevents him from giving thanks to God. It rather leads him into uncleanliness like a pig, bringing delight to him and evil thoughts of the Enemy, and making him a stranger both to life and to God.'

[E150] Somebody said: 'I see myself all the time with my head full of dust and I beseech God to pardon my sins, for they are numerous.'

[E151] An elder said: 'If you are arrogant you are a devil, if you are sorrowful, you are like a son to him; and if you are preoccupied with many things, repose will be removed from you.'

[E152] Said Abba Cronios of Mount Panahon: 'I know a brother in Scete, whom [evil] thoughts tormented by saying: "Why do you not work hard?" He answered the thoughts thus: "Does the work of my hands sustain me? Not at all! It is God who provides for me." The brother said [again] to his thoughts: "Behold, I will neither work nor eat nor drink until I have seen for myself whether I sustain myself, or God." And he went to a mountain and stayed there for eight days without eating, drinking, or working. As he continued to fast, neither eating nor drinking, he grew more feeble. Then, exhausted, he noted with his own eyes a dish beside him full of honey and he said: "Behold, God gave me honey instead of bread." He ate some of it and recovered his strength.' Abba Cronios said: 'I saw the dish of honey with my own eyes and ate some of it. [So did] some other brothers.'

[E153] That brother also said to me: 'Abba Cronios told me: "When I left Scete, I went into the wilderness in the land of Egypt and stayed there.

While I was there and plaiting palm leaves, an army of terrifying and impure spirits arrived, and some entered my dwelling and said: 'Arise and go, the king summons you.' I said to them: 'I will not go!' They grasped the plait in my hand and said to me: 'Come on, arise, we say to you, the king is calling you, and you remain here plaiting!' They smote me and dragged me outside by force. I looked up and saw someone seated on a throne and they said to me: 'Bow down to the king!' I said: 'I will not bow down', and they smote me again and left me on the ground for dead. When I fell to the ground, they left me and went away. Then somebody came to me, shook me, and said: 'Rise up, I am yours.' When he lifted me, I regained my strength and rose, but could see no scar or wound on my body. I said to him: 'Where have you been until now?' He answered 'I was here, but I left you to see if you would stand fast or not.'''

[E154] An elder said: 'Mortification of the body brings forth purity of the body and the purity of the body binds the heart to God. Blessed be God who has bound my heart to him.'

[E155] Abba Sisoes of Petra, [a disciple] of Abba Antony, said: 'Fasting is the mother of all virtues, because it gives birth to them and leads man to all of them. But humbleness of spirit is the greatest of all virtues.'

[E156] An elder said: 'Solicitude[85] prevails over all desires.'

[E157] An elder said: 'Do you see the prison with its thieves, robbers, wicked people, and sinners? This is the eternal prison of people's bodies. But the prison of free men and of believers is the fever that makes them give thanks to God when they suffer pain, so that they receive blessings from the living God.'

[E158] Said Abba Poemen: 'Why cannot we get rid of the heavy burden on our shoulders and accept a small burden and find relief?'[86] He said of the heavy burden: 'If you make accusations against your brother and extol yourself, that is a heavy burden. And a light burden is when you make accusations against yourself and extol your brothers.'

---

[85] Or: *understanding*. διάκρισις, discernment? 'Le discernement vainc tous les désirs', Dom Lucien.
[86] Cf. Mt 11:30.

[E159] That brother also said to me: 'I said to Abba Poemen: "Why are we, brothers of these days, not victorious and do not succeed like our predecessors?" The elder answered: "Because the word of God has left you and you do not proclaim it. You proclaim the insignificant words of this world which are not God's. That is why we are not victorious and make no progress."'

[E160] That brother also said to me: 'I said to Abba Poemen: "What is humility of the spirit?" He said to me: "That you should set your wishes behind you, meaning that you should restrain your wishes and put them behind your brother's. This is the perfect humility of spirit – which is godly."'

[E161] A brother said: 'I asked an elder about some matter and said to him: "Behold, we are searching for good deeds yet we do not perform them; instead we do evil ones. We just speak about the words of God, but we do not do them."'

[E162] An elder said: 'Is it not strange that we commit our hearts to possessions, to our families, to [our] desires and our works in the world: to those very things that caused us to turn our backs on the world? But we do not observe what is useful to us on account of God and *that* is the [proper] work of the monk.'

[E163] Abba Poemen said: 'I know a brother of Scete who fasted every second day for three years and still was not triumphant. When he stopped fasting every second day and deliberately fasted [every day] until evening, from that time on he always prevailed.' And to me Abba Poemen said: 'Eat and do not eat, drink and do not drink, sleep and do not sleep. Act with wisdom and you will find repose.'

[E164] A brother said to me: 'Isaac of Harahu told me: "I visited Abba Sisoes of Petra, [a disciple] of Abba Antony, and asked of him a favour saying: 'Tell me a word by which I should live.' He said to me: 'Go, abide by these three things, and you will live. Accept contempt as an honour, misery as wealth; and love your neighbour as yourself. God will dwell with you and will strengthen you against your enemies.'"'[87]

---

[87] Cf. *APalph*, Macarius the Egyptian 20.

[E165] A brother said to me: 'When I was going to Abba Poemen, that he might rejoice with me, I told another brother that the elder was very gentle. The brother said to me: "Take me too so I can see him" and I took him there, to the elder. However, the elder grew very angry. The brother said to Abba Poemen: "You have always rejoiced with me, so what is wrong now?" Abba Poemen said to him: "He who does not know joy does not know grief either."'

[E166] Abba Agueras said to me: 'I once went to Abba Poemen and said to him: "I have been wandering everywhere in order to settle down, but have not found rest; where do you wish me to settle?" And he said to me:[88] "In these days there is no wilderness. Go, seek for yourself [a place of] many people and settle among them. Behave as someone who does not exist and say: 'I have no worry', and you will find great rest."'

[E167] An elder told me: 'Three favours come to a man: two of them God is not pleased with and one favour God is pleased with.' I said to the elder: 'What are those two favours God is not pleased with, and what is the one God is pleased with?' The elder said to me: 'There is a good thing which the thought of man gives birth to, but it is not due to God. And there is another favour that evil spirits bring upon man and which is not from God. And there is [yet] another favour that is from God, which comes to man but he understands it not and does not put his heart into it. If the man does not take his *melote*,[89] and does not go to [find] a Man of God, he will not know that he is a Man of God. He will reveal to him all his thoughts and he will answer: "This favour that came upon you is from God" and he will [also] tell him: "With this favour, God is pleased." Now, the monk's toil is in vain if he does not visit the servants of God to learn what is profitable to his soul. Amen.'

These are the words and deeds of the elders.[90]

---

[88] The Eth. text has erroneously [?]: 'to him'.

[89] Eth. *meleṭur* [also: *məluṭār, maleṭo, maliṭo, maluṭā, məleṭo*, etc.] < Gr. μηλωτή – sheepskin, monk's mantle, cover[ing].

[90] In the manuscript published by V. Arras, after this saying there follows the benediction request for the manuscript producers: 'May their [i.e., the elders'] prayers and blessings be with the one who ordered the writing [of this book], with the scribe, with the reader, with the translator, and with the listener to these words, for ever and ever. Amen, amen, and amen.'

Patericon Aethiopice

[E168] One of the elders said: 'It is a great and wondrous thing when we stand to say a prayer, as if God were watching us, and as if he were with us listening to our words. But when we sin [it is] as if God does not see us, and as if he does not know our deeds.'
[83] 76⁹¹

[E169] One of the wise said: 'I see no rest except in renouncing the world. There is no peace except in toil⁹² and deliverance from bondage [is attained] by not seeking the wealth of people, by renouncing the body, by the remembrance of death, by a scattering love,⁹³ by abandoning slander, by good ways of living, and by learning wisdom. [There is no] deliverance from [the infernal] fire [except by] renouncing desires.'⁹⁴
[110] 99

[E170] [An elder] said again: 'Who[ever] does not attack, or afflict,⁹⁵ or revile people, he pursues the work of angels. And who[ever] attacks people, and is angry [with them], but immediately returns to become reconciled⁹⁶ with his brother and repents for having left him, that is truly the act of a champion. But who[ever] makes his neighbours sad⁹⁷ and holds a grudge in his heart, he is a brother of Satan and cannot ask God for forgiveness. If he asks for [it], he will not receive it as long as he does not forgive and pardon his brother.'
[145]

[E171] [An elder] said: 'He who does not toil with his body and does not suffer in his heart is like a body without a soul. So [it is with] one who performs manual labour and suffers with a good intention in his heart on account of God. Hardship will befall him and he will say: "I am negligent in God's service" but he is eager to serve, so that he might reaffirm the law of God. Through his suffering, he will come to understand that he is not perfect and he will fight to make his soul right in the commandments of God. He will increase his toil, while saying in his heart: "I am

---

⁹¹ Ethiopian numbering, not always provided.
⁹² Eth. *ṣəmunā*; perhaps 'solitary life' is meant.
⁹³ 'Seed of love'; perhaps 'alms' are meant.
⁹⁴ The saying seems to be corrupt. The translation is tentative.
⁹⁵ Read *waʾiyāḥazzən* [not: *waʾiyaḥāzzən*].
⁹⁶ Read *yətʾarak* [not: *yətʾāraq*].
⁹⁷ Read *yāḥazzənomu* [not: *yaḥāzzənomu*].

worthless and a sinner." He will become one who toils with his body and suffers in his heart and therefore he will serve in humility, and will toil in his heart.'
[162]

[E172] Abba Clement said: 'He who does not have the voice of the fear of God in his heart should know that his soul is dead.'
[168] 131

[E173] Again he said: 'God does not condemn us if we have not performed miracles or if we have not learned mysteries or if we have not been educated in the speech of the forefathers or of theology. He will only judge us if we do not continue to mourn and weep all our days on account of our sins. For that, he will condemn us.'
[169]

[E174] Concerning the triumph over the Enemy: If we humble ourselves, God will repel the Enemy. We should always be on guard: this is a victory over Satan.
[179] 155

[E175] About the three virtues that are the best of all, the fathers said: 'These three virtues are precious and whoever holds them fast can dwell among people or [in] the wilderness or wherever he wishes. The first is renunciation of oneself, [the second] rejection of desires, and [the third] that [one] regard oneself as below all creatures.'
[180] 156

[E176] A man[98] came to an elder in order to receive from him a rule [of life]. He answered him saying: 'My son, let your rule be that you should sit and consider in your mind the fear of God, and say: "How can I find God?" and: "How have I passed my days in idleness? From now on I shall repent, because my death is approaching. I shall patiently put up with my neighbour[s] and every affliction and sorrow they may cause, so that the Lord may know [all that I am experiencing] and show me mercy and may give me understanding to abandon wrath and that he may expel from me envy towards the sons of the lying Enemy." Since the larger part of your days that were sufficient for penitence have passed, try to find in

---

[98] Another Ms: 'a brother'.

your mind [the strength] to resist [the Enemy], that he may not bring affliction upon you; and that you may instruct [your] spiritual children in the fear of God and in the memory of their sins, even though you cannot be sure yourself [of these things], being a man on probation.'
[183]

[E177] A brother approached an elder and asked him: 'What should I do, abba?' The elder answered him: 'Weep and lament until the day you die, because when you are sorrowful and you lament, you do not go from one sorrow to another, but to gladness; because God does not lead [people] from one sorrow to another, but to joy.'
[203]

[E178] The holy Abba Poemen said: 'Follow the good way, do justice, flee from this world entirely.'
[204]

[E179] And he said: 'If you love what does not grow old, do not seek what grows old. And if you love life that does not pass away, ponder death every day.'
[205]

[E180] And he said: 'Abhor the disputes of this world, because great is their [power of] destruction.'
[206]

[E181] And [Abba Macarius]⁹⁹ said to us: 'One day my soul was troubled by hunger and I said to it: "Die and be angry" and: "May your soul pass away, because when it wants food outside the proper time or earlier, I will not give [it] to you."'¹⁰⁰
[208]

[E182] Some brothers asked Abba Agathon saying: 'Which work is better in searching for the goodwill of God and which is more beneficial to our Lord?' He said to them: 'A meek heart and sincere prayer in fear and trembling; know [pl.] that you will stand before God and he will examine you and will know what is in your hearts.'
[219]

---

⁹⁹ His name occurs in the previous saying [which is not translated here].
¹⁰⁰ The text of this saying is corrupt; translation tentative.

[E183] [Thieves] plundered the possessions of a wise monk, but he did not get angry and did not search [for the perpetrators]. The one who robbed him said to him: 'Why are you not angry?' He answered saying: 'Because, for me, you are like a death that tears away a man from his possessions. But the monk should not be angry, nor speak ill of anyone, nor pay back evil with evil.'
[220]

[E184] Abba John said: 'We have left the true service and tormented our souls. We have begun to serve transitory things and to venerate [our] bodies.'
[222]

[E185] A monk said: 'If there is a servant who serves with care, God will require that he not bind himself to the goods of the world, which may lead him astray. [Otherwise] there will remain [only] a memory of his name and lamentation for the remission of his sins.'
[318] 221

[E186] [That elder[101]] also said: 'He who fills his belly with food and drink neglects prayer and cannot carry on the fight in his mind. Hunger and vigilance cleanse the heart of evil thought and the body from the attacks of the Enemy, so that the Holy Spirit will dwell in him.'
[322]

[E187] Prayer is the shield[102] and sword of the monk. If there is no pure prayer there is no sword with which to fight.
[324]

[E188] A monk asked an elder saying: 'What should I do that I may be saved?' And the elder answered: 'The work of your hands together with divine service will deliver you.'
[329]

[E189] [Gregory][103] said: 'May your work be clean before God and not [only] in appearance.'
[348]

---

[101] Supposedly the same as in the former saying, no. 321 [which is not translated here]: 'one of the elders'.

[102] A possible meaning, Eth. *waḍan* – an otherwise unknown word.

[103] The author of the former saying [no. 347].

WITOLD WITAKOWSKI

WITOLD WITAKOWSKI

[E190] Abba Poemen said:[104] 'For all the works that you do, take counsel, because it is written: "Work without advice is stupidity." If someone asks you, respond to him; and if not – it is better to remain silent.'
[350] 220

[E191] Abba Philip said: 'He who loves silence will not be pierced by the arrows of the Enemy; but the one who dwells among the people will receive many wounds.'
[353] 231

[E192] [That elder[105]] also said: 'If you love the salvation of your soul, always pray (as is written) with fear and trembling in your heart, knowing that you have evil enemies who will lie to you, [place before you] a stumbling block, and who will set an ambush for you.'
[386]

[E193] An elder said: 'There is nothing more rotten than a sinful man: neither dog, nor pig, nor jackal, because they are beasts and they keep to what is theirs. But man, who was created in the image of God, did not keep [God's] law. Woe to the soul which became accustomed to sins, like a dog that has become accustomed to the smell of fat and, [even though] they beat him and chase him away, withdraws a little but returns and does not want to go away until they kill him.'
[416] 265

[E194] He also said: 'We do not fear God as we fear dogs.' His disciple said to him: 'Why are you blaspheming like that against God?' And he said: 'Because we commit sins in the night and return when we hear the sound of dogs, and not because of fear of God.'
[417]

[E195] By Epiphanios, the bishop: He gave orders to his disciples, when his soul was leaving him, saying: 'Listen, understand, and keep these words of me, a sinner: Do not love the wealth of this world, so that you may find relief and joy on the last day. Do not rail against your brothers, so that the suffering brought by Satan may not endure in you. Beware of the desires of this world which arouse [bad] thoughts about the body and be aware that [they are] from Satan, since [when] the body is at rest, the

---

[104] Here: Eth. *Bāwmin*.
[105] The same as in the former saying [no. 384].

heart thinks about vain things. Watch over your thoughts and remember the name of God in order the better to withstand the attack of the Enemy.'[106]

[424] 269

[E196] An elder said: 'He who meditates in his soul and makes right his deeds builds for himself a strong fortress.'

[431] 274

[E197] Blessed is the man who endures an affliction and becomes strong without anger.

[437]

[E198] Humility means leaving anger aside and he who dwells in his[107] goodness will be filled with spiritual good things.

[438]

[E199] [You possess] humility when you detest sins, but remember your former sins.

[440]

[E200] A brother said to an elder: 'I want to take a little more food because of my illness' and he said to him: 'Do as you wish.' But when the brother returned, he said: 'Did you really tell me the truth?' To which the elder replied: 'If you really want the truth, "Cast your thoughts on God and he will feed you."'[108]

[444] 279

---

[106] This saying is also extant in Greek [*PG* 41:108] and in Arabic, *Orientalia Christiana Periodica* 30 (1964), p. 500.

[107] God's? It is not clear.

[108] Cf. Ps 55:22.

Glossary

Non-English words retained in the translation

Abba   Father, a senior monk, but not necessarily an *old* one.

Accidie (*akêdia*)   'Sloth, torpor, especially as a condition leading to listlessness and want of interest in life' (*OED*), probably akin to depression.

Agapê   Literally, 'love', used to designate a common meal shared by monks on special occasions (hence 'love-feast') possibly originally made possible by some freewill offering (*agapê*); also a charitable donation, alms.

Amma   Mother.

Anchorite   One who withdraws: one who has abandoned 'the world' for the desert or (more usually) has left a community to live alone.

Apatheia   Literally, 'unfeeling'; indifference to physical conditions, a term found rarely in the *Apophthegmata* but common in later monastic writing.

Askêsis   Literally, 'a formation', usually meaning the practice of asceticism: the discipline associated with the monastic way of life, often translated: 'spiritual discipline'.

Askêtês   One who practices *askêsis*.

Coenobion (*koinobion*)   Literally, 'common life'. A place or a community in which monks live together with shared worship, meals and responsibilities (a convent) under the supervision of a *koinobiarch*, here translated 'superior', or *higoumen*.

Dynamis   The healing 'power' believed to be given off by holy persons and their relics etc. as in Mark 5:30.

Hêsychia (*hêsuchia*)   Not merely (or necessarily) silence [*siôpê*] but an interior silence characterized by a tranquil acquiescence in the will of God, producing a profound calm and great peace within.

Higoumen (*hêgoumenos*, f. *hêgoumenissa*)   The head of a monastic community.

Leviton   i.e. 'Levite's'; the monk's garment worn only for prayer and for burial, usually white.

Logismos, pl. *logismoi*   Literally, 'thought[s]', is a word of many meanings. It can simply mean one's thinking process, but it can also mean everything that goes on in that process, good, bad, and indifferent, from a mere whim to a severe temptation.

Porneia   Any illicit sexual activity of thought, word or deed; the most dreaded of all *logismoi*, variously (incorrectly) translated by fornication, immorality, unchastity, uncleanness etc.

Synaxis   Literally, 'a congregating', means an act of worship, either of one or a few monks (the 'little synaxis', also called *liturgy*) or of an entire community (e.g. at weekends and festivals) at a central location. The Holy Eucharist ('Offering') is often called *synaxis*.

English words used with specific meanings

Alienation, voluntary exile, and *expatriation*   Translate Greek *xeniteia*, Latin *perigrinatio*; making oneself a 'stranger and sojourner' (1 Pet 2:11), usually in an uninhabited place or in a strange land.

Ascetic, -ism   *askêtês, askêsis*, the practitioner and practice of spiritual discipline, perceived as a training or formation in traveling the way to perfection.

Burnt-faced-one   *Aithiops* (from which 'Ethiopian'): a devil or demon.

Dried loaf   *paxamas*, 'biscuit', named after the baker Paxamos: a bread-roll that has been sun-dried or baked hard.

Elder   Here translates *gerôn,* often misleadingly rendered 'old man', but age is not necessarily implied (cf. 'elder' among North-American Indians). An elder is one advanced, not so much in age, as in experience; hence a senior monk, as opposed to a junior (brother).

Expatriation   See *Alienation, voluntary exile* and *expatriation*.

Loose-talk   *parrhêsia*, 'outspokenness', 'familiarity', also in a good sense: 'freedom of access', e.g. to the Deity: see 1 John 2:28 etc.

Lord-and-master   Translates *despotês*.

Monastery   'Is the name of a dwelling and means nothing more than a place, a lodging that is, for monks' (even for only one monk), Cassian, *Conf.* 18.10.

Poverty   Here inadequately translates *aktêmosynê*, literally, 'without possessions'. In the *Apophthegmata* the word means not only the voluntary abandonment of material possessions but, a fortiori, indifference to possessions even when they are accessible.

Sheepskin   *mêlôtê*, the 'mantle' of 2 Kgs 2, something each monk appears to have possessed, but the word can also designate his few possessions.

Sorrow for sin   Here translates *katanyxis*, sometimes rendered 'compunction'.

Spiritual discipline   Here indicates ascetic practice, e.g. fasting, meditating (i.e. reciting), keeping vigil etc.

Spiritual gift   Here translates *charisma*.

Worldling   'One who is devoted to the interests and pleasures of the world' (*OED*). This obsolete English word that has been resurrected to represent the Greek *kosmikos*, a person 'of the world' as opposed to one 'of the desert', i.e. 'non-monk', is sometimes translated 'layman', a 'non-clergyman' (but very few monks were clerics), sometimes 'secular', but that usually means a cleric who is not a monk; almost no worldlings were clerics.

Proper names

Where there is an English equivalent, this has been used, e.g. John, Peter, James, Theodore, Elijah (for *Élias*) and so forth.

The usual Latin forms have been used where there is an accepted transliteration (e.g. Macarius, Syncletica); otherwise names have been transliterated directly.

Where words are found in square brackets in the translation, these are words that are not found the text, but are desirable or necessary to make the meaning clear.

Index of Persons

Index of Places

General Index

Discernment G17, A82, C10, E156
Disciple, unsatisfactory one retained
    A65
Discretion L10, E4, E18
Doctor A1
Dog[s] S82, E10, E193, E194
Door C18, E7
Dragon A74, C2
Dream G11, A72

Education E173
End of the world C36, C45
Eucharist L21
Eunuch S59
Example, teaching by G70, S26
Exhaustion S20
Eye, evil C33, C42

Fasting G22, G23, L9, E135, E152, E155,
    E163
Favours, three E167
Fig[s] C2
Food E148
Fool E103
Forgetting G61
Forgiveness S25, S31, S34, E60, E146, E170
Forty-day fast A11
Fox[es] C44, E113
Friendship S78, A16

Gazelles S86
General A17
Gluttony E38, E186
Gold G54, G55, A17, A71
Greeks A39

Hand in the fire C24
Handmaid of God L65
Harvest L60, A25, C1
Haven of rest S44
Head of the *logismoi* L39
Hesychia G8, G39, G56, G69, A68
Honey G26, E124, E125
Hood A80
Hospitality C17
Humility G18, G20, G29, G46, G49, L15,
    L31, L64, L88, L89, C50, S26, A57,
    A60, A61, E58, E155, E160, E198,
    E199
Hunter[s] E7

Infancy, raised in desert from L62, A59
Insane E52

Judging G37, G38, S10, S17

Keeping quiet L46, L48, L50
Key E80
King of Egypt, new E19
Kneeling A58
Know yourself S88

Lentils L21
Letter, handwritten A7
Linen, -working G50, S22
Lion[s] C44, C35, E10
Liturgy G64
Lives of the Fathers G67
Love your neighbour E85

Mat of Eulalius unburnt L67
    sitting on to work E51
Meditation[s] / recitation L60, C10, C29, E13,
    E43, E46, E55, E196
Memento mori S48, A52, E46, E179
Moderation A37
Monastic habit C61

Nails, burning A76
Nakedness G3, G4, G41, A35, E61
Nazirite S21
Nostalgia L85, S53*, C36, E16, E22, E27, E47,
    E70, E110, E115, E159, E161, E162,
    E184

Obedience G1, G2, S26, S72, C24, C30
Oil L61
Ostrich C32, C41, E7

Parable of wealth E62
Patient endurance C26
Peacemakers E74
Persian[s] G23
Porches of Solomon E141
Precepts, Seven L94
Prison E157
Porneia G3, G14, G25, G27, G28, G41, G45,
    L63, S16, S30, S31, S84, S97, S99, A8,
    A13, A14, A15, E33, E119, E124, E126,
    E127, E144, E148, E149
    brother in G73
Possess Christ L42
Possessions L18, L25, S96
Poverty E3, E27
Prayer S101–109, E187, E192
Prayer of the assembly S7
Priest taken in adultery G41